Study Guide
to accompany
Crooks and Stein

Psychology:
Science, Behavior, and Life
second edition

Prepared by
Cheryl Hale
Jefferson College
Missouri

Holt, Rinehart and Winston, Inc.

Fort Worth   Chicago   San Francisco   Philadelphia
Montreal   Toronto   London   Sydney   Tokyo

ISBN: 0–03–053264–7

Address Editorial Correspondence to: Harcourt Brace Jovanovich, Inc.,
                                              301 Commerce Street, Suite 3700, Fort Worth, TX 76102

Address Orders to: Harcourt Brace Jovanovich, Inc.,
                            6277 Sea Harbor Drive, Orlando, Florida 32887.
                            1–800–782–4479, or 1–800–433–0001 (in Florida)

PRINTED IN THE UNITED STATES OF AMERICA

2 3 4   054   9 8 7 6 5 4 3 2

Harcourt Brace Jovanovich, Inc.
The Dryden Press
Saunders College Publishing

CONTENTS

How To Use This Study Guide

"Miracles do not happen. People work to accomplish what seems to be miraculous."
from the Chanukah Blessing

Students beginning a course in general psychology have varying preconceptions. Some students believe that because psychology is a science, it will be difficult for them to understand. Other students believe that because psychology is about people, it will be an easy course simply because they are a person and the course is about them. Most students fall somewhere in between these two extremes. This Study Guide is designed to assist all types of students successfully complete their general psychology course. Students who feel (for whatever reason) that the course will be easy or difficult for them will benefit from the structure of and exercises included in this Study Guide. If, as you read this introduction at the beginning of the semester (or you just bought this Study Guide after performing poorly on your first exam), you believe that it would take a miracle for you to receive an A, B, or C (choose one) in this course, reread the quote at the top of the page. The quote is about *work* not miracles. This Study Guide will help you work to master the material covered in your general psychology course. If you work by reading the text, attending class and taking notes, reading and doing the exercises in the Study Guide, and incorporating all of this information in your studying, your work will be rewarded with considerable knowledge concerning psychology. Further, this knowledge should be reflected in your course grade.

The introduction to the Study Guide has two main sections. The first section describes the major features of the Study Guide and provides information on how to effectively use it. The second section presents general information on effective studying and test-taking that is relevant for all your courses. You may have already noticed from the Table of Contents in the textbook that psychologists study such topics as learning, thinking, and memory. The second section of this introduction will refer you to specific sections of the textbook that are directly relevant to study and problem-solving skills that would be helpful for you to read at the beginning of the semester.

ORGANIZATION OF EACH CHAPTER

Each chapter in this Study Guide is divided into nine parts:

I. Learning Objectives
II. Overview
III. Key Terms/Matching Exercizes
IV. True–False Statement
V. Multiple-Choice Questions
VI. Summary Tables
VII. Thought Questions/Critical Thinking
VIII. Applications
IX. Summary Tables Solutions

This organization uses a number of methods to assist you in mastering the information presented in the textbook: highlights of or introduction to the material (Part I. and Part II.), questions to assess your basic knowledge of the material (Part III.–Part V.), and exercises designed to encourage critical thinking, by stimulating or challenging you to analyze, evaluate, and apply the principles discussed in the textbook in a variety of ways (Part VI–Part VIII.). For your convenience, Part I.–Part V. are divided into sections that correspond to the major sections in the textbook. Let's look at each part individually.

Part I. Learning Objectives

The learning objectives highlight all the major topics discussed in the chapter, and should be used in three different ways. First, read the learning objectives before reading the text and attending class lectures so that you will be aware of the important topics, concepts, and terms you should be focusing on. Second, after reading the chapter and attending class lectures you should be able to discuss each learning objective. Page references follow each learning objective. If you are having difficulty with a particular learning objective, refer to the textbook and reread the appropriate pages. Third, the learning objectives are phrased in a way that is suitable for essay questions, in studying for an exam practice composing answers to each. It is useful to put an asterisk (*) beside those learning objectives your instructor emphasized in class and devote extra attention to these learning objectives. Similarly, if your instructor did not assign the entire chapter, you should cross off any learning objectives associated with the material in the text that was not assigned. (Caution: Do not cross off learning objectives that your instructor assigned but did not emphasize in class lectures, you are still responsible and may be questioned concerning that material.)

Part II. Overview

The overview contains a brief summary of the material presented in the chapter. The overview serves two functions. As with the learning objectives, you should read the overview before reading the text and attending class to prepare for the material that will be presented. The second function of the overview is that because it is brief it presents a concise overview (or global view) of how the different topics in the chapter relate to each other. Thus it is helpful to reread the overview after reading the chapter and when studying for your exams.

Part III. Key Terms/Matching Exercises

The matching exercises are designed to assess your knowledge of the basic concepts (and for some chapters, individuals) discussed in the text. The matching questions are organized by topic, therefore the terms are often closely related. The matching exercises focus your attention on subtle similarities and differences between related terms. Check your answers against the Answer Key. If you have difficulty with some of the concepts, the Answer Key includes page references to assist you in accurately learning each. You might want to consider first answering the matching exercises (and also the true-false statements and multiple-choice questions) on a separate sheet of paper enabling you to go back over these exercises and give yourself a retest(s) of the material.

Part IV. True-False Statements

True–false statements are included to assess your knowledge concerning definitions, facts, and concepts and also to focus on distinctions between related concepts. I have found that many students find true–false items (where there is a 50 percent probability of guessing correctly) more difficult than multiple-choice questions (where there is only a 25 percent chance of guessing correctly). In multiple-choice questions the correct answer is directly stated and the student's task is to select it from among the choices presented. You can visualize a true–false item as a multiple-choice question that only provides one choice (a). The student has to decide for himself or herself what choices b, c, and d would be and then decide which choice is correct. Carefully examine all terms in each true-false item before answering. Check your responses against the Answer Key. Space is provided for you to go back to the false statements and supply a revised statement that is true. This part of the true–false exercise can be very helpful in "finetuning" your knowledge of the material. For false items there are usually a number of ways to change the statement into a true statement: For example, if the statement is basically a definition you could either change the term so that it matches the definition provided or change the definition so that it matches the term. The Answer Key supplies a page reference for each item. Those that are true are described on the referenced page. The page reference for false statements supplies at least one correct (or true) version of a related statement.

Part V. Multiple-Choice Questions

Many instructors include some multiple-choice questions on their exams. The multiple-choice questions in this Study Guide are similar to the type of multiple-choice questions you may encounter on your exams. Some of the multiple-choice questions are straightforward and refer specifically to the terms, facts, and concepts described in the text, whereas other questions require you to apply information from the text to new situations or examples. Answering these questions should give you a good estimate of how well prepared you are for the exam. You might want to take this "practice" multiple-choice test after you have started to review for the exam. Check your answers against the Answer Key, which has page references included. Allow yourself enough study time to be able to review the material related to those questions you missed or were unsure of the correct answer. For each chapter five multiple-choice questions have annotated answers provided. These annotations contain detailed information explaining why the correct answer *is* correct and also explain why the remaining choices are incorrect. The questions that receive the annotated answers are not necessarily the trickiest or even most difficult questions, rather they are questions selected to cover a variety of topics from each chapter and to illustrate a number of different styles of multiple-choice questions.

Part VI. Summary Tables

Each chapter in the Study Guide has between one and four Summary Tables for you to complete. These tables take a variety of forms including listing and describing related concepts, summarizing a number of related theories, and summarizing a large body of information from the chapter in a concise manner. The Summary Tables serve two purposes. First, in order to complete these tables you will need to think about the information in the textbook and organize your thoughts. If you have carefully prepared for your exam, you should be able to fill in the information without constantly referring to the text and your notes for "hints." If you encounter difficulty with a Summary Table (or a substantial part of a table) it indicates an area of weakness that you should review. Part IX. Summary Tables Solutions, at the end of the chapter, provide completed tables for you to compare with your completed tables. Second, the completed tables are well suited for use to quickly review the material.

Part VII. Thought Questions/Critical Thinking

Research has shown that memory for material is enhanced through critical thinking. Critical thinking involves analyzing, evaluating, reorganizing, and relating information to a larger body of information. These questions ask you to really think about the principles of psychology that are discussed in the textbook. I doubt that many of the thought questions included in the Study Guide will appear on your exams. However, by thinking about and preparing answers to these questions you will gain an increased understanding of the principles of psychology discussed in the textbook.

Part VIII. Applications

To encourage you to continue to think critically, each chapter typically concludes with two applications. These applications fall into two general categories: research-based applications and everyday-life applications. Research-based applications ask you to examine your own behavior (for example, keep a sleep diary), examine the behavior of others (for example, the strategies they use to solve problems), and design experiments to illustrate or test some of the concepts discussed in the textbook. Everyday-life applications ask you to, for example, suggest possible diagnoses for individuals with psychological disorders, develop a stress test to determine the amount of stress experienced by college students, and evaluate television commercials. I strongly suggest that you do at least one of the applications for each chapter in the Study Guide. These exercises will help you to master the material in the textbook and will also give you a more complete "feel" for the science of psychology and how it relates to the behavior and mental processes of individuals.

HOW TO STUDY AND TAKE EXAMS

SQ3R Method

The SQ3R method developed by educational psychologist Francis Robinson is a well-known and effective strategy for studying written material. There are five steps in the SQ3R method: Survey, Question, Read, Recite, and Review.

Survey. Before you begin to read and study a chapter, quickly scan or survey the chapter in order to get a general outline of the material to be discussed. Look at the main headings and subheadings and examine the tables and figures. The purpose of the survey is to provide you with general information concerning the chapter that you will expand upon later.

Reading the learning objectives and chapter overview in this Study Guide would also be part of your survey.

Question. Before beginning to read the chapter stop and write questions concerning the results of your survey. You could start by turning each chapter heading into a question (use key words such as who, what, when, where, why, and how). You might add to your list of questions after you begin to read the chapter. Asking a number of questions prepares you for the next step.

Read. Actively read the chapter searching for the answers to the questions you formulated. Your comprehension of the chapter will be increased because your active reading has a purpose (answering specific questions). This approach is very different from passive reading ("Only 10 more pages to go") which often is not associated with gaining an understanding of the information.

Recite. After you have read the first section of the chapter stop. Close your textbook or look away from it and recite (mentally, out load, or in writing) the main points of the section. These main points should be the answer to the first questions you asked. After checking your recited answer with the text, make any necessary corrections to your answer and recite it again. Then proceed to read and recite for the next section of the chapter.

Review. After you have read all the new information (whether it is a chapter or a shorter daily reading assignment), go back over all the new material and review it and the material from previous assignments. This review step increases your retention of the information and also helps to clarify how the individual sections of the chapter relate to each other.

Helpful Hints from Your Text

Three short sections in the textbook provide specific information directly related to studying and taking exams in your general psychology course and other classes. I encourage you to read the following sections of the text now.

1. In your classes it is frequently necessary to memorize information. The chapter on memory (Chapter 7, pp. 238–240) discusses six different mnemonic devices or memory systems to enhance your retention of specific information.
2. The memory chapter also includes a section titled "Strategies for Improving Academic Memory" (pp. 261–264), which discusses nine different strategies to improve the efficiency of your studying.
3. Chapter 13 (Intelligence) discusses (pp. 484–485) six steps involved in solving multiple-choice-type problems, and the characteristics of students who perform poorly and well on these types of problems. The text outlines strategies for how to improve your performance on multiple-choice problems.

Class Notes

Attending class lectures is good, listening attentively is better, and taking a good set of class notes is best. We will discuss notetaking from two perspectives, during class and after class.
In Class
1. Keep all of your notes for one class in a large notebook. Begin each day's notes with the date and topic or chapter that will be discussed.
2. Do not try to save money by conserving paper. When the instructor starts to lecture on a new chapter start a new page in your notebook. Only write on the front of each sheet. Do not write on every line and do not write across the entire length of any line. Do leave plenty of blank space so that you can add information later or make notes on your notes.

3. Do not try to write down everything the instructor says (it's impossible and not everything is important). Do try to summarize in your own words what the instructor says. When you study, your "own words" will make more sense to you than the instructor's.

4. Take notes in an outline format. Make certain that major topics or concepts stand out and are not buried within smaller details. List details under major topics in an orderly fashion.

5. If the instructor cares enough to write or draw something on the chalkboard, include it in your notes. Frequently information presented on the chalkboard appears on exams.

6. Include examples in your notes. One of the main advantages an instructor has over a textbook author is that the instructor can supply many more examples to illustrate a concept than would be possible for the author. Don't just listen to these "extra examples or stories" write them down in your notes. Often examples are well remembered, by writing the example in your notes you will hopefully not only remember the example but also remember what concept it was designed to illustrate.

After Class

1. Review your notes as soon after class as possible, while the lecture is still relatively fresh in your mind. Fill in information or details (remember all that blank space you left) to supplement the notes you wrote down during class, rephrase information that is unclear, copy over words that are illegible (if you can barely read it today, it will be incomprehensible when studying for an exam). Also review your notes for accuracy and, if necessary, correct your notes.

2. Develop a system to cross-reference your class notes, text, and this Study Guide. There are a number of possibilities to accomplish this. For example, if your instructor gives a novel example to illustrate a concept (about his grandfather in World War I) note "Grandfather's war story" at the appropriate place in the text. You may find it helpful to write down in the text which days' lectures go with which sections of the text (and vice versa). You might also find it helpful to write in your notes which chapter learning objective is related to each section of the lecture material.

Test-Taking Strategies

General Strategies

1. Before you begin to answer the test questions:
- If there is no clock in the classroom, wear a watch on exam days.
- Read all instructions for the entire test. If instructions are not clear to you, ask your instructor to explain.
- Note how many points each question (and each section of the exam) is worth.
- Decide how much time you will need to complete each section of the test and budget your time accordingly. You will want to devote more time to a 20-point essay question than to a 5-point short-answer question.

2. During the test:
- Periodically check the time to see if you are "on schedule." Do not allow yourself to spend too much time on any particular question. At times it is necessary to "move along." If you spend too much time staring at a difficult question at the beginning of the test, you might not have time to answer the easy questions at the end of the test.
- Use all of the time you are alotted. If a few minutes are left after you finish the test, use this time to double-check that you answered all questions, to look for careless mistakes, to proofread your written answers, and to ponder those difficult questions.

Strategies for Multiple-Choice Tests

1. Do not jump or skip around through the questions. Answer all questions in order. If you are unsure of an answer, make an educated guess and mark that question so that you can go back and devote more attention to evaluating it carefully after you have finished the remainder of the test.

2. Read the main body of each question (the question stem) carefully and try to supply the answer before you read the choices. This prepares you to read the responses intelligently. Then read *all* the alternative responses to find the one *best* answer to the question. Examine each alternative and eliminate those that are obviously incorrect first.

3. Questions using words such as *not* and *least likely* may be tricky. Use extra care in reading these questions and the alternative responses.

4. Finally, your first "guess" on a multiple-choice question is usually correct. If you change your answer, have a good reason for doing so.

Strategies for Essay Tests

1. For exams that contain both essay and objective questions, read the essay questions first, but answer them last. You will probably find some information that will help you on the essay questions in the other sections of the test.

2. Read the questions carefully. Pay close attention to key words such as *define*, *evaluate*, and *illustrate*. Make sure that you answer the question that your instructor asked.

3. Answer the essay questions that you know best first, then answer the remaining questions.

CHAPTER 1

The Nature and Origins of Psychology

PART I. LEARNING OBJECTIVES

When you finish studying this chapter you should be able to:

Psychology Defined

1. Give a complete definition of psychology. **(4)**

2. Explain why psychology is a science. **(4)**

3. Explain why psychology studies both behavior and mental processes. **(5)**

4. Explain why psychology studies animal as well as human behavior. **(6)**

Psychology's History

5. Discuss the two roots (philosophy and physiology) of psychology: What did each contribute to the new science of psychology? **(8)**

6. Describe how Wundt, Titchener, and other structuralists would define and study psychology. **(9)**

7. Describe how James' approach—functionalism—would define and study psychology. **(10)**

8. Explain why Watson and other behaviorists believed it was impossible to study the mind scientifically. Describe the approach to psychology supported by behaviorists. **(10)**

9. Describe the Gestalt approach to the study of psychology. **(11)**

10. Discuss Freud's psychoanalytic approach and explain how it fundamentally differed from the other early approaches to psychology. **(11)**

11. Describe the approach taken by humanistic psychologists. Discuss how its approach differs from that of Freud and the behaviorists. **(11-12)**

12. Explain how cognitive psychology and information processing led to a renewed interest in mental processes. **(12)**

Fields of Specialization in Psychology Today

13. Compare and contrast clinical psychology and counseling psychology. **(13, 15)**

14. Explain the differences between clinical psychologists and psychiatrists. **(15)**

15. Describe the work of experimental psychologists, and explain why it is misleading to consider experimental psychology to be a separate field. **(15)**

16. Describe and give an example of the types of questions or fields of study that would interest neuropsychologists. **(16)**

17. Describe and give an example of the types of questions or fields of study that would interest educational and school psychologists. **(16)**

18. Describe and give an example of the types of questions or fields of study that would interest industrial/organizational psychologists. **(16)**

19. Describe and give an example of the types of questions or fields of study that would interest engineering psychologists. **(17)**

20. Describe and give an example of the types of questions or fields of study that would interest developmental psychologists. **(17)**

21. Describe and give an example of the types of questions or fields of study that would interest social psychologists. **(17)**

22. Describe and give an example of the types of questions or fields of study that would interest personality psychologists. **(17-18)**

23. Briefly describe five new areas of specialization in psychology. **(18)**

24. Discuss the changing face of psychology and the current tension between scientifically oriented and health-care provider oriented psychologists. **(19)**

25. Identify the three goals of psychology. **(20-21)**

PART II. OVERVIEW

Psychology is the scientific study of behavior and mental processes of humans and other animals. The goals of psychology are to understand, predict, and control behavior and mental processes. The subject matter of psychology is very broad and includes internal physiological responses, behavior, and complex mental processes such as perceiving, thinking, and creativity.

The combined influence of two distinct fields led to the beginning of psychology in the late 1800s. Philosophers were concerned with the mind and attempted to understand it through the application of logical reasoning. Physiologists, on the other hand, relied on the scientific method to study bodily processes.

The new science of psychology had many different beginnings or approaches. Structuralism (Wundt and Titchener) tried to identify the basic elements of conscious experience through the use of introspection. Functionalism (James) was concerned with the adaptive functions of different conscious processes. While the structuralists were interested in the parts or structure of the mind, the functionalists were more interested in what the mind was capable of doing. Behaviorism (Watson) took a very different approach and rejected mental processes from study and concentrated on observable behaviors. Gestalt psychology (Wertheimer, Köhler, and Koffka) believed that "the whole is different from the sum of its parts" and was interested in how people organize experiences and perceive patterns. Freud's psychoanalytic approach emphasized the role of the unconscious mind in the development of human personality.

A large number of areas of specialization exist in psychology today. Some psychologists perform activities that help individuals cope with difficulties in their daily life (clinical, counseling, and school) whereas others are concerned with making the work environment more satisfying (industrial/organizational) or well designed for efficiency (engineering). Educational psychologists are involved in the study and application of teaching methods. In many of the other areas of specializations, psychologists concentrate on studying basic psychological processes (developmental, neuropsychological, personality, and social).

PART III. KEY TERMS/MATCHING EXERCISES

Match the following concepts and/or individuals with the appropriate descriptions. Check your answers against the Answer Key.

Psychology Defined

Concepts

_e._ 1. psychology **(4)**

_c._ 2. scientific method **(5)**

_b._ 3. behavior **(6)**

_g._ 4. mental processes **(6)**

_d._ 5. theories **(22)**

_a._ 6. hypothesis **(22)**

_h._ 7. American Psychological Association (APA) **(20)**

_f_ 8. American Psychological Society (APS) **(20)**

Descriptions

a. Scientific assumptions that can be directly subjected to empirical tests

b. An internal physiological response or activity of an organism that can be observed

c. Provides reliable information as opposed to subjective opinions

d. Tentative attempts to organize and explain a body of data, facts, or observations

e. The scientific study of the behavior and mental processes of humans and other animals

f. Organization with the stated purpose of representing the academic and research interests of psychology

g. Internal activity of an organism that cannot be directly observed

h. A large and well-established organization that today is more closely aligned with applied as opposed to academic psychology

Answer Key   1. e   2. c   3. b   4. g   5. d   6. a   7. h   8. f

Psychology's History

Concepts

_b._ 1. behaviorism **(10)**

_f._ 2. cognitive psychology **(12)**

_e._ 3. functionalism **(10)**

_a._ 4. Gestalt psychology **(11)**

_g._ 5. humanistic psychology **(11-12)**

_c._ 6. psychoanalysis **(11)**

_d._ 7. structuralism **(9)**

Descriptions

a. Believes the relationship between the parts is more important than the individual part

b. Rejected the study of mental processes and emphasized the study of the relationship between stimuli and responses

c. Emphasized the role of the unconscious mind and sexual urges in influencing human behavior

d. Attempts to reduce conscious experience into its basic elements

e. Emphasizes the practical nature of the mind

f. Resulted in renewed interest in mental processes such as thinking, problem solving, and creativity

g. Emphasizes the role of free choice and conscious rational choices have on human behavior

Answer Key   1. b   2. f   3. e   4. a   5. g   6. c   7. d

Individuals

_b._ 1. Freud **(11)**

_g._ 2. James **(10)**

_e._ 3. Maslow and Rogers **(11-12)**

_a._ 4. Titchener **(9)**

_c._ 5. Watson **(10)**

_f._ 6. Wertheimer, Köhler, and Koffka **(11)**

_d._ 7. Wundt **(9)**

Descriptions

a. Carried on in Wundt's tradition and labeled the approach "structuralism"

b. Developed his approach as a result of treating emotionally disturbed individuals

c. Pioneered the stimulus–response approach to psychology and emphasized objectively verifiable phenomena

d. Used introspection to study mental processes

e. Believed that people have a natural tendency to strive for self-actualization or the attainment of their fullest potential

f. Believed that the whole of an experience was different from the sum of its parts

g. Was strongly influenced by Darwin's Theory of Natural Selection

Answer Key   1. b   2. g   3. e   4. a   5. c   6. f   7. d

Fields of Specialization in Psychology Today

Concepts

_d_ 1. clinical (**13, 15**)   _f_ 6. industrial/organization (**16-17**)

_c_ 2. counseling (**15**)   _e_ 7. neuropsychology (**16**)

_j_ 3. developmental (**17**)   _h_ 8. personality (**17-18**)

_g_ 4. educational (**16**)   _b_ 9. social (**17**)

_a_ 5. engineering (**17**)   _i_ 10. school (**16**)

Descriptions

a. Concerned with the relationship between the working environment, equipment, and people

b. Would be interested in topics such as interpersonal attraction, conformity, and group processes

c. Focuses on adjustment problems that are not serious psychological problems

d. Concerned with the diagnosis and treatment of serious psychological problems

e. Focuses on the relationship between physiological processes and behavior

f. Concerned with using psychological concepts to make the workplace a more satisfying environment for employees and management

g. Focuses on the study and application of teaching methods and learning

h. Focuses on the uniqueness of individuals and the key elements that provide the foundation of human personality

i. Concerned with evaluating and resolving learning and emotional problems as they relate to school activities

j. Concerned with factors that influence behavior and development throughout the life cycle

Answer Key   1. d   2. c   3. j   4. g   5. a   6. f   7. e   8. h   9. b   10. i

New Areas of Specialization

Concepts

_b_ 1. artificial intelligence (**19**)   _c_ 4. health psychology (**18-19**)

_e_ 2. environmental psychology (**18**)   _a_ 5. quantitative psychology (**19**)

_d_ 3. forensic psychology (**18**)

Descriptions

a. Develops mathematical models of complex relationships between behavior and its causes

b. Develops computer models that simulate complex human cognitive processes

c. Concerned with how psychological and physical factors relate to the treatment and prevention of illness

d. Works with the legal system in a variety of ways

e. Has interests that are in many ways similar to engineering psychology

Answer Key   1. b   2. e   3. d   4. c   5. a

PART IV. TRUE-FALSE STATEMENTS

Fill in the blank before each statement with either a T (true) or an F (false). Check your answers against the Answer Key. Then go back to the items that are false and make the necessary change(s) to the statements to convert the items into true statements.

Psychology Defined

_____ 1. Psychology is a science because it deals with both animal and human behavior.

_____ 2. One reason why psychologists study animal behavior is that, occasionally, ethical considerations would prohibit the use of human subjects in a research project.

Psychology's History

_____ 3. One of the main benefits that the science of psychology received from its roots in philosophy, is that philosophy emphasizes the use of observation to acquire knowledge.

_____ 4. According to Wundt and Titchener, psychology should attempt to study the structure of the conscious mind.

_____ 5. Gestalt psychologists had major disagreements with the principles of structuralism, although they were in general agreement with the principles of behaviorism.

_____ 6. Humanistic psychology emphasizes the role of the unconscious processes in determining human behavior.

Fields of Specialization in Psychology Today

_____ 7. Counseling psychologists focus on relatively minor psychological problems; clinical psychologists focus on more serious psychological problems.

_____ 8. Neuropsychologists might investigate the effects of both drugs and brain damage on behavior.

_____ 9. In order to increase employee productivity, an industrial/organizational psychologist would likely assist in the design of a new fast-food restaurant.

_____

_____

_____ 10. Health psychology is a new area of specialization in psychology that has received widespread interest and is recognized as an important field of study.

_____

_____

The Goals of Psychology

_____ 11. The goals of psychology are to understand, predict, and control (or influence) behavior and mental processes.

_____

_____

Answer Key			
1. F **(4)**	5. F **(11)**	9. F **(16-17)**	
2. T **(6)**	6. F **(11-12)**	10. T **(18-19)**	
3. F **(8)**	7. T **(13-15)**	11. T **(20)**	
4. T **(9)**	8. T **(16)**		

PART V. MULTIPLE-CHOICE QUESTIONS

Choose the best answer to each question. Circle your choice. Check your answers against the Answer Key. Questions marked with an asterisk (*) include annotated answers.

Psychology Defined

1. Which of the following terms or phrases is *not* included in the definition of psychology?

a. Behavior and mental processes
b. Subjective study
c. Scientific study
d. Humans and other animals

2. Which of the following pairs of terms are both mental processes?

a. Sleeping and dreaming
b. Fear and breathing
c. Anger and remembering
d. Talking and deciding

*3. You want to study the effects of the presence of red-filtered background lighting on resting heart rate. Originally, you might choose to perform the study with animals rather than humans because

a. ethical considerations would prohibit the use of human subjects in this experiment.
b. you could obtain information about the genetic background of animals but not humans.
c. animals can be obtained at very little expense.
d. animal studies allow you to have more control.

4. The roots of modern psychology may be traced to

    a. philosophy and physics.
    b. philosophy and physiology.
    c. psychoanalysis and physiology.
    d. physics and philanthropy.

5. The "root" of psychology that used logical thought processes to reach conclusions was

    a. philosophy.
    b. psychoanalysis.
    c. physiology.
    d. physics.

6. An approach to psychology that attempted to break down experience into its basic elements was

    a. structuralism.
    b. psychoanalysis.
    c. functionalism.
    d. behaviorism.

7. If you take a sip of a soft drink and concentrate on what you are experiencing (cold, bubbly, sweet, etc.), you would be utilizing the technique of

    a. empiricism.
    b. functionalism.
    c. behaviorism.
    d. introspection.

8. The approach to psychology that emphasized the practical nature of the mind and believed that processes such as consciousness helped people adapt was

    a. Gestalt psychology.
    b. functionalism.
    c. humanistic psychology.
    d. structuralism.

9. The fact that behavior can be observed and quantified and feelings cannot is the basis of

    a. structuralism.
    b. behaviorism.
    c. functionalism.
    d. Gestalt psychology.

10. Which individual is incorrectly paired with an approach to psychology?

    a. Titchener—structuralism
    b. Maslow—humanistic psychology
    c. Watson—Gestalt psychology
    d. James—functionalism

11. Gestalt psychology focused on

    a. the most basic elements of our experiences.

    b. gaining an understanding of the unconscious mind.

    c. the relationship between environmental stimuli and an organism's response to them.

    d. the way people perceive patterns and organize experiences.

12. Which approach to psychology could explain why some individuals interpret "IX" as the letters "I" and "X", and other individuals interpret it as the number 9?

    a. Humanistic psychology

    b. Functionalism

    c. Gestalt psychology

    d. Structuralism

*13. As discussed in the text, one basic difference between Freud's psychoanalytic approach and other early approaches to psychology is that

    a. Freud's approach was subjective whereas the others were objective.

    b. Freud's approach generated more research than other approaches.

    c. Not everyone agreed with Freud's approach whereas there was universal agreement concerning the other approaches.

    d. Freud's approach only concerned people whereas all the other approaches dealt with both animals and people.

14. You act impulsively, then wonder why. Freud would tell you that your behavior was influenced by your

    a. irritation.

    b. unconscious mind.

    c. immaturity.

    d. inability to think fast.

*15. Which of the following is a *false* statement?

    a. Humanistic psychologists emphasize the role of free choice.

    b. Humanistic psychologists view people as being controlled by events in their environment.

    c. Humanistic psychologists have interest in topics such as self-esteem and personal fulfillment.

    d. Humanistic psychologists deemphasize the influence of unconscious processes.

16. An individual who subscribes to the information-processing perspective would most appropriately also be considered as a proponent of

    a. educational psychology.

    b. neuropsychology.

    c. behaviorism.

    d. cognitive psychology.

Fields of Specialization in Psychology Today

17. You are studying to be a psychologist. The chances are greater than 50 percent that you will specialize in

     a. experimental psychology.
     b. industrial psychology.
     c. education.
     d. clinical or counseling psychology.

*18. Which of the following types of psychologists would be *least likely* to study the development of the ability of children to work appropriately on group projects in school?

     a. School psychologist
     b. Educational psychologist
     c. Developmental psychologist
     d. Social psychologist

19. Which of the following professionals can prescribe medications?

     a. Psychiatrists
     b. Clinical psychologists
     c. Counseling psychologists
     d. Both a and b are correct.

20. An _____ psychologist would be concerned with the workplace being organized for optimal efficiency; an _____ psychologist would be concerned that the workplace provided a satisfying environment.

     a. engineering | environmental
     b. engineering | industrial/organizational
     c. industrial/organizational | engineering
     d. industrial/organizational | environmental

21. You see an article titled "The Effect of Hawaiian Vacations on the Remission of Cancer." The psychologist who conducted this research was most likely a(n)

     a. forensic psychologist.
     b. medical psychologist.
     c. environmental psychologist.
     d. health psychologist.

*22. A cognitive psychologist would be *least likely* to conduct research in the area of

     a. educational psychology.
     b. quantitative psychology.
     c. information processing.
     d. artificial intelligence.

23. In the case of Charles Whitman (who murdered 14 people on the campus of the University of Texas) the most satisfactory explanation was provided from which of the following fields of specialization?

     a. Clinical psychology
     b. Forensic psychology
     c. Neuropsychology
     d. Personality psychology

24. Educational psychologists differ from school psychologists in that educational psychologists are more likely to

   a. assist students with special problems.
   b. help students with learning problems.
   c. engage in research.
   d. consult with parents and teachers.

25. A "human factors psychologist" is also known as a(n) _____ psychologist.

   a. engineering
   b. environmental
   c. social
   d. personality

26. You see an article titled "The Effect of Peer Pressure on Alcohol Consumption by Teenagers." The psychologist who conducted this research was most likely a(n) _____ psychologist.

   a. social
   b. educational
   c. environmental
   d. personality

27. John Hinkley's (President Reagan's attempted assassin) psychological profile would probably have been performed by a(n) _____ psychologist.

   a. personality
   b. forensic
   c. social
   d. organizational

28. In recent years the number of individuals receiving doctorates in psychology has

   a. increased in social, personality, and neuropsychology and decreased in clinical, counseling, and school psychology.
   b. increased in clinical, counseling, and school psychology and decreased in social, personality, and neuropsychology.
   c. increased dramatically in all areas of psychology.
   d. not changed since the 1950s.

29. The goal of psychology that is sometimes perceived as controversial is

   a. understanding behavior.
   b. generating behavior.
   c. controlling behavior.
   d. predicting behavior.

30. _____ generate predictions or _____ that may be subjected to empirical tests.

   a. observations | beliefs
   b. hypotheses | theories
   c. theories | hypotheses
   d. facts | theories

Answer Key

1. b	(4)	7. d	(9)	•13. a	(11)	19. a	(15)	25. a	(17)
2. c	(5)	8. b	(10)	14. b	(11)	20. b	(17)	26. a	(17)
•3. d	(6)	9. b	(10)	•15. b	(11-12)	21. d	(18-19)	27. b	(18)
4. b	(8)	10. c	(10)	16. d	(12)	•22. b	(19)	28. b	(19-20)
5. a	(8)	11. d	(11)	17. d	(13)	23. c	(16)	29. c	(21)
6. a	(9)	12. c	(11)	•18. a	(16)	24. c	(16)	30. c	(22)

Annotated Answers

3. The correct choice is d. With human subjects it would be more difficult to control the activities subjects engaged in prior to the experiment that could have an effect on resting heart rate.
   a. It would be ethical to conduct this experiment with human subjects.
   b. While there may be a potential genetic influence on resting heart rate, it does not appear to be a major consideration in this research.
   c. The cost of doing this research with human subjects would not be a major consideration in this experiment.

13. The correct choice is a. While the other approaches were objective and could be tested in the laboratory, it is not generally possible to test Freud's subjective approach in the laboratory.
    b. Freud's approach did not generate as much research as the other approaches.
    c. There was no universal agreement concerning the other approaches; for example, Gestalt psychologists were very critical of both structuralism and behaviorism.
    d. Some of the other approaches (for example, structuralism and humanistic psychology) were also solely concerned with humans.

15. The correct choice is b. Behaviorists support this statement.
    a. Humanistic psychologists emphasize that people have free choice.
    c. Humanistic psychologists are very interested in topics such as self-esteem and personal fulfullment.
    d. Because humanistic psychologists emphasize conscious choices they deemphasize the influence of the unconscious.

18. The correct choice is a. School psychologists are primarily interested in helping individual children resolve learning and emotional problems. Additionally, they typically do not conduct research.
    b. An educational psychologist might study this behavior from the perspective of gaining insight into how to best organize or coordinate group projects.
    c. A developmental psychologist might study this behavior from the perspective of discovering at what age children can appropriately handle group projects.
    d. A social psychologist might study this behavior from the perspective of observing the dynamics of group processes and the social roles involved in group projects.

22. The correct choice is b. Quantitative psychology involves the development of mathematical models of the relationships between complex behaviors and its causes.
    a. Although answer a is probably the "best" incorrect choice, the interests of cognitive and educational psychologists overlap.
    c. Information processing is a cognitive process.
    d. Artificial intelligence involves developing computer models that simulate cognitive processes.

PART VI. SUMMARY TABLES

To test your understanding of the material discussed in this chapter complete the following tables. Check your answers with those supplied in PART IX.

Approaches to Psychology

Approach	Individuals	What Should Psychology Study?	Methods of Study and/or Specific Areas of Interest
Structuralism	Wundt Titchener	identify the basis elements of conscious exper.	introspection
Functionalism	James	The practical nature of cons. experience	How mental processess help people Adapt
Behaviorism	Watson	Relationship B/T environ. events (stimuli) + responses	objective phen. (behavior)
Gestalt psychology	Wertheimer Kohler Koffka	How we organize exp. + perceive patterns	Relationship B/T parts is more import. than the indiv. parts
Psychoanalytic	Freud	How the uncons. mind urges influences on person.	subjective study, treating emotionally dist. patients,
Humanistic psychology	Maslow Rogers	Role of FREE Choice	topics such as love, self esteem, personal fulfillment
Cognitive psychology		Mental process.	Thinking, Perceiving, problem solving + Creativity

A number of speciality areas in psychology have interests that overlap. Fill in the following table to indicate those areas of specialization that have overlapping interests. Place an "X" in the grid if there is significant overlap between the fields. Place a "/" in the grid if there is some overlap but it is not extensive. Because completing this table is not a completely objective task, do not expect to be in total agreement with the solution supplied in PART IX. However, if there are major discrepancies between your solution and the solution in this *Study Guide* (for example, an "X" appears where you left a blank) reevaluate your answers and review the areas of specialization in the text.

Overlap of Speciality Areas

	CLIN	COUN	DEV	ED	ENG	ENV	FOR	HEA	I/O	NEU	PER	SOC	SCH
CLIN													
COUN													
DEV													
ED													
ENG													
ENV													
FOR													
HEA													
I/O													
NEU													
PER													
SOC													
SCH													

Key: CLIN = clinical, COUN = counseling, DEV = developmental, ED = educational, ENG = engineering, I/O = industrial/organizational, NEU = neuropsychology, PER = personality, SOC = social, SCH = school.

PART VII. THOUGHT QUESTIONS/CRITICAL THINKING

Prepare answers to the following discussion questions.

1. Many people would argue that psychology is not really a science but just common sense. These individuals might say that we all know that "Opposites attract," "You should look before you leap," and "Absence makes the heart grow fonder." How would you explain to these people that a science of psychology is necessary? Would your argument be strengthened if you mentioned that we also know "Birds of a feather flock together," "He who hesitates is lost," and "Out of sight, out of mind"?

2. If you had been an aspiring young psychologist when psychology was first becoming established, which school of psychology (structuralism, functionalism, behaviorism, Gestalt psychology, or psychoanalysis) do you think you would have been *most likely* to join? Explain your choice.

3. If you had been an aspiring young psychologist when psychology was first becoming established, which school of psychology do you think you would have been *least likely* to join? Explain your choice.

4. The areas of specialization in psychology overlap with other disciplines. If you were interested in a specific area of psychology but did not want to go on to graduate school in psychology, where else could you continue your education?

for example   clinical psychology _____ medical school (psychiatrist)

industrial/organizational _____

forensic _____

neuropsychology _____

engineering _____

health _____

educational _____

5. The text discusses the tension between empirically based or academic psychologists and applied or human-service provider psychologists. This tension is illustrated by the founding of a new organization (APS) in 1988 that broke off from APA. Do you think it is a good idea or a bad idea (or doesn't it matter) for there to be more than one major national organization of psychologists?

PART VIII. APPLICATIONS

1. Imagine that Wundt, James, Watson, Wertheimer, and Freud are members of a panel at the First International Convention of Psychology. The topics on the agenda for discussion include: How should psychology be defined? What methods should psychologists use to gain information? What are two or three critical issues for psychology to address? The discussion would probably be very lively. On the different issues, who are the psychologists with opinions that are in general agreement? With opposing opinions?

After the panel discussion is over do you think that any of the five panel members would leave together to discuss their similarities over lunch? If so, who and why? Would any of the psychologists be likely to eat lunch alone? If so, who and why?

2. Imagine that you are the head of a major corporation. You have assembled a group of 10 psychologists (a clinical, cognitive, developmental, educational, engineering, environmental, health, industrial/organizational, personality, and social psychologist) to participate in a roundtable discussion to address the following issues or problem areas.

a. You desire to implement a no-smoking policy in the office and manufacturing areas of your corporation.

b. Your corporation manufactures VCRs. You are aware that many people (the stereotype would be grandparents) have difficulty learning to operate VCRs. You are also aware that young children (who are not hesitant to operate VCRs) frequently experience problems in operating the VCR. You believe that if you can develop a "Grandma-proof" and/or "child-proof" VCR your company's profits will increase dramatically.

c. Although most of your managers do not report any difficulties with the weekly staff meetings they have with the employees, 20 percent of the managers report that these meetings are not generally productive and that the employees seem to enter the meetings with a negative attitude.

d. It will be necessary for a group of your employees to travel to an isolated work site for two weeks where they will work in a cramped, temporary facility (a house trailer) under the supervision of a recently hired female employee, who is quickly moving up the corporate ladder.

e. At the recent company picnic you observed that while many of your employees and their families wore seatbelts, a significant number did not. It appeared that there might be some age-related (for example, individuals over age 50 were less likely to wear seatbelts than those under age 30) and sex-related (women were more likely to wear seatbelts than men) differences in seatbelt use. You think 100 percent seatbelt use is a worthy task for your company to encourage.

f. Due to safety concerns you feel it is necessary to start a random drug-test program for some of your employees. Obviously you want your employees to accept the testing program, therefore you do not want the results of a positive drug test to be excessively punitive in nature.

What would the individual psychologists identify as critical features to be addressed in each example? What action would they recommend taking to accomplish your goals? For each example, which psychologist(s) would you put in charge of overseeing the accomplishment of your goals?

PART IX. SUMMARY TABLES SOLUTIONS

Approaches to Psychology

Approach	Individuals	What Should Psychology Study?	Methods of Study and/or Specific Areas of Interest
Structuralism	Wundt Titchener	Identify the basic elements of conscious experience	Introspection
Functionalism	James	The practical nature of conscious experience	How mental processes help people adapt
Behaviorism	Watson	Relationship between environmental events (stimuli) and responses	Objective phenomena (behavior)
Gestalt psychology	Wertheimer Köhler Koffka	How we organize experience and perceive patterns	Relationship between parts is more important than the individual parts
Psychoanalytic	Freud	How the unconscious mind and sexual urges influence personality	Subjective study from treating emotionally disturbed individuals
Humanistic psychology	Maslow Rogers	Role of free choice in determining human behavior	Self-actualization and topics such as love, self-esteem, personal fulfillment
Cognitive psychology	—	Mental processes	Thinking, perceiving, problem solving, and creativity

Overlap of Speciality Areas

	CLIN	COUN	DEV	ED	ENG	ENV	FOR	HEA	I/O	NEU	PER	SOC	SCH
CLIN	—	X	/				X	X		/	X	/	/
COUN	X	—	/				/	X			X	/	/
DEV	/	/	—	X				/		/	/	/	/
ED			X	—		/						/	/
ENG					—	X			X	/	/		
ENV				/	X	—			X	/	/	/	
FOR	X	/					—			/	/	/	
HEA	X	X	/					—			/	/	
I/O					X	X			—		/	/	
NEU	/		/		/	/	/			—			/
PER	X	X	/		/	/	/	/	/		—	/	/
SOC	/	/	/	/		/	/	/	/		/	—	/
SCH	/	/	/	/						/	/	/	—

Key: CLIN = clinical, COUN = counseling, DEV = developmental, ED = educational, ENG = engineering, I/O = industrial/organizational, NEU = neuropsychology, PER = personality, SOC = social, SCH = school.

CHAPTER 2

The Methods of Psychology

PART I. LEARNING OBJECTIVES

When you finish studying this chapter you should be able to:

Reasons for Conducting Research

1. Explain three reasons for conducting research. **(28)**

Research Methods

2. Describe the experimental method and discuss the advantages of this research method. **(32)**

3. Define independent variable and dependent variable and explain how the two terms are related. **(32)**

4. Describe and explain the functions of experimental and control groups in research. **(33)**

5. Discuss two limitations of the experimental method. **(34)**

6. Discuss the APA's ethical guidelines for conducting research. **(37)**

7. Explain why survey research uses relatively small samples. Explain the difference between representative and random samples. **(38)**

8. Compare and contrast the use of interviews and questionnaires in survey research. **(40)**

9. Discuss the limitations of the survey method of research. **(40)**

10. Describe the observational method and discuss the advantages of this research method. **(41)**

11. Discuss two potential drawbacks of the observational method. **(41-42)**

12. Describe the case-study method and discuss the advantages of this research method. **(42-43)**

13. Discuss the limitations of the case-study method of research). **(43-44)**

14. Describe the correlational method and explain the terms positive correlation and negative correlation. **(44)**

15. Discuss why the correlational method does not allow for conclusions concerning cause-and-effect relationships. **(45-46)**

Describing and Interpreting Research Findings

16. Explain the function of descriptive statistics. **(46)**

17. Discuss the function of measures of central tendency and define the mean, median, and mode. **(46)**

18. Discuss the function of measures of variability and define the range and standard deviation. **(46-47)**

19. Explain the function of inferential statistics and the difference between descriptive and inferential statistics. **(48)**

20. Define operational definition and discuss why operational definitions are essential in scientific communication. **(48)**

What to Believe: A Statement of Perspective

21. Discuss six questions that should be considered when critically evaluating a research study. **(49)**

PART II. OVERVIEW

This chapter discusses three reasons for conducting scientific research: (1) to test a hypothesis or tentative explanation concerning a possible relationship between variables; (2) to solve a specific problem; and (3) to replicate or confirm the results of previous research. Replication studies allow researchers to have more confidence in research findings if results are consistent with the results of other studies.

Psychologists use a variety of research methods. The choice of which method to use in a particular study depends in large part on the type of information desired. Because the experimental method offers the most control over conditions that might influence the behavior being studied, it is often the method selected in psychological research. When conducting an experiment, the researcher changes or manipulates one factor (the independent variable) and then observes whether there is a corresponding change in a second factor (the dependent variable). The simplest experiments contain two groups of subjects. The experimental group receives or is exposed to the independent variable, while the control group is not. By comparing the two groups' behavior (as measured by the dependent variable) the researcher may infer a cause-and-effect relationship between the independent variable and the change in the dependent variable.

Psychologists also use a number of other research methods. Survey methods, which include questionnaires and interviews, allow the researcher to describe and summarize the behaviors, attitudes, and values of large groups of people. Because every member of the population of interest cannot be included in a survey, the researcher selects a smaller number of individuals (a sample) to survey. Observational methods allow researchers to directly observe and describe the behaviors of individuals. Often individuals are observed behaving in their normal environment. Case studies are frequently used to provide detailed information concerning a specific individual. Frequently, individuals who provide a "good example" of a particular problem behavior are used for case studies. A final research method, correlational studies, allows the researcher to determine if there is a consistent relationship between two variables. Additionally, the researcher can determine the strength of the relationship between the variables. If two variables show a positive correlation, an increase in one variable would be accompanied by an increase in the second variable. In a negative correlation, an increase in one variable would be accompanied by a decrease in the second variable. Unlike experimental studies, correlational studies do not allow the researcher to infer a cause-and-effect relationship between the two variables.

A description of the ethical guidelines for conducting research is also included in this chapter. Ethical guidelines cover topics such as informed consent, the protection of the subject's confidentiality, and the treatment of animals. Ethical guidelines also describe when it is appropriate to use deception in experiments.

Chapter 2 concludes with a brief discussion of statistics. Descriptive statistics help to reduce the data into a form that is more easily understood. The three measures of central tendency (mean, median, mode) provide different methods to describe the typical score. Measures of variability (range, standard deviation) provide information about how closely together or spread out the scores are. Inferential statistics are typically more sophisticated mathematical techniques that allow the researcher to infer or conclude if the results obtained in the experiment are the result of the experimental manipulation (independent variable) or the result that could have been obtained by chance alone.

PART III. KEY TERMS/MATCHING EXERCISES

Match the following concepts and/or individuals with the appropriate descriptions. Check your answers against the Answer Key.

Research Methods (Overview)

Concepts

_d_ 1. case study (**42-43**)   _c_ 4. observational (**42**)

_e_ 2. correlational (**44**)   _b_ 5. survey (**38**)

_a_ 3. experimental (**34**)

Descriptions

a. Allows for conclusions about cause-and-effect relationships

b. Provides information concerning attitudes and behaviors

c. Eliminates the possibility of inaccurate reports supplied by the subjects either intentionally or unintentionally

d. Commonly focuses on a specific individual

e. Provides information concerning the relationship between two variables

Answer Key   1. d   2. e   3. a   4. c   5. b

Research Methods (Experimental and Survey)

Concepts

_e_ 1. independent variable **(32-33)**   _a_ 6. sample **(38-39)**
_i_ 2. dependent variable **(32-33)**   _j_ 7. representative sample **(39)**
_d_ 3. experimental group **(33)**   _f_ 8. random sample **(39)**
_c_ 4. control group **(33)**   _h_ 9. questionnaire **(40)**
_g_ 5. ethical guidelines **(37)**   _b_ 10. interview **(40)**

Descriptions

a. Used because it is usually impossible to study all members of the group or population of interest to the researcher

b. Allows the researcher to clarify confusing questions

c. Subjects who do not receive the independent variable

d. Subjects who receive the independent variable

e. Condition or factor that the researcher manipulates

f. May not accurately reflect or "mimic" the characteristics of the entire population of interest to the researcher

g. Associated with deception, debriefing, and the protection of confidentiality

h. Involves an individual answering a written list of questions

i. Measure of behavior

j. Would include individuals who reflect or "mimic" the characteristics of the entire population of interest to the researcher

Answer Key   1. e   2. i   3. d   4. c   5. g   6. a   7. j   8. f   9. h   10. b

Research Methods (Observational, Case Study, and Correlational)

Concepts

_c_ 1. naturalistic observation **(41)**   _a_ 4. coefficient of correlation **(44)**
_f_ 2. observer bias **(42)**   _e_ 5. positive correlation **(44)**
_b_ 3. observer effect **(42)**   _d_ 6. negative correlation **(45)**

Description

a. Varies between −1.00 and +1.00

b. The tendency of individuals to modify their behavior because of the researcher's presence.

c. Assesses behavior in a natural setting

d. Indicates that an increase in one variable is accompanied by a decrease in a second variable

e. Indicates that an increase in one variable is accompanied by an increase in a second variable

f. Tendency of a researcher to misinterpret behavior

Answer Key   1. c   2. f   3. b   4. a   5. e   6. d

Describing and Interpreting Research Findings (Statistics)

Concepts

_f_ 1. descriptive statistics **(46)**   _c_ 4. measures of variability **(46-47)**

_b_ 2. inferential statistics **(48)**   _a_ 5. operational definition **(48)**

_d_ 3. measures of central tendency **(46)**   _e_ 6. statistics **(46)**

Descriptions

a. Specifies the procedures or techniques used to measure or observe a variable

b. Mathematical methods used to draw conclusions about the meaning of data

c. Reflects the distribution of scores from a group of scores

d. Reflects the middle, average, or typical score from a group of scores

e. Mathematical methods used to describe and interpret data

f. Reduce a quantity of data to a form that is more understandable

Answer Key   1. f   2. b   3. d   4. c   5. a   6. e

Concepts

_e_ 1. mean **(46)**   _f_ 5. range **(47)**

_g_ 2. median **(46)**   _b_ 6. standard deviation **(47)**

_c_ 3. mode **(46)**   _d_ 7. statistical significance **(48)**

_a_ 4. normal distribution **(46)**

Descriptions

a. Exists when the three measures of central tendency are close together

b. Takes into account all scores in a group of scores and indicates how closely individual scores are clustered around the average score

c. Most frequently occurring score in a group of scores

d. Mathematical measure that allows the researcher to determine, with a high level of confidence, if the independent variable was responsible for the difference in scores between the experimental and control group

e. Arithmetic average of a group of scores

f. Difference between the highest and lowest scores in a group of scores

g. Score that falls in the middle of a distribution of a group of scores

Answer Key   1. e   2. g   3. c   4. a   5. f   6. b   7. d

PART IV. TRUE-FALSE STATEMENTS

Fill in the blank before each statement with either a T (true) or an F (false). Check your answers against the Answer Key. Then go back to the items that are false and make the necessary change(s) to the statements to convert the items into true statements.

Research Methods

_____ 1. A replication study would be conducted in order to solve a problem.

_____

_____

_____ 2. The research method that allows the researcher the greatest amount of control over relevant factors is the case study method.

_____

_____

_____ 3. In the experimental method, the control group does not receive the experimental manipulation (the IV).

_____

_____

_____ 4. The ethical guidelines for conducting research with humans state that it is never appropriate to deceive the subject.

_____

_____

_____ 5. A main consideration for researchers conducting survey research involves the manner by which subjects are selected from the population to participate in the survey.

_____

_____

_____ 6. Observer bias relates to the potential drawback of observational studies characterized by participants altering their behavior as a result of the researcher's presence.

_____

_____

_____ 7. One major limitation of case studies is that it is often difficult to generalize findings from the individual used to other individuals.

_____

_____

_____ 8. If you are interested in uncovering cause-and-effect relationships between two variables, you would use the correlational method.

_____

_____

Describing and Interpreting Research Findings

_____ 9. Descriptive statistics involve measures of central tendency, measures of variability, and measures of significance.

_____

_____

_____ 10. The standard deviation is a more sensitive measure of variability than the range.

_____

_____

_____ 11. Inferential statistics allow researchers to draw inferences of conclusions concerning the effect of the experimental manipulation.

_____

_____

Answer Key	1. F **(29)**	5. T **(40)**	9. F **(46)**
	2. F **(32)**	6. F **(42)**	10. T **(47)**
	3. T **(33)**	7. T **(43)**	11. T **(48)**
	4. F **(37-38)**	8. F **(45-46)**	

PART V. MULTIPLE-CHOICE QUESTIONS

Choose the best answer to each question. Circle your choice. Check your answers against the Answer Key. Questions marked with an asterisk (*) include annotated answers.

Reasons for Conducting Research

1. Which of the following is _not_ a reason to conduct research?

 a. To confirm previous findings
 b. To uncover serendipity
 c. To solve a problem
 d. To test an hypothesis

2. Because results of a study may vary considerably depending on the exact experimental conditions and research method used, _____ studies serve an important purpose.

 a. experimental
 b. redundant
 c. replication
 d. control

3. The results of previous research and the psychologist's observations of behavior are two common sources of

 a. operational definitions.
 b. serendipity.
 c. hypotheses.
 d. theories.

Research Methods

4. One problem with research methods used in psychology—with the exception of the experimental method—is that they

   a. take too long.
   b. require more effort.
   c. cost more.
   d. do not allow for precise control over factors influencing the outcome.

5. If a researcher is interested in an in-depth study concerning the long-term consequences physical disabilities have on psychological adjustment, this researcher would most likely use the *case-study* method.

   a. case-study
   b. interview
   c. observational
   d. experimental

6. If a researcher is interested in the relationship between birth order (first, second, third born) and popularity, this researcher would most likely use the *correlational* method.

   a. experimental
   b. survey
   c. correlational
   d. observational

7. Normally, which scientific method of research is used to learn about people's opinions, attitudes, and values?

   a. Survey
   b. Experimental
   c. Naturalistic observation
   d. Case study

8. A number of techniques such as observation, questionnaires, interviews, and experimentation may be utilized by a researcher using the *case-study* method.

   a. clinical
   b. survey
   c. inferential
   d. case-study

9. A researcher is interested in the effects of vitamin W on physical endurance. The control group would

   a. receive a different vitamin (for example, vitamin C).
   b. not receive vitamin W.
   c. receive vitamin W.
   d. not be measured on the dependent variable.

*10. In the example described in question 9, the researcher needs to

    a. identify the research method used.

    b. correlate physical endurance with the dependent variable.

    c. measure the behavior of both the experimental and control groups on the independent variable.

    d. supply an operational definition of physical endurance.

11. Which of the following pairs of terms do *not* belong together?

    a. Independent variable, control group

    b. Independent variable, experimental group

    c. Dependent variable, control group

    d. Dependent variable, experimental group

12. The condition or factor that an experimenter manipulates is the _indep._ variable.

    a. representative sample

    b. dependent

    c. independent

    d. critical

*13. In Milgram's obedience to authority study described in the text, the dependent variable was

    a. whether or not the subjects had sadistic personalities.

    b. whether or not the subjects really believed they were administering shocks to the other individual.

    c. whether or not the subjects experienced stress when administering the shocks.

    d. how many painful shocks the subjects administered.

14. The most controversial of the ethical guidelines for conducting research with humans concerns

    a. debriefing.

    b. deception.

    c. the protection of confidentiality.

    d. informed consent.

15. Survey research includes both

    a. public opinion polls and case studies.

    b. interviews and case studies.

    c. questionnaires and interviews.

    d. questionnaires and observational studies.

16. Which type of sample would *least likely* be demographically biased?

    a. Representative sample

    b. Natural sample

    c. Random sample

    d. All of the above would show demographic bias.

17. One advantage the survey method of questionnaires has over interviews is that questionnaire studies

  a. are more flexible.
  b. usually provide more detailed information about an individual subject.
  c. allow the researcher to clarify confusing questions.
  d. usually take less time to complete.

18. When researchers want to explore a question concerning a large population they must

  a. use every individual in the population.
  b. select a research sample of the population.
  c. use only a correlational approach.
  d. use the help of census takers.

19. Secretly observing people in a fast-food restaurant and noting each time someone bites into a hamburger is an example of the _____ method.

  a. experimental
  b. case-study
  c. naturalistic observation
  d. survey

20. If correctly used, the observational method frequently results in the researcher

  a. calculating the coefficient of correlation.
  b. developing hypotheses to be examined more completely through the use of other research methods.
  c. interpreting why the observed behaviors occurred.
  d. concluding that his or her original hypothesis was correct.

21. Children assigned arbitrary labels of normal, emotionally disturbed, or intellectually impaired were rated by their teachers. These ratings were clearly influenced by the labels applied to each child. This problem is called

  a. observer bias.
  b. observer effect.
  c. human nature.
  d. case study.

22. Which of the following is *not* a limitation of the case-study method?

  a. The research project may last for months or even years
  b. The researcher lacks investigative control over all potentially relevant variables
  c. Not all relevant data or information are directly observed by the researcher
  d. The potential of bias by the researcher

*23. Which of the following pairs of variables would you expect to show the highest positive correlation?

  a. The stock market/interest rates
  b. How many semesters a student has been at college/a student's overall grade-point average (GPA)
  c. The age of a child/his or her height
  d. The amount of allowance a child receives each week/how old the family car is

24. A high correlation (either positive or negative) indicates that

    a. the scores on the two variables are nearly identical.

    b. a change in one variable caused a change in the second variable.

    c. a third factor or variable was always responsible for the observed relationship between the variables.

    d. There was a high level of consistency in the relationship between the two variables.

Describing and Interpreting Research Findings

*25. In addition to your test score, your professor will give you only one piece of information concerning your test performance relative to that of your classmates. Which of the following statistics would give you the most useful information?

    a. Mean

    b. Percentile

    c. Standard deviation

    d. Median

26. Which of the following terms does *not* belong with the others?

    a. Range

    b. Mode

    c. Measures of central tendency

    d. Mean

27. A distribution of scores in which most scores fall relatively close to the mean score would have a

    a. low standard deviation.

    b. high standard deviation.

    c. low range.

    d. There is not enough information given to allow for a conclusion.

28. In the following distribution of scores—1, 4, 4, 5, 6, 8, 8, 8, 10—the median score is

    a. 6

    b. 7

    c. 8

    d. 9

29. In the distribution of scores listed in question 28 the mode is

    a. 6

    b. 7

    c. 8

    d. 9

30. The distance between extreme measures of scores is referred to as the

    a. average.

    b. range.

    c. mean.

    d. median.

31. Inferential statistics allow the researcher to

a. determine measures of variability.

b. calculate correlations.

c. determine if differences between groups of subjects are due to experimental manipulation or to chance.

d. reduce a quantity of data to a form that is more easily understood.

What to Believe: A Statement of Perspective

*32. The most important question to ask when evaluating a survey study is:

a. Was there a control group?

b. Was there bias in the selection of subjects?

c. Have there been other surveys that confirm the results of this study?

d. Did a reputable professional conduct the survey?

Answer Key

1. b	(28)	8. d	(42-43)	15. c	(40)	21. a	(42)	27. a	(47)
2. c	(30)	9. b	(33)	16. a	(38-39)	22. a	(43)	28. a	(46)
3. c	(28)	*10. d	(48)	17. d	(40)	*23. c	(44)	29. c	(46)
4. d	(32)	11. a	(33)	18. b	(39)	24. d	(44)	30. b	(47)
5. a	(42-43)	12. c	(32-33)	19. c	(41)	*25. b	(48)	31. c	(48)
6. c	(44)	*13. d	(36)	20. b	(41)	26. a	(46)	*32. b	(40)
7. a	(38)	14. b	(37)						

Annotated Answers

10. The correct choice is d. The researcher needs to specify exactly how physical endurance will be measured.

a. The research will obviously be an experimental study because there is a control group.

b. Physical endurance is the dependent variable and would not be correlated with itself.

c. The independent variable is the experimental manipulation, it is the dependent variable that is the measure of behavior.

13. The correct choice is d. Milgram recorded the number and severity of shocks administered.

a. The personalities of the subjects were not examined in this study.

b. Although some of the subjects may have had doubts concerning whether or not they were really administering painful shocks, Milgram did not address this issue in this experiment.

c. Milgram did notice that many of the subjects experienced stress, but this stress was neither the central feature of the experiment nor the behavior Milgram measured.

23. The correct choice is c. Because children become taller not shorter, there has to be a positive correlation. To get a feel for how strong or high the correlation would be think of a typical newborn, 2-year-old, 6-year-old, and 10-year-old, and compare their heights.

a. As was described in the text the correlation between the stock market and interest rates is a negative correlation.

b. While there probably is a positive correlation between semesters of college and GPA, it does not seem likely to be as strong a relationship as that between age and height.

d. Most likely there is a negative correlation between allowance and how old the family car is. The less money a family has the smaller the allowance and older the car.

25. The correct choice is b. Your percentile would indicate your relative class standing by supplying information concerning what percentage of classmates received scores lower than yours.

a. The mean would only allow you to know if your score was above or below average.

c. The standard deviation tells you how closely together scores in the distribution are to the mean, but if you do not know what the mean is (as is the case in this example), the standard deviation would provide no useful information.

d. The median would only allow you to know if your test score was in the top half or bottom half of the class.

32. The correct choice is b. If there was significant bias in the sample it would invalidate the results of the study. For example, if a researcher was surveying sexually active teenage girls to determine if they used a form of birth control regularly, he or she would get very different results if the survey was only given to girls at an abortion clinic or only at planned parenthood or to a representative sample.

a. Control groups are not used in survey studies.

c. Although the existence of other surveys with comparable results might give more credibility to this survey's findings, it is not the most important question to ask in this example.

d. Who conducted the survey is a relevant question to ask, but it is not the most important consideration. A very good survey study could be conducted by an individual without extensive scientific training.

PART VI. SUMMARY TABLES

To test your understanding of the material discussed in this chapter complete the following tables. Check your answers with those supplied in PART IX.

Research Methods

Method	How Conducted	Advantages	Limitations
Experimental			
Survey			
Observational			
Case study			
Correlational			

Descriptive Statistics

	(Place a √ in Correct Column) Measure of		How Is It Calculated?
	Central Tendency	Variability	
Mean			
Median			
Mode			
Range			
Standard deviation			See Research Appendix in the text

PART VII. THOUGHT QUESTIONS/CRITICAL THINKING

Prepare answers to the following discussion questions.

1. Different research methods vary greatly in the way information is gathered, the type of information collected, and how the information is compiled or interpreted. Frequently a researcher has some degree of choice in selecting the appropriate method. For example, if a researcher was interested in studying "helping behavior" he or she might:

    a. Design an experimental situation in which one person would need help and then measure under what conditions other people would be most likely to give assistance
    b. Conduct a survey asking people about how frequently and under what circumstances they have helped others in the past
    c. Use the observational method to observe helping behaviors
    d. Conduct a case study with "good samaritans"
    e. Correlate helping behavior with certain personality traits

    Identify some of the critical features of a research topic that would argue for and/or against the selection of each of the research methods used by psychologists.

2. If you had a choice of research methods to use in order to study a particular problem, which research method would you select? (Do not automatically select the experimental method because it offers the researcher greater control.) Select the method that you feel would supply the mose useful or relevant information or the method that would be most satisfying or interesting for you to conduct. Explain the reasons for your selection.

3. Some adolescents and adults are more popular than others. Imagine that you are interested in asking if "popularity" is also an appropriate concept to use to describe young children. You have unlimited access to a class of third-graders. You have made the following list of questions to study:

a. What, if any, factors are related to popularity in third-graders?

b. Do children differ in popularity?

c. What effect does popularity (and unpopularity) have on a child's schoolwork?

In what order (first, second, third) would you address these questions? Which research method would you use to study each question?

4. Many people do not like complex mathematical calculations. These people might say, "Because descriptive statistics give a researcher a lot of information, why do we need inferential statistics?" How would you explain to these people why scientific research needs inferential statistics?

PART VIII. APPLICATIONS

1. You would like to lose 25 pounds. In the local newspaper you see advertisements for two weight-loss programs:

    a. The "Say Goodbye to Fat, Inc." ad explains that their medically approved diet supplement (which is eaten before each meal) plan results in rapid weight loss when used along with a vigorous exercise program. The ad quotes a woman who says she lost over 100 pounds in the past year as a result of the diet supplement and two hours of exercise each day.

    b. The "Quick Weight Loss, Limited" ad explains that by using hypnosis and post-hypnotic suggestions your desire to eat will be cut in half and the pounds will fade away. The ad quotes a woman who says that since her first orientation session last week she has lost 11 pounds and can't wait to see the results after four or six months.

    You decide to check out each of the programs before you decide to sign up with one. At the "Say Goodbye to Fat" meeting you overhear someone say that in addition to the diet supplement and exercise she has also stopped having her traditional bedtime snack. You also notice one of the assistants telling a group member that she had "better shape up" or she would lose her deposit. At the "Quick Weight Loss" meeting you overhear someone say that they have also started to eat a commercially available instant breakfast.

    Evaluate each of the programs for strengths and weaknesses. Which program would you be more likely to join? It would be a hard decision to make solely on the information provided. In order to make the best-informed decision possible, prepare a list of questions that you would ask the director of each of the programs.

2. The text notes that the experimental method is often the research method of choice for psychologists. Imagine that instead of being a student in general psychology, you are a lab assistant in charge of the laboratory sections of the general psychology class. Periodically throughout the semester you would like to use the students in the lab sections as subjects in experiments designed to illustrate the different topics discussed in class. You decide to introduce the experimental method by conducting an experiment on either the effect of amount of time studying a list of Spanish vocabulary words on how much information is learned or the effect of exercise on heart rate.

    a. What is your hypothesis?

    b. Write a paragraph explaining exactly what procedure you will use to conduct the experiment.

    c. Identify the independent variable.

d. Identify the dependent variable and explain how it will be measured.

e. Identify the experimental group(s).

f. Identify the control group.

g. Explain how you would assign subjects to the experimental and control groups.

h. Provide any necessary operational definitions.

i. Evaluate your experiment in regards to the APA's ethical guidelines. Even though this experiment is only a classroom exercise and not a "real" experiment, you must adhere to the guidelines.

j. How would you compare the experimental and control groups on their performance on the dependent variable? Using only descriptive statistics, how would you present the results (that is, would you calculate means, percentiles, or whatever)?

k. Predict what differences in behavior you would find if your hypothesis was confirmed by the results of the experiment.

PART IX. SUMMARY TABLES SOLUTIONS

Research Methods

Method	How Conducted	Advantages	Limitations
Experimental	Manipulate IV and look for a change in the DV	Precise control Can infer cause and effect	Artificial situation Not all variables can be manipulated
Survey	Use questionnaires and interviews to ask people about attitudes, behaviors, and values	Supplies a lot of information with relative ease	Sample may be biased Accuracy of reports Can't examine individuals in detail
Observational	Observe ongoing behavior frequently in a natural setting	Behavior is not "artificial" Direct observation by researcher	Observer bias Observer effect
Case study	In-depth study of one individual (or group of individuals)	More insight into individual is possible	Lack of experimental control Bias by researcher May be difficult to generalize to other individuals
Correlational	Measure relationship between two variables	Can study variables that would be impossible to manipulate in an experiment	Cannot infer a cause-and-effect relationship

Descriptive Statistics

	(Place a √ in Correct Column) Measure of		How Is It Calculated?
	Central Tendency	Variability	
Mean	√		Add up all scores and divide by the number of scores
Median	√		Arrange all scores in order from lowest to highest and select the score that falls in the middle of the distribution
Mode	√		Select the most frequently occurring score
Range		√	Subtract the lowest score from the highest score
Standard deviation		√	See Research Appendix in the text

CHAPTER 3

Biological Foundations of Behavior

PART I. LEARNING OBJECTIVES

When you finish studying this chapter you should be able to:

Overview of the Nervous System: Organization and Function

1. Briefly describe the major components and functions of the central nervous system (CNS) and peripheral nervous system (PNS). **(56)**

Neurons: Basic Units of the Nervous System

2. Define neuron and describe the functions of the three classes of neurons. **(56, 58)**

3. Identify the four main parts of a neuron and describe the functions of each part. **(58)**

4. Describe the electrical changes that result in a neuron firing an impulse and describe the resting potential, graded potentials, and action potential. **(59)**

5. Explain two factors that affect the speed at which an impulse travels through a neuron. **(60-61)**

6. Describe the process by which neurotransmitters excite and inhibit the transmission of neural impulses between neurons. **(64)**

7. Discuss evidence indicating that neurotransmitters may be directly related to schizophrenia, depression, and drug-related behaviors. **(64)**

8. Define endogenous opiates and discuss some of the brain functions these are believed to influence. **(66)**

The Brain and the Spinal Cord

9. Describe the overall appearance of the human brain. **(66, 68)**

10. Describe the structure and functions of the spinal cord and spinal nerves. **(68-69)**

11. Describe the functions and location in the brain of the medulla, pons, cerebellum, and reticular formation. **(69-71)**

12. Identify the general functions of the limbic system and describe the specific functions of its components: amygdala, hippocampus, and septal area. **(72-73)**

13. Describe the location and functions of the hypothalamus. **(75-76)**

14. Describe the location and functions of the thalamus. **(76)**

15. Describe the physical structure and primary functions of the cerebral cortex and identify the sensory, motor, and association cortex. **(76-77)**

16. Name and identify the location of the four lobes of the cortex and indicate the specialized functions of each lobe. **(77-80)**

17. Define lateralization of function and describe the amount of lateralization of function that exists in the cortex. **(80)**

18. Describe the split-brain procedure and discuss the effects this procedure has on the overall functioning of the brain. **(80-83)**

19. Discuss whether or not it is appropriate to consider one hemisphere of the cortex to be dominant. **(83)**

20. Name and describe three invasive techniques used to study the brain. **(85-86)**

21. Name and describe four noninvasive techniques used to study the brain. **(86-89)**

The Peripheral Nervous System

22. Discuss the functions of the somatic and autonomic nervous systems. **(89-91)**

23. Compare and contrast the functioning of the sympathetic and parasympathetic nervous systems. **(89-91)**

The Endocrine System

24. Briefly describe the major components and functioning of the endocrine system. **(91-93)**

25. Discuss how the nervous and endocrine systems work together to govern behavior. **(92-93)**

26. Identify the functions of the pituitary gland, thyroid gland, adrenal glands, and the gonads. **(93-94)**

PART II. OVERVIEW

Two systems—the nervous system and the endocrine system—combine to govern internal physical responses, behaviors, and mental processes. Chapter 3 describes the structure and function of both systems.

The nervous system sends messages between parts of the body through an electro-chemical process. The basic unit of the nervous system is the neuron. The main parts of the neuron are: the dendrites (which receive impulses from other neurons); the cell body (which handles the cell's metabolic functions); the axon (which transmits the impulse away from the cell body toward other neurons); and at the end of the axon the terminal buttons (which secrete neurotransmitters into the synapse [the space between neurons] where the impulse will begin to stimulate the dendrites of the next neuron). The process by which a neuron "decides" to transmit a neural impulse is electrical in nature. A neuron that is not receiving any neural impulses is at the resting potential. As a neuron receives input, electrical changes or graded potentials occur. When the neuron receives a critical amount of input, the electrical state of the neuron again changes and the neuron fires its action potential or impulse down the axon to the terminal buttons. The process that allows the impulse to cross the synapse from one neuron to stimulate the next neuron is chemical in nature and controlled by the presence of neurotransmitters.

The nervous system has two main divisions. The first division, the central nervous system (CNS), consists of the brain and spinal cord. The cerebral cortex, which is responsible for higher mental processes, is described in detail. The text also describes the location and functions of a number of other brain structures (medulla, pons, cerebellum, reticular formation, limbic system, hypothalamus, and thalamus).

The second main division of the nervous system is the peripheral nervous system (PNS). The PNS consists of the somatic nervous system that controls the major skeletal muscles and transmits information to and from the CNS. The autonomic nervous system, which controls the internal organs and glands, is divided into two divisions that have opposing effects. The sympathetic nervous system (which assumes control in emergency situations) tends to influence a number of organs to operate at their upper limits (for example, heart rate is increased) to help deal with an emergency situation. The parasympathetic nervous system tends to influence organs to operate at reduced or "normal" levels of functioning.

The endocrine system consists of a number of glands that influence internal physical responses by secreting hormones into the bloodstream. These hormones affect specific organs or functions of the body. The pituitary gland is an important endocrine gland that exerts an influence on many other endocrine glands. The functioning of the pituitary gland is controlled by the hypothalamus in the CNS. The text also describes the functions of the thyroid gland, adrenal gland, and gonads.

PART III. KEY TERMS/MATCHING EXERCISES

Match the following concepts and/or individuals with the appropriate descriptions. Check your answers against the Answer Key.

Overview of the Nervous System

Concepts

_c_ 1. peripheral nervous system **(56)**

_d_ 2. sympathetic nervous system **(89, 91)**

_b_ 3. central nervous system **(56)**

_e_ 4. parasympathetic nervous system **(89, 91)**

_a_ 5. interneuron **(58)**

_g_ 6. motor (efferent) neuron **(58)**

_f_ 7. sensory (afferent) neuron **(56, 58)**

Descriptions

a. Present in the spinal cord and brain

b. Plays a central role in coordinating and integrating all bodily functions

c. Consists of the somatic and autonomic nervous systems

d. Activated in emergency situations and causes heart rate and breathing to increase

e. Counteracts the responses described in d above.

f. Relays or sends messages from the body to the spinal cord and brain

g. Relays or sends messages from the brain and spinal cord to the muscles and glands

Answer Key   1. c   2. d   3. b   4. e   5. a   6. g   7. f

Neurons

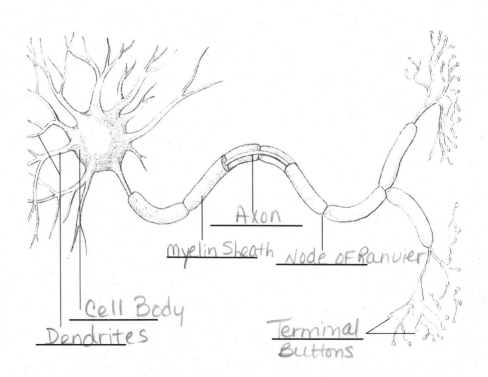

Cell Body

Dendrites

Axon

Myelin Sheath   Node of Ranvier

Terminal Buttons

In addition to the standard matching exercise, label the diagram on page 40 with the correct numbers.

Concepts

_e_ 1. node of Ranvier **(61)**   _a_ 4. cell body **(58)**

_c_ 2. axon **(60)**   _b_ 5. dendrites **(58)**

_f_ 3. terminal buttons **(59)**   _d_ 6. myelin sheath **(61)**

Descriptions

a. Controls the metabolic functions of the neuron

b. Receives information from other neurons

c. Sends the action potential toward other neurons

d. Composed of insulating glia cells

e. Exposed or uninsulated areas of the axon

f. Release neurotransmitters

Answer Key   1. e   2. c   3. f   4. a   5. b   6. d

Check your labeled diagram against Figure 3.2 on page 58 in the text.

Neurotransmission

Concepts

_c_ 1. graded potentials **(60)**   _e_ 4. synapse **(62)**

_b_ 2. neurotransmitters **(62)**   _d_ 5. resting potential **(59)**

_a_ 3. action potential **(60)**

Descriptions

a. Electrical state that occurs in an all-or-none manner

b. Chemicals that move between two neurons

c. Vary in relation to the intensity of stimulation and distance from the point of stimulation

d. Polarized electrical state of a neuron when it is not receiving information or impulses from other neurons

e. Relates to where neurotransmission is primarily a chemical process

Answer Key   1. c   2. b   3. a   4. e   5. d

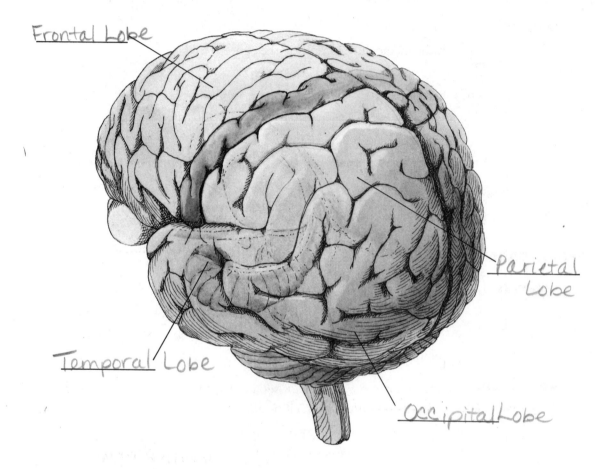

Brain Structures

Concepts

_i_ 1. cerebellum **(71)**   _c_ 6. medulla **(69)**
_f_ 2. cerebrum **(76-77)**   _e_ 7. pons **(69)**
_d_ 3. corpus callosum **(80)**   _h_ 8. reticular formation **(71)**
_a_ 4. hypothalamus **(75-76)**   _g_ 9. thalamus **(76)**
_b_ 5. limbic system **(72)**

Descriptions

a. Involved in basic motivation, emotional expression, and control of the endocrine system
b. Contains the amygdala, hippocampus, and septal areas; also involved in emotional expression
c. Controls vital functions such as breathing, heart rate, and blood pressure
d. Nerve fibers that connect the two cerebral hemispheres
e. Controls species-specific behaviors and influences facial expressions
f. Composed of the "gray matter" and "white matter"
g. Directs sensory information to the appropriate areas of the cortex
h. Plays a critical role in arousal or alertness
i. Provides fine-tuning or control of body movements

Answer Key   1. i   2. f   3. d   4. a   5. b   6. c   7. e   8. h   9. g

The Cerebral Cortex

In addition to the standard matching exercise, label the diagram on page 42 with the correct numbers associated with the four lobes of the cortex.

Concepts

_e_ 1. temporal lobe **(79)**   _d_ 4. frontal lobe **(77-78)**
_f_ 2. parietal lobe **(78-79)**   _c_ 5. lateralization of function **(80)**
_a_ 3. association cortex **(77)** _b_ 6. occipital lobe **(79)**

Descriptions

a. Involved in higher mental functions and consists of 75 percent of the cortex
b. Contains the visual cortex
c. Degree to which a particular function is controlled by only one side of the cortex
d. Contains the motor cortex, Broca's area, and is involved in emotional expression
e. Contains the auditory cortex and Wernicke's area
f. Contains the somatosensory cortex

Answer Key   1. e   2. f   3. a   4. d   5. c   6. b

Check your labeled diagram against Figure 3.6 on page 70 in the text.

The Endocrine System

Concepts

_____ 1. adrenal gland (**93-94**)   _____ 4. hormones (**91**)

_____ 2. endocrine system (**91**)   _____ 5. pituitary gland (**93**)

_____ 3. gonads (**94**)   _____ 6. thyroid gland (**93**)

Descriptions

a. Chemicals secreted into the bloodstream that influence target organs

b. Secretes hormones that act in association with the sympathetic nervous system and also increase metabolism

c. Releases a number of hormones that influence other glands

d. Another way, along with the nervous system, that the body governs behavior

e. Regulates metabolism

f. Secrete estrogens and/or androgens

Answer Key   1. b   2. d   3. f   4. a   5. c   6. e

PART IV. TRUE-FALSE STATEMENTS

Fill in the blank before each statement with either a T (true) or an F (false). Check your answers against the Answer Key. Then go back to the items that are false and make the necessary change(s) to the statements to convert the items into true statements.

Neurons

_F_ 1. The terminal buttons of one neuron secrete neurotransmitters into the synapse where they stimulate the axon of a second neuron.

_____

_____

_T_ 2. When the sum of all the graded potentials reaches a threshold, an action potential is triggered.

_____

_____

_F_ 3. Axons insulated with myelin sheaths conduct the action potential at a faster rate than uninsulated axons.

_____

_____

_T_ 4. Neurotransmitters may have either an excitatory or inhibitory effect on the postsynaptic membrane.

_____

_____

The Brain and the Spinal Cord

_T_ 5. The pons is the lowest part of the brain and is located directly above the spinal cord.

_____

_____

_T_ 6. Considerable damage to the frontal lobe would be likely to affect the emotional life of an individual.

_____

_____

_F_ 7. The cerebellum is the brain structure responsible for higher mental processes such as perceiving, thinking, and remembering.

_____

_____

_F_ 8. Approximately 75 percent of the human cortex consists of the motor and sensory cortex.

_____

_____

_F_ 9. Many of the new techniques to study the brain do not require surgery and are therefore considered to be noninvasive.

_____

_____

The Peripheral Nervous System

_F_ 10. The somatic nervous system controls the smooth muscles, internal organs, and glands of the body.

_____

_____

_T_ 11. Following the body's response to an emergency situation, the parasympathetic nervous system resumes control of bodily functions, such as heart rate and digestion.

_____

_____

The Endocrine System

_T_ 12. Some of the chemical substances in the body function as both hormones and neurotransmitters.

_____

_____

_F_ 13. The pituitary gland is considered the "master gland" because it secretes hormones that stimulate the hypothalamus to release additional hormones.

_____

_____

_____ 14. The activation of the encodrine system has a more immediate effect on behavior than does activation of the nervous system.

_____

_____

Answer Key

1. F **(59)**	6. T **(78)**	11. T **(91)**
2. T **(60)**	7. F **(71)**	12. T **(91-92)**
3. T **(61)**	8. F **(77)**	13. F **(93)**
4. T **(64)**	9. T **(86)**	14. F **(91-92)**
5. F **(69)**	10. F **(89)**	

PART V. MULTIPLE-CHOICE QUESTIONS

Choose the best answer to each question. Circle your choice. Check your answers against the Answer Key. Questions marked with an asterisk (*) include annotated answers.

Overview of the Nervous System

1. The two major divisions of the nervous system are the

  a. brain and spinal cord.
  b. central nervous system and endocrine system.
  c. central nervous system and peripheral nervous system.
  d. central nervous system and autonomic nervous system.

Neurons

2. Afferent nerves send messages _toward_ the spinal cord and brain.

  a. away from
  b. toward
  c. within
  d. slowly away from

3. The part of the neuron that receives impulses from other neurons is the

  a. axon.
  b. dendrites.
  c. synapse.
  d. terminal buttons.

*4. Which is the last part of the neuron to be involved in the transmission of a neural impulse toward the next neuron?

  a. Axon hillock
  b. Cell body
  c. Dendrites
  d. Terminal buttons

5. The process by which neural impulses are transmitted within the central nervous system is

    a. not chemical in nature.
    b. seen only in the brain.
    c. electrochemical in nature.
    d. the same as electricity through a wire.

*6. As a neuron is receiving an excitatory impulse from another neuron the cell membrane becomes

    a. depolarized.
    b. polarized.
    c. impermeable to ions.
    d. a graded potential.

7. Which of the following follows the all-or-none law?

    a. Graded potentials
    b. Electrical potentials
    c. Resting potentials
    d. Action potentials

8. Two factors that relate to the perceived intensity of a stimuli are how many neurons are firing action potentials and

    a. if the axons have myelin sheaths.
    b. the voltage associated with each action potential.
    c. the rate at which these neurons are firing.
    d. whether the supply of neurotransmitters is exhausted.

9. If IPSPs did not exist

    a. it would be "easier" for a neuron to fire its action potential.
    b. it would be "harder" for a neuron to fire its action potential.
    c. there would be no effect on the ease with which a neuron fires its action potential.
    d. it would be impossible for neural impulses to travel across the synapse.

10. Some psychologists hypothesize that schizophrenia may be linked to

    a. the presence of substances that mimic neurotransmitters.
    b. the levels of or sensitivity to a specific neurotransmitter.
    c. faulty neural connections in the brain.
    d. the presence of substances that prevent the transmission of a neural impulse across the synaptic gap.

11. Which of the following has an effect on the body similar to morphine?

    a. Serotonin
    b. Acetylcholine
    c. Dopamine
    d. Endorphins

12. Which of the following has *not* been associated with the presence of endogenous opioids?

    a. A counteracting of the negative effects of stress.
    b. A sense of well-being and euphoria.
    c. A greater sensitivity to painful stimuli.
    d. Changes in food and liquid intake.

The Brain and the Spinal Cord

13. Basic reflexive behaviors, such as the quick withdrawal of a hand from a hot stove, are controlled by the

    a. lower brain centers.
    b. spinal cord.
    c. limbic system.
    d. cortex.

14. Sensory input from the eyes is relayed to the visual cortex by the

    a. thalamus.
    b. hypothalamus.
    c. pons.
    d. reticular activating system.

15. If an animal's amygdala is electrically stimulated, that animal would

    a. go into a blind rage.
    b. experience a sensation that could be labeled "pleasure."
    c. become aroused or alert.
    d. enter a comalike sleep.

*16. If a person had an auto accident and suffered brain damage, and afterward had awkward, jerky, and uncoordinated movements, the damaged part of that person's brain would most likely be the

    a. motor cortex.
    b. spinal cord.
    c. cerebellum.
    d. myelin sheaths.

17. The reticular formation plays a role in

    a. life-supporting functions such as breathing and heartbeat.
    b. the fine-tuning of motor messages.
    c. coordinating and regulating motor movements.
    d. controlling levels of arousal and alertness.

18. Over which of the following does the hypothalamus *not* exert control?

    a. The endocrine system
    b. Emotional expression
    c. Arousal and alertness
    d. Basic motivations (eating, drinking, sexual behavior)

19. The association cortex is another name for the

   a. area of the cortex involved with higher mental processes and integrating sensory and motor messages.
   b. area of the cerebrum that is underneath and directly associated with the cerebral cortex.
   c. sensory and motor cortex.
   d. frontal lobe.

20. If you were to electrically stimulate a person's occipital lobe they would most likely

   a. have difficulty recalling their phone number.
   b. report a visual experience.
   c. move a part of their body.
   d. report an auditory experience.

21. Individuals with damage to _Broca's area_ have difficulty articulating speech, while individuals with damage to _Wernicke's area_ have difficulty comprehending speech.

   a. cortex | reticular formation
   b. Broca's area | Wernicke's area
   c. Wernicke's area | Broca's area
   d. central fissure | corpus callosum

22. If a split-brain operated patient sees "airxplane" briefly while focusing on the "x," he or she would say they saw the word

   a. plane.
   b. airplane.
   c. air.
   d. That patient would report that he or she did not see a word.

23. Research on lateralization of function suggests that the right hemisphere is better than the left in

   a. tasks involving the use of logic.
   b. perceiving spatial relationships.
   c. math.
   d. verbal ability.

24. Which of the following is an invasive technique used to study the functions of the brain?

   a. Positron emission tomography (PET)
   b. Electroencephalography (EEG)
   c. Neurometrics
   d. Electrical recording

The Peripheral Nervous System

25. The two major divisions of the peripheral nervous system are the ___somatic autonomic___ nervous systems.

   a. afferent and efferent
   b. sympathetic and parasympathetic
   c. somatic and parasympathetic
   d. somatic and autonomic

26. Which of the following is *not* controlled by the autonomic nervous system?

a. The major skeletal muscles
b. Digestion
c. Pupil size
d. Heart rate

27. If you hit your thumb with a hammer, which nervous system sends the pain message to your brain?

a. Somatic nervous system
b. Central nervous system
c. Autonomic nervous system
d. Corpus callosum

28. Our normal state (somewhere between extreme excitement and complete relaxation) is maintained by

a. the sympathetic nervous system.
b. the parasympathetic nervous system.
c. a balance between the sympathetic and parasympathetic nervous systems.
d. the reticular activating system.

*29. One major difference between the sympathetic and parasympathetic nervous systems is that the sympathetic nervous system

a. increases the level of functioning in all the affected bodily systems.
b. decreases the level of functioning in all the affected bodily systems.
c. stimulates the different parts of the body independently of one another.
d. simultaneously stimulates the different parts of the body.

The Endocrine System

30. The brain structure that most directly influences the endocrine system is the

a. thalamus.
b. hypothalamus.
c. temporal lobe.
d. limbic system.

*31. While the nervous system originally turns on the body's response to an emergency situation, the endocrine system

a. returns the body's response to normal after the emergency is over.
b. controls our cognitive reaction to the emergency situation.
c. sustains the body's response.
d. moderates or limits the body's response.

32. The pituitary hormones

a. have a variety of target organs.
b. have the thyroid as their only target organ.
c. directly influence the hypothalamus to begin secreting hormones.
d. become neuropeptides.

33. The part of the endocrine system that is most closely associated with activation of the sympathetic nervous system is the

   a. gonads.
   b. pituitary gland.
   c. adrenal medulla.
   d. adrenal cortex.

34. The thyroid gland secretes thyroxine, which

   a. is also called growth hormone.
   b. is associated with fear and rage.
   c. regulates metabolism.
   d. is responsible for the development of secondary sex characteristics during puberty.

35. Which of the following does *not* exert a strong influence on the fertility cycle of women?

   a. Progesterone
   b. Androgens
   c. Estrogens
   d. Ovaries

Answer Key

1. c	(56)	8. c	(60-61)	15. a	(72)	22. a	(82-83)	*29. d	(91)
2. b	(56, 58)	9. a	(64)	*16. c	(71)	23. b	(83)	30. b	(92)
3. b	(58)	10. b	(64)	17. d	(71)	24. d	(85)	*31. c	(91-92)
*4. d	(59)	11. d	(66)	18. c	(75-76)	25. d	(89)	32. a	(93)
5. c	(59)	12. c	(66)	19. a	(77)	26. a	(89)	33. c	(93)
*6. a	(60)	13. b	(69)	20. b	(79)	27. a	(89)	34. c	(93)
7. d	(60)	14. a	(76)	21. b	(80)	28. c	(89)	35. b	(94)

Annotated Answers

4. The correct choice is d. The terminal buttons on the transmitting end of the axon release neurotransmitters into the synapse.
   a. The axon hillock is a part of the cell body near the base or beginning of the axon.
   b. The cell body is in the middle of the neuron and is not therefore the last part of the neuron involved in neurotransmission.
   c. The dendrites are the first part of the neuron involved in the transmission of the neural impulse.

6. The correct choice is a. Depolarized relates to the cell membrane becoming less negative, which is what occurs when a neuron receives excitatory impulses.
   b. The membrane is said to be polarized when it is at the resting potential.
   c. If the cell membrane was to become impermeable to ions, these could not pass through the cell membrane and the electrical changes necessary for the neuron to fire its action potential could not occur.
   d. While the situation described in this question would result in a graded potential, the cell membrane does not become a graded potential.

16. The correct choice is c. The cerebellum functions to fine-tune muscle movements that are broadly under the control of higher brain centers.

a. Damage to the motor cortex would leave the person paralyzed in the affected body parts and not just with a lack of smoothness of movement.

b. First, the spinal cord is not part of the brain. Second, damage to the spinal cord would leave the person paralyzed in the affected body parts.

d. Although the absence of myelin sheaths is associated with loss of motor control (as in MS), myelin is not a brain structure and would not be subject to damage in an auto accident.

29. The correct answer is d. Because the primary action of the SNS is to help us respond to emergency situations, it is important that the body reacts quickly and therefore the SNS stimulates the different body parts simultaneously.

a. The SNS does not increase the functioning of all the affected body parts, digestion is decreased.

b. The PNS does not decrease the functioning of all the affected body parts, digestion is increased.

c. It is the PNS that stimulates the different body parts independently.

31. The correct choice is c. The hormones secreted by the adrenal medulla in response to an emergency situation have the effect of continuing the responses initiated by the nervous system.

a. The parasympathetic nervous system is primarily responsible for the return to normal functioning.

b. Our cognitive response is primarily determined by the cortex.

d. The endocrine system does not moderate the reactions caused by the nervous system, but sustains or reinforces the nervous system's reaction.

PART VI. SUMMARY TABLES

To test your understanding of the material discussed in this chapter complete the following tables. Check your answers with those supplied in PART IX.

Parts of a Neuron

	Description	Location	Function
Dendrites	Resembles branches of a tree	At the end of neuron	Receives messages from other neurons
Cell body	Largest part of neuron in nucleus	In the middle of neuron	Handles metabolic functions of neuron
Axon	Slender extended fiber length varies greatly	end of neuron oppos. Dendrites	Transmits the action potent. toward other neurons
Terminal buttons	Bulb like structures	At transmitting end of Axon	Release neurotransmitter into synapse.

Brain Structures

Structure	Location	Primary Functions
Medulla	Directly above Spinal CORD	breathing, pulse rate, heart rate, blood pressure
Pons	Lower brain, directly above medulla	Fine tunes motor messages
Cerebellum	under back part of Cerebral hemisp.	Coordinates + Regulates body movement
Reticular formation	Fibers extend from lower brain to thalamus	Controls arousal + alertness
Limbic system	Central CORE of Brain	emotional expression, motivation, learning + memory
Hypothalamus	Beneath cerebrum + thalamus	motivations, hot + cold temp reg., controls Endoc.
Thalamus	Beneath cerebrum	Relays sensory messages to cortex
Cerebral cortex	outer layer of cerebrum	Resp. for higher mental processes

Fill in the following diagram to visualize the separate divisions of the nervous system. Two of the lowest-level components of the nervous system are described. (**Hint:** Work backwards to complete the diagram.)

Overview of the Nervous System

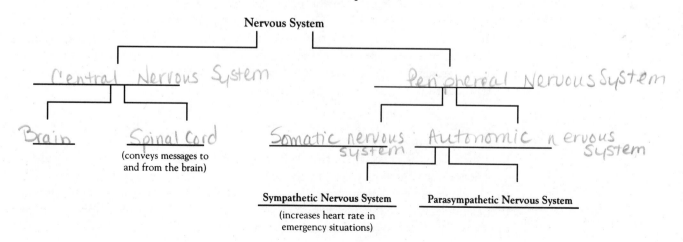

PART VIII. THOUGHT QUESTIONS/CRITICAL THINKING

Prepare answers to the following discussion questions.

1. A computer model is frequently used to describe the functioning of the nervous system. Both a computer and the nervous system receive input, perform internal activities or decision-making functions, and provide output. Using a computer analogy (input, internal activities, output) describe what controls the decision-making process an individual neuron goes through when "deciding" whether to fire its action potential (or output).

2. Following brain damage an individual may show a number of behavioral deficits and symptoms. For each of the following symptoms identify which brain structure(s) or area(s) of the brain is (are) most likely to have been damaged. Explain to justify your choices.

   a. Following a stroke a person has difficulty performing tasks involving logical thought processes and is partially paralyzed on the right side of the body.
   b. A person is unable to effectively control or regulate his or her food intake and gains 50 pounds in a short period of time.
   c. A tiger is no longer capable of effectively stalking and killing its prey.
   d. A person undergoes a significant change in personality and has difficulty coping with simple problems associated with daily life.
   e. A person is in a comalike sleep for a period of weeks or months.
   f. A person (like Charles Whitman [discussed in Chapter 1]) who appeared to be fairly normal, goes on a violent killing spree.

3. Your body has two primary systems for sending messages: the nervous system and the endocrine system. If you wanted to get a message from one place to another quickly (or by "express mail") which system would you use? If you wanted to be constantly reminded of a message (or by "a string on your finger") which system would you use? Explain your answers.

PART VIII. APPLICATIONS

1. At the beginning of a discussion on the nervous system, its functioning is often described by using an analogy to the electrical wiring of a house. However, because a message progresses through the nervous system via an electrochemical process and the wiring of a house is strictly electrical, the analogy is incomplete. The analogy is also incomplete for at least one other reason. Develop an analogy to the functioning of the nervous system that would describe the functioning of a house's electrical system as if it was also controlled by an electrochemical process.

2. Neurologists use a variety of specialized techniques (EEG, CAT, PET, MRI) to diagnose the location and extent of possible brain damage. However, the neurologist can frequently isolate the areas where they believe the brain damage is located by the behavioral deficits or symptoms shown by the patient. Try to develop simple behavioral tests that could be used to determine the location of damage to a variety of brain structures. (For example, if the individual has a problem memorizing and recalling a list of phone numbers, you might suspect damage to the hippocampus.)

3. We know that many parts of the cerebral cortex have specific functions (motor, somatosensory, visual, and auditory cortex); we also have data indicating lateralization of function regarding abilities such as language, perceiving spatial relationships, and math. It is appropriate to conclude that many areas of the brain are involved in specific functions. This idea—that different areas of the brain have specific "jobs"—is not a new idea. In the early 1800s a "science" of phrenology was developed by Joseph Gall with the intent of identifying the location of brain areas associated with specific personality traits or abilities. Gall believed that the brain was very similar to a muscle and if a specific area of the brain (associated with a specific function) received a lot of "exercise" that area would enlarge and result in a detectable bump or bulge on the skull. Gall went around feeling the skulls of individuals known to show specific traits (pickpockets, people with high sex drives or sadistic personalities, etc.) in an effort to find bumps that could be associated with the specific "talents" of the individuals. Gall developed a complex map of the skull showing the areas associated with the different abilities. (For example, the tendency to steal was just above the ears, and sexuality was at the back of the skull.) For a time, phrenology was a very popular "science" but ultimately it fell into disfavor because it was not accurate. Based on the information from this chapter and Chapter 2 concerning the methods of science, discuss why phrenology was a "bad science" and doomed to failure.

PART IX. SUMMARY TABLES SOLUTIONS

Parts of a Neuron

	Description	Location	Function
Dendrites	Resembles the branches of a tree	At one end of the neuron	Receives messages from other neurons
Cell body	Largest part of the neuron, contains nucleus	In the middle of the neuron	Handles metabolic functions of the neuron
Axon	Slender extended fiber length varies greatly	At end of neuron opposite dendrites	Transmits the action potential toward other neurons
Terminal buttons	Bulblike structures	At the transmitting end of the axon	Releases neurotransmitters into the synapse

Brain Structures

Structure	Location	Primary Functions
Medulla	Directly above the spinal cord	Critical functions such as breathing, heart rate, blood pressure
Pons	Lower brain, directly above medulla	Fine-tunes motor messages prior to cerebellum involvement species-typical behaviors
Cerebellum	Under back part of cerebral hemispheres	Coordinates and regulates motor movements
Reticular formation	Fibers extend from lower brain (near spinal cord) to the thalamus	Controls arousal and alertness
Limbic system	Central core of brain along innermost edges of cerebral hemispheres	Emotional expression, motivation, learning, memory
Hypothalamus	Beneath cerebrum and thalamus	Homeostasis, motivations, emotions, controls endocrine system
Thalamus	Beneath cerebrum	Relays sensory messages to appropriate areas of cortex
Cerebral cortex	Outer layer of cerebrum	Responsible for higher mental processes

Overview of the Nervous System

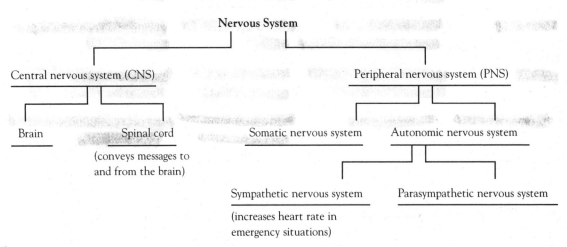

CHAPTER 4

Sensation and Perception

PART I. LEARNING OBJECTIVES

When you finish studying this chapter you should be able to:

Principles of Sensation and Perception

1. Define sensation and perception and explain the relationship between the processes. **(99)**

2. Describe the process of transduction. **(100)**

3. Define threshold and differentiate between absolute and difference thresholds. **(102)**

4. Explain how sensory thresholds, attention, and adaptation prevent us from perceiving the occurrence of many stimuli or events. **(102-104)**

5. Define signal detection theory and discuss how background noise and cognitive processes affect the detection of a stimulus. **(105)**

Vision

6. Describe how brightness, hue, and saturation are related to the physical properties of a light stimulus. **(108)**

7. Describe the structure, and explain the functions of each part of the human eye. **(108)**

8. Describe how visual information from the eye is transmitted to and interpreted by the visual cortex. **(112)**

9. Describe the general processes involved in color vision, and summarize two major theories of color vision. **(114)**

Hearing

10. Describe how loudness, pitch, and timbre are related to the physical properties of a sound stimulus. **(120)**

11. Describe the structure, and explain the functions of each part of the human ear. **(120, 123-124)**

12. Summarize the place theory and frequency theory of pitch discrimination. **(124)**

13. Explain the process by which we locate the source of a sound. **(125)**

14. Describe the two major types of hearing loss. **(125-126)**

The Chemical Senses: Taste and Smell

15. Describe how the sensation of taste occurs and identify the four different taste sensations. **(126-127)**

16. Describe how the sensation of smell occurs and summarize one widely held theory of how transduction takes place. **(128-130)**

The Skin Senses | The Body Senses

17. Describe the receptors for, and briefly describe the three different components of the sense of touch. **(131)**

18. Explain why it is difficult to gain a scientific understanding of pain and describe the gate-control theory of pain perception. **(131-132)**

19. Describe the two body senses (kinesthesis and equilibrium), and indicate the structures that are involved in the transduction of the stimuli these respond to. **(133)**

Perceiving the World

20. Explain what is meant by perceptual organization, and describe several principles that influence how people organize sensations. **(134)**

21. Define selective attention, and describe several characteristics of stimuli that influence which of a number of stimuli are attended to. **(135)**

22. Describe several binocular and monocular cues that aid our perception of distance. **(138)**

23. Describe the visual cliff and summarize the results of experiments that show that depth perception is innate in many species. **(141)**

24. Define perceptual constancy and describe four types of perceptual constancies. **(142)**

25. Differentiate between physical and perceptual illusions and explain the mechanisms responsible for a number of perceptual illusions. **(144)**

26. Define perceptual set and explain how a perceptual set influences our perception of a stimulus. **(146)**

PART II. OVERVIEW

The processes of sensation and perception relate to how individuals become aware of stimulus events in the environment and how they interpret those events. The term sensation refers to the response of a sense organ to a stimulus. Sensory systems transduce physical energy from the environment into electrochemical energy. Perception involves how the nervous system interprets or gives meaning to a sensation. Even though our sensory systems supply us with a vast amount of information, we do not sense—and therefore do not perceive—all events equally well.

Visible light is composed of electromagnetic radiation. Brightness, hue, and saturation are the three properties of light that are perceived. The structures of the eye can be described by an analogy to a camera and film. Structures such as the cornea, iris and pupil, and lens are comparable to a camera. The retina, which contains the photoreceptor cells (rods and cones), is comparable to the film. Two theories of color vision are described.

Sound waves consist of rhythmic changes in air pressure. Loudness, pitch, and timbre are the three properties of sound that are perceived. The ear consists of the outer ear (which collects the sound), the middle ear (which amplifies the sound), and the inner ear (which transduces the sound into electrochemical energy). Two theories of pitch discrimination are described. Additionally, the two primary types of hearing loss are described.

The chemical senses (taste and smell), the skin or touch senses (pressure, temperature, and pain), and body senses (kinesthesis and equilibrium) are briefly described.

The process of perception is discussed in detail. Gestalt psychologists identified a number of principles of perceptual organization including figure ground, perceptual grouping (proximity, similarity, and good continuation) and closure. Selective attention is the process that describes how we come to focus our attention on only some sensations while "screening out" others. Both binocular (two eyes) and monocular (one eye) cues that are used to perceive distance are described. Perceptual constancy is the tendency to perceive an object as unchanging even if the sensations transmitted through the nervous system change. The four types of perceptual constancies are size, shape, color, and brightness. Finally, because perception is a cognitive process of interpreting sensations, additional subjective factors (perceptual sets) that influence our perceptions are outlined.

PART III. KEY TERMS/MATCHING EXERCISES

Match the following concepts and/or individuals with the appropriate descriptions. Check your answers against the Answer Key.

Principles of Sensation and Perception

Concepts

_a_· 1. absolute threshold **(102)**

_e_· 2. difference threshold **(102–103)**

_b_· 3. perception **(99)**

_a_· 4. sensation **(99)**

_g_· 5. signal detection theory **(105)**

_c_· 6. transduction **(100)**

_f_· 7. Weber's law **(103)**

Descriptions

a. Response of a sensory receptor to a simulus event

b. Response of organizing or interpreting a stimulus event

c. Occurs when sensory input in the form of energy is transformed into electro-chemical energy

d. Weakest intensity of a stimulus that can be perceived 50 percent of the time

e. Equivalent to a just noticeable difference (JND)

f. Quantifies the relationship between the intensity of a stimulus and the just noticeable difference (JND)

g. Utilizes the concepts of noise and response criterion

Answer Key   1. d   2. e   3. b   4. a   5. g   6. c   7. f

Vision (The Eye)

Concepts

_a_ 1. brightness (**108**)
_c_ 2. saturation (**108**)
_e_ 3. rods (**110**)
_g_ 4. lens (**108**)
_i_ 5. trichromatic theory of color vision (**116**)

_j_ 6. opponent-process theory of color vision (**116-118**)
_h_ 7. iris (**108**)
_f_ 8. cones (**109**)
_d_ 9. retina (**108**)
_b_ 10. hue (**108**)

Descriptions

a. Related to the intensity of a light stimulus

b. Related to the wavelength of a light stimulus

c. Related to the proportion of chromatic to achromatic light present in a light stimulus

d. Contains photoreceptor cells

e. Sensitive to low intensities of light and primarily responsible for peripheral vision

f. Concentrated in the fovea and responsible for color vision

g. Functions to project a focused image of a visual stimulus on the back of the eye

h. Functions to control the amount of light that enters the eye through the pupil

i. Supported by evidence that different types of cones are most sensitive to one of three wavelengths

j. Supported by the phenomenon of negative afterimages and cases of color blindness.

Answer Key   1. a   2. c   3. e   4. g   5. i   6. j   7. h   8. f   9. d   10. b

Hearing (The Ear)

Concepts

_h._ 1. place theory (**124**)

_j._ 2. sensorineural hearing loss (**125**)

_e._ 3. ossicles (**121**)

_b._ 4. pitch (**121**)

_d._ 5. tympanic membrane (**121**)

_i._ 6. volley theory (**124-125**)

_K_ 7. conduction hearing loss (**126**)

_a_ 8. loudness (**121**)

_c._ 9. timbre (**121**)

_g._ 10. auditory hair cells (**123**)

_f._ 11. cochlea (**123**)

Descriptions

a. Related to the intensity of a sound stimulus

b. Related to the frequency of a sound stimulus

c. Helps to explain why a musical note sounds different when played on a clarinet and a saxophone

d. Commonly referred to as the eardrum

e. Consists of the malleus, incus, and stapes

f. Contains the basilar membrane, organ of Corti, and is filled with fluid

g. transduces sound stimuli into electrochemical energy

h. Explains the ability to discriminate pitches that are higher than 4000 Hz

i. Associated with the frequency theory of pitch discrimination

j. Would result from damage to the hair cells or auditory nerve

k. Can be compensated for by the use of a hearing aid

Answer Key 1. h 2. j 3. e 4. b 5. d 6. i 7. k 8. a 9. c 10. g 11. f

The Chemical Senses: Taste and Smell | The Body Senses

Concepts

_b._ 1. olfaction (**129**)

_d._ 2. kinesthesis (**133**)

_a._ 3. gustation (**127**)

_e._ 4. equilibrium (**134**)

_c._ 5. gate-control theory (**131-132**)

Descriptions

a. Greatly enhanced by our sense of smell

b. Researchers have not identified the most basic or primary sensations associated with this sense

c. Proposes an explanation concerning the experience or perception of pain

d. Allows us to be aware of the relative placement or location of our body parts

e. Dependent on the semicircular canals and vestibular sacs

Answer Key 1. b 2. d 3. a 4. e 5. c

Perceiving the World (Perceptual Organization | Depth Perception)

Concepts

___d___ 1. binocular (retinal) disparity (**138-139**)

___g___ 2. linear perspective (**140**)

___b___ 3. perceptual grouping (**135**)

___a___ 4. figure-ground patterns (**134**)

___i___ 5. visual cliff (**141**)

___c___ 6. closure (**135**)

___h___ 7. texture gradients (**140**)

___e___ 8. convergence (**139**)

___f___ 9. overlap (**140**)

Descriptions

a. Principle that explains why some ambiguous figures may be perceived in more than one way

b. Includes proximity, similarity, and good continuation

c. Relates to the tendency to perceive incomplete figures as complete

d. Based on the fact that each eye sees a slightly different view of the world

e. Binocular depth-perception cue that results from the tension created by rotation (or crossing) of one's eyes

f. Observation that closer objects obstruct one's view of more distant objects

g. Observation that parallel lines appear to converge off in the distance

h. Observation that farther elements appear more dense than closer elements

i. Has been utilized to suggest that depth perception is innate in many animals

Answer Key 1. d 2. g 3. b 4. a 5. i 6. c 7. h 8. e 9. f

Perceiving the World (Selective Attention, Perceptual Constancy, and Illusions)

Concepts

___a___ 1. perceptual constancy (**142**)

___e___ 2. perceptual set (**146**)

___c___ 3. shape constancy (**142**)

___d___ 4. illusion (**144**)

___b___ 5. size constancy (**142**)

___f___ 6. selective attention (**135**)

Descriptions

a. Tendency to perceive stimuli as unchanging even though the images projected onto the retina may change

b. Involves the use of distance cues

c. Critical factor involved in the Ames room

d. False perception in that it differs from the actual physical state of the perceived object

e. Related to expectancies and selective perception

f. Influenced by factors such as contrast, novelty, and intensity

Answer Key 1. a 2. e 3. c 4. d 5. b 6. f

PART IV. TRUE-FALSE STATEMENTS

Fill in the blank before each statement with either a T (true) or an F (false). Check your answers against the Answer Key. Then go back to the items that are false and make the necessary change(s) to the statements to convert the items into true statements.

Principles of Sensation and Perception

_____ 1. A given stimulus will always result in the same perception.

_____

_____

_____ 2. A stimulus, sufficiently intense to activate a sensory process 50 percent of the time, is the absolute threshold for that sensory system.

_____

_____

_____ 3. The simplest explanation of why we become accustomed to a foul-smelling environment, and after a while do not notice it, is offered by signal detection theory.

_____

_____

Vision

_____ 4. The wavelength of a light stimulus is related to the hue we perceive the stimulus to be.

_____

_____

_____ 5. Light energy is transduced into electrochemical energy by the lens.

_____

_____

_____ 6. Additive color mixing relates to mixing or combining lights of different wavelengths.

_____

_____

Hearing

_____ 7. The function of the pinna and auditory canal is to amplify the intensity of a sound stimulus.

_____

_____

_____ 8. The place theory of pitch discrimination proposes that high frequency sounds are detected or sensed near the oval window, whereas lower frequency sounds are detected farther from the oval window.

_____

_____

_____ 9. A person suffering from conduction hearing loss would still be able to hear through bone conduction.

_____

_____

Perceiving the World

_____ 10. The major principles of perceptual organization were identified by the humanistic psychologists.

_____

_____

_____ 11. The two binocular depth-perception cues are binocular disparity and overlap.

_____

_____

_____ 12. The psychological principle that states that we would tend to focus on a stimulus that is difficult is selective attention.

_____

_____

Answer Key	1. F **(99)**	5. F **(110)**	9. T **(126)**
	2. T **(102)**	6. T **(115-116)**	10. F **(134)**
	3. F **(104)**	7. F **(121)**	11. F **(138-139)**
	4. T **(107)**	8. T **(124)**	12. T **(138)**

PART V. MULTIPLE-CHOICE QUESTIONS

Choose the best answer to each question. Circle your choice. Check your answers against the Answer Key. Questions marked with an asterisk (*) include annotated answers.

_____

Principles of Sensation and Perception

1. The process of interpreting and organizing the nervous system's response to a stimulus is

    a. adaptation.
    b. sensation.
    (c.) perception.
    d. psychophysics.

2. Which one of the following can be referred as a "raw material"?

    a. An illusion
    (b.) A sensation
    c. A perception
    d. A figure-ground

3. The process by which sensory organs transform mechanical, chemical, or light energy into the electrochemical energy of neuron transmission is

   a. transduction.
   b. sensation.
   c. adaptation.
   d. psychophysics.

4. When a child receives a hearing test at school and responds when he or she can first hear a soft sound, this test is determining his or her _absolute_ threshold.

   a. auditory
   b. difference
   c. absolute
   d. intensity

5. Probably when you were a teenager listening to the stereo at home, your mother told you to "Turn down that racket." After you turned down the volume your mom yelled at you for not doing what she told you to do. Why didn't your mother think you turned down the volume?

   a. Although you had adapted to the reduced volume, your mother had not.
   b. Because she is older, your mother's ears are less sensitive than yours.
   c. You probably did not lower the volume enough to exceed the auditory threshold.
   d. You probably did not lower the volume enough to exceed the difference threshold.

6. The discovery that the difference threshold tends to be a constant fraction of the stimulus is called

   a. Weber's law
   b. threshold consistency.
   c. adaptation.
   d. the attention factor.

*7. Signal detection theory states that as noise increases,

   a. a just noticeable difference becomes smaller.
   b. it would be more difficult to detect a signal.
   c. "hits" would probably increase.
   d. it would become less difficult to detect a signal.

Vision

*8. Which of the following terms does *not* belong with the others?

   a. Saturation
   b. Hue
   c. Wavelength
   d. Brightness

9. Which of the following structures does light energy pass through first?

   a. Aqueous humor
   b. Retina
   c. Vitreous humor
   d. Pupil

10. While _cones_ are responsible for color vision, _rods_ allow us to see in dim light.

    a. cones | rods
    b. rods | cones
    c. photoreceptor cells | bipolar cells
    d. rods | reels

11. A person with poor peripheral vision would most likely have a problem associated with his or her

    a. lens.
    b. optic nerve.
    c. cones.
    d. rods.

12. A person whose lens cannot correctly focus an image on his or her retina has a problem associated with

    a. maintaining the proper pupil size.
    b. accommodation.
    c. convergence.
    d. adaptation.

*13. The dual processes of dark and light adaptation are related to

    a. the activity of the cones.
    b. the activity of the rods.
    c. the chemical response of the photopigments in the photoreceptor cells.
    d. pupil size.

14. The one type of sight-destroying or sight-limiting problem that medical procedures cannot compensate for or overcome is damage to the

    a. optic nerve.
    b. visual cortex.
    c. cornea.
    d. lens.

15. The three primary colors of additive light are

    a. red, white, and black.
    b. blue, green, and yellow-green.
    c. red, blue, and yellow.
    d. red, blue, and green.

16. The opponent-process theory is supported at the level of the _ganglion cells_ ; and the trichromatic theory is supported at the level of the _cones_ .

    a. lateral geniculate nucleus | cortex
    b. ganglion cells | cones
    c. cones | ganglion cells
    d. rods | optic nerve

17. The fact that we never perceive such shades as greenish-red or bluish-yellow supports which theory of color vision?

- **a.** The opponent-process theory
- **b.** The trichromatic theory
- **c.** The Young theory
- **d.** The Young-Helmholtz theory

Hearing

18. Sound waves are really

- **a.** changes in the concentration of photons.
- **b.** changes in the complexity of air molecules.
- **c.** changes in air pressure.
- **d.** a bending of the cilia of hair cells.

19. If the frequency of a sound stimulus changes you would perceive a change in

- **a.** timbre.
- **b.** saturation.
- **c.** loudness.
- **d.** pitch.

20. The retina of the eye is analogous to the ___organ of Corti___ of the ear.

- **a.** hair cells
- **b.** cochlea
- **c.** organ of Corti
- **d.** oval window

21. The function of the middle ear is to ___amplify the___ ; the function of the inner ear is to ___transduce the sound into sound electrochemical energy___.

- **a.** amplify the sound | transduce the sound into electrochemical energy
- **b.** transduce the sound into electrochemical energy | amplify the sound
- **c.** register the sensation | perceive the stimulus
- **d.** collect the sound | amplify the sound

22. The place theory of pitch discrimination best explains how ___high___ frequency sounds are sensed.

- **a.** low
- **b.** medium
- **c.** high
- **d.** No frequencies of sounds—the place theory is no longer accepted.

23. The ___volley___ theory proposes a mechanism that combines with the more global ___frequency___ theory to account for the ability to distinguish tones in the 1000–4000 Hz range.

- **a.** frequency | volley
- **b.** volley | frequency
- **c.** place | frequency
- **d.** volley | place

24. The two factors that allow us to locate the place of origin of a sound stimulus are

    a. frequency and complexity.

    b. arrival time and closure.

    c. intensity and kinesthesis.

    d. intensity and arrival time.

*25. The reason that you can hear sounds of higher frequencies than your parents and grandparents is that they

    a. have deterioration of the auditory nerve.

    b. have sensorineural hearing loss.

    c. have conduction hearing loss.

    d. do not have as effective a bone conduction as you.

Taste and Smell | The Body Senses

26. The chemical senses include

    a. gustation and olfaction.

    b. touch and pain.

    c. vision and hearing.

    d. kinesthesis and equilibrium.

27. Which of the following is *not* one of the four main sensations that can be distinguished by our sense of taste?

    a. Bitterness

    b. Sourness

    c. Saltiness

    d. Spiciness

28. The receptor for smell is the

    a. basilar membrane.

    b. olfactory membrane.

    c. organ of Corti.

    d. auditory nerve.

29. Temperature receptors for cold _____ , while the receptors for heat _____ .

    a. are closer to the skin's surface | are farther away from the skin's surface

    b. are farther away from the skin's surface | are closer to the skin's surface

    c. use myelinated fibers | use unmyelinated fibers

    d. are stimulated by increasing pressure to the skin | are stimulated by decreasing pressure to the skin

30. The gate-control theory of pain suggests that

    a. pain is inevitable.

    b. acupuncture does not work.

    c. chemicals induce the perception of pain.

    d. competition from other sensations may block one's perception of pain.

31. Astronauts experiencing weightlessness in space do not know when they are upside-down because the absence of gravity would disrupt their _____ sense(s).

  a. vestibular
  b. kinesthesis
  c. equilibrium and kinesthesis
  d. olfactory

Perceiving the World

32. The tendency to perceive a pile of change as being composed of pennies, nickels, and dimes is the result of

  a. closure.
  b. similarity.
  c. proximity.
  d. selective attention.

33. The process of selective attention would most likely cause you to perceive which of the following while driving on a highway?

  a. The blue car that you have been passing and been passed by for the last hour
  b. The exit signs for the next city, which is not your destination
  c. A small airplane being towed by a truck
  d. A road sign that says you are 300 miles from your destination

34. The feeling of tension in the eye muscles provides a binocular cue for depth when attempting to focus on a nearby object. This is referred to as

  a. retinal disparity.
  b. size constancy.
  c. convergence.
  d. motion parallax.

*35. When watching a travelogue video of the Grand Canyon you perceive depth as a result of

  a. only monocular cues.
  b. only binocular cues.
  c. both monocular and binocular cues.
  d. relative size, aerial perspective, and motion parallax.

36. A newly hatched chick would be likely to

  a. "fall off" a visual cliff.
  b. only "fall off" a visual cliff one time.
  c. not cross over from the shallow side to the deep side of a visual cliff.
  d. cross over to the deep side of a visual cliff if food were available on the deep side.

37. The _____ viewpoint concerning the reason why perceptual constancies exist is illustrated by the Ames room.

  a. environmental cues'
  b. physical responding of the receptors in the eye
  c. unconscious inferences'
  d. selective attention

38. When you incorrectly perceive that two lines are the same length when they are not, you are experiencing a(n)

  a. Muller-Lyer effect.
  b. hallucination.
  c. illusion.
  d. delusion.

39. Subjective factors (such as your expectancies and preconceived ideas) that influence your perceptions are referred to as

  a. perceptual constancies.
  b. perceptual set.
  c. subjective perceptions.
  d. objective perceptions.

Answer Key

1. c	**(99)**	9. a	**(108)**	17. a	**(116)**	*25. b	**(125)**	33. c	**(136)**
2. b	**(99)**	10. a	**(110)**	18. c	**(118)**	26. a	**(126)**	34. c	**(139)**
3. a	**(100)**	11. d	**(110)**	19. d	**(121)**	27. d	**(126-127)**	*35. a	**(138)**
4. c	**(102)**	12. b	**(108)**	20. c	**(123)**	28. b	**(128)**	36. c	**(141)**
5. d	**(103)**	*13. c	**(110-111)**	21. a	**(121, 123)**	29. a	**(131)**	37. a	**(143)**
6. a	**(103)·**	14. b	**(112)**	22. c	**(124)**	30. d	**(133)**	38. c	**(144)**
*7. b	**(105)**	15. d	**(115)**	23. b	**(124)**	31. c	**(133)**	39. b	**(146)**
*8. c	**(108)**	16. b	**(117-118)**	24. d	**(125)**	32. b	**(135)**		

Annotated Answers

7. The correct choice is b. An increase in noise would have the effect of overshadowing the signal and would become less noticeable and more difficult to detect.
  a. According to Weber's law the JND would not change.
  c. Because a "hit" is defined as the correct detection of a signal, hits would tend to decrease.
  d. This choice is the exact opposite of the correct choice.

8. The correct choice is c. Wavelength is the unit of measurement used to describe a physical characteristic of a light stimulus; a, b, and d are all qualities related to how we interpret or perceive a light stimulus.

13. The correct choice is c. The photopigments in both the rods and cones respond to light energy. In dark adaptation, the resulting change is relatively slow to complete; and in light adaptation, the changes occur more rapidly. a and b are both incomplete because they each relate to only one type of photoreceptor cell.
  d. Although pupil size does change when going from a light to a dark environment (and vice versa), changes in pupil size are not sufficient to account for the changes that occur in light and dark adaptation. For example, pupil size would increase quickly when entering a dark environment and could not explain why the process of dark adaptation takes 30 minutes to complete.

25. The correct choice is b. The most common form of sensorineural hearing loss is the gradual loss of the ability to hear high frequencies that occurs with aging.
  a. The auditory nerve does not typically deteriorate with age.

c. Conduction hearing loss would typically result in a reduction of sensitivity to all frequencies—not just high frequency sounds.

d. The effectiveness of bone conduction does not significantly change as a result of aging.

35. The correct choice is a. Because the video was shot with only one camera, the image on the screen is monocular in nature and binocular cues would not be present.

b. Binocular cues would not be available.

c. This choice is incorrect because b is incorrect.

d. The cues listed are monocular cues; other monocular cues, such as overlap and linear perspective, would also be available.

PART VI. SUMMARY TABLES

To test your understanding of the material discussed in this chapter complete the following tables. Check your answers with those supplied in PART IX.

Theories of Color Vision

Theory	Assumptions	Supporting Evidence	Weaknesses
Trichromatic or Young-Helmholtz			
Opponent process			

Theories of Pitch Discrimination

Theory	Assumptions	Supporting Evidence	Weaknesses
Place			
Frequency			

Perceptual Organization

Principle	Description	Number of Corresponding Figure in Textbook as Example
Figure-ground		
Proximity		
Similarity		
Good continuation		
Closure		

Depth Perception Cues

Cue	Monocular/Binocular	Description
Aerial perspective		
Binocular disparity		
Convergence		
Height of plane		
Linear perspective		
Overlap		
Relative size		
Texture gradient		
Relative motion		

PART VII. THOUGHT QUESTIONS/CRITICAL THINKING

Prepare answers to the following discussion questions.

1. Discuss the principles of sensation and perception that help explain each of the following observations.

    a. If you close your eyes and press on your eyelids you "see lights."

    b. If the walls and/or the floors of a room (usually a bathroom) are composed of small rectangular tiles that form a repeating square pattern (such as shown), you almost cannot help but try to decide which group of "squares" go together to make up a larger piece or tile. Additionally, as soon as you think you have figured it out ("These four make a big tile"), you decide you're wrong ("No, it's those four").

c. If you hit your thumb with a hammer and it hurts, when you hold your thumb and squeeze it your thumb doesn't hurt nearly as bad.

d. You never mistake a car down the road for a toy car, but if you look down from the twentieth floor of a building the cars on the street below do look like toy cars.

e. You've been home all day and haven't noticed anything unusual, but as soon as your roommate walks in the door she says, "There's a gas leak in the house." She's correct!

2. Discuss how sensory thresholds, selective attention, and signal detection theory combine to influence our perceptions of the world.

3. a. Draw and label a diagram showing the structure of the eye and ear.

    b. For each of the following structures of the eye identify the structure of the ear that has a comparable function.

        rods and cones _____

        retina _____

        cornea _____

        lens _____

4. When you're driving and hear a siren, sometimes you immediately know where the siren is coming from (usually the left or right); other times it's much harder to determine where the sound is coming from (usually the front or back). Explain why it is easier to locate a sound coming from the left or right than sound coming from the front or back (and also from above and below).

5. I'm not saying that flying saucers exist or not, but if two people see the same "flying saucer" they often give very different descriptions. One person might say, "It was huge, the size of a city block and about 3000 feet above the ground." The second person might say, "Oh no, it was hovering just above the treetops and about the size of a small airplane." Explain why their descriptions differ so widely. (**Hint:** How big is a flying saucer? How high do flying saucers usually fly?)

PART VIII. APPLICATIONS

1. Imagine that in addition to the five senses (vision, hearing, smell, taste, and touch), people have a sixth sense. Design this sensory system: What type of energy will be sensed? How would that energy be transduced into electrochemical energy? What would the receptor cells be like? How would different qualities of that energy (such as loudness, pitch, and timbre) be sensed? How would the brain organize and interpret the sensation? Design one of the following sensory systems:

    a. A temperature-sensing system that would be more complete than the cold and heat receptors in the skin we already have. This sensory system would allow people to know the exact temperature of their environment. If you decide that it would be beneficial for this sensory system to supply information concerning humidity and the wind-chill factor how would these factors be incorporated into the functioning of the system?

    b. An ultraviolat-radiation-sensing system that would allow us to limit damage to our skin associated with excessive ultraviolet radiation.

    c. A bacteria- or virus-sensing system that would allow us to limit our exposure to health threats.

    d. A "sensory system" for a computer network that would allow the computer to detect the presence of a computer virus or unauthorized user.

2. You are in charge of a lab section of general psychology, and it's time for you to design an experiment to illustrate the principles of sensation and perception. Decide whether the experiment will involve: a comparison of the relative effectiveness of monocular and binocular depth-perception cues; whether one's perception of taste is enhanced by their sense of smell (see p. 127 in the text); or whether people are better at locating a sound source from the left and right or front and back (see Thought Question #4). Answer and/or describe the following:

    a. What is your hypothesis?

    b. Write a paragraph explaining exactly what procedure you will use to conduct the experiment.

    c. Identify the independent variable.

    d. Identify the dependent variable and explain how it will be measured.

    e. Identify the experimental group(s).

    f. Identify the control group.

    g. Explain how you would assign subjects to the experimental and control group(s).

    h. Provide any necessary operational definitions.

    i. Evaluate your experiment as it regards the APA's ethical guidelines. Even though this experiment is only a classroom exercise and not a "real" experiment, you must adhere to the guidelines.

    j. How would you compare the experimental and control group(s) on their performance on the dependent variable? Using only descriptive statistics, how would you present the results (that is, would you calculate means, percentiles, or whatever)?

    k. Predict what differences in behavior you would find if your hypothesis was confirmed by the results of the experiment.

PART IX. SUMMARY TABLES SOLUTIONS

Theories of Color Vision

Theory	Assumptions	Supporting Evidence	Weaknesses
Trichromatic or Young-Helmholtz	Three types of cones for red, blue, and green	Evidence of three types of cones most sensitive to blue, green, and yellow-green; genes have been identified for the three types of cones	Does not explain color blindness, negative afterimages
Opponent process	Three types of receptors each respond to pairs of colors: red-green, blue-yellow, and black-white	Cannot see reddish-green; color blindness; negative afterimages; and supported by the functioning of the ganglion cells and lateral geniculate nuclei	No major weaknesses when combined with the trichromatic theory

Theories of Pitch Discrimination

Theory	Assumptions	Supporting Evidence	Weaknesses
Place	Different frequencies displace different regions of the basilar membrane: high frequencies closest to the oval window	Predictions consistent with displacement of basilar membrane for high and medium frequencies	Predictions not supported for low frequency sound; cannot explain how very small differences in frequency can be perceived
Frequency	Frequency is determined by the frequency of impulses in the auditory nerve	For frequencies below 1000 Hz the firing of individual auditory nerve fibers match the frequency; with volley theory can explain frequencies between 1000–4000 Hz	Unnecessary for frequencies above 4000 Hz, which can be explained by the place theory

Perceptual Organization

Principle	Description	Number of Corresponding Figure in Textbook as Example
Figure-ground	When perceiving a stimulus, attention is focused on the figure and everything else becomes the ground (or background)	See Figure 4.24
Proximity	Objects that are close to each other are perceived as belonging together	See Figure 4.25A
Similarity	Objects that are alike are perceived as belonging together	See Figure 4.25B
Good continuation	Objects or elements that flow smoothly together are perceived as belonging together	See Figure 4.25C
Closure	We tend to perceive incomplete figures as closed or completed	See Figure 4.26

Depth Perception Cues

Cue	Monocular/Binocular	Description
Aerial perspective	Mono	Distant objects appear hazy or fuzzy
Binocular disparity	Bino	Each eye sees a slightly different view of the world
Convergence	Bino	The awareness of tension in the eye muscles
Height of plane	Mono	More distant objects appear to be higher than closer objects
Linear perspective	Mono	Parallel lines appear to converge in the distance
Overlap	Mono	Closer objects block the view of more distant objects
Relative size	Mono	Closer objects appear larger than more distant objects
Texture gradient	Mono	Closer objects appear less dense than more distant objects
Relative motion	Mono	Nearby objects appear to move a greater distance and faster than more distant objects

CHAPTER 5

States of Consciousness

PART I. LEARNING OBJECTIVES

When you finish studying this chapter you should be able to:

The Nature of Consciousness

1. Define consciousness, and differentiate between the terms conscious, preconscious, and unconscious. **(152)**

2. Describe "normal," alternative, and altered states of consciousness, and discuss five ways alternative and altered states qualitatively differ from the "normal" state of consciousness. **(153)**

Sleep and Dreaming

3. Describe the differences between REM (rapid eye movement) and NREM (nonrapid eye movement) sleep. **(154)**

4. Describe the four stages of sleep and include how brain waves, eye movements, and muscular activity differ in each stage. **(154-155)**

5. Describe the sleep cycle (the pattern of changes in stages of sleep throughout a night's sleep). **(155-157)**

6. Explain the connection between REM sleep and dreaming and changes in brain activity and muscular activity associated with REM sleep. **(157-158)**

7. Describe the changes in sleep patterns that occur as one ages. **(158)**

8. Describe the results of sleep-deprivation experiments with both humans and animals as subjects. **(158-159)**

9. Outline four theories that explain why we need to sleep. **(160-161)**

10. Describe the results of dream-deprivation experiments with both humans and animals as subjects. **(161-62)**

11. Outline four theories that explain why we dream. **(162-164)**

12. Describe lucid dreaming. **(164)**

13. Describe five sleep disorders and discuss the factors thought to be responsible for each disorder. **(166-169)**

Meditation

14. Describe meditation, and list some mental and physical benefits that have been associated with meditation and relaxation. **(169-170)**

Hypnosis

15. Explain how a hypnotic state differs from a normal waking state, and discuss a number of phenomena that have been associated with hypnosis. **(171-172)**

16. Describe the conflicting theories concerning hypnosis proposed by Hilgard and Barber. **(174-175)**

Drugs That Alter Consciousness

17. Define psychoactive drugs and describe tolerance, physiological dependence, and psychological dependence. **(175)**

18. Describe the physiological and psychoactive effects of depressants (sedatives, opiates, and alcohol) and give examples of each type of drug. **(176-178)**

19. Discuss a variety of reasons why people drink alcohol excessively, and evaluate two methods to treat alcohol addiction. **(178-180)**

20. Describe the physiological and psychoactive effects of stimulants (caffeine, nicotine, amphetamines, and cocaine). **(180-183)**

21. Describe the physiological and psychoactive effects of hallucinogens (LSD, PCP, and marijuana). **(183-186)**

PART II. OVERVIEW

There are a number of states of consciousness or different states of awareness. The "normal" state of consciousness involves being alert and concentrating on something. Alternative states of consciousness are natural states of consciousness such as daydreaming, sleep, and dreaming. Deliberate changes in consciousness through meditation, hypnosis, or psychoactive drugs are referred to as altered states of consciousness.

Sleep consists of two types of sleep, REM (rapid eye movement) sleep is associated with dreaming. NREM (nonrapid eye movement) sleep is further divided into four stages that differ in how "deep" the sleep is and in brain wave patterns. Throughout a night's sleep an individual goes through a complete sleep cycle (NREM and REM) every 90 minutes. A number of theories have been proposed to explain why we sleep and dream; and a number of sleep disorders are described, ranging from sleepwalking and nightmares to insomnia, sleep apnea, and narcolepsy.

Meditation is the practice of altering consciousness to achieve a state of tranquillity, relaxation, and inner peace. Meditation is associated with numerous physiological changes such as decreases in heart rate and respiration and a change in brain wave patterns. Hypnosis is a state of relaxation during which the hypnotized individual is highly suggestible to the instructions of the hypnotist.

Psychoactive drugs alter consciousness by interferring with the normal functioning of neurotransmitters in the CNS (central nervous system). These drugs may result in an individual developing either a physiological, psychological—or both—dependence. There are three major groups of psychoactive drugs. Depressants decrease the activity of the CNS. Depressants include sedatives, opiates, and alcohol. Stimulants increase the transmission of nervous impulses in the CNS. Stimulants include caffeine, nicotine, amphetamines, and cocaine. Hallucinogens produce changes in sensory perceptions, thinking processes, and emotions. Hallucinogens include LSD, PCP, and marijuana.

PART III. KEY TERMS/MATCHING EXERCISES

Match the following concepts and/or individuals with the appropriate descriptions. Check your answers against the Answer Key.

The Nature of Consciousness

Concepts

_c_ 1. altered states of consciousness (**153**)

_f_ 2. alternative states of consciousness (**153**)

_e_ 3. conscious (**152**)

_b_ 4. "normal" state of consciousness (**153**)

_d_ 5. preconscious (**152**)

_a_ 6. unconscious (**152**)

Descriptions

a. Contains thoughts, perceptions, and memories that you cannot easily bring to your awareness

b. Occurs when you are awake and alert

c. Results from deliberate efforts to change your state of consciousness

d. Contains thought, perceptions, and memories that you can easily bring to your awareness

e. Contains the thoughts, perceptions, and memories that you are aware of at a given time

f. Includes daydreaming, sleep, and dreaming

Answer Key   1. c   2. f   3. e   4. b   5. d   6. a

Sleep and Dreaming

Concepts

_f_ 1. stage 1 sleep **(155)**   _c_ 6. manifest content **(164)**

_g_ 2. stage 4 sleep **(155)**   _a_ 7. narcolepsy **(168)**

_b_ 3. REM sleep **(154)**   _d_ 8. sleep apnea **(168)**

_i_ 4. NREM sleep **(154)**   _e_ 9. insomnia **(166)**

_h_ 5. latent content **(164)**

Descriptions

a. Associated with the inappropriate loss of muscle tone and immediate onset of REM sleep

b. Is commonly associated with dreaming

c. According to Freud, the "plot" of a dream

d. Occurs when an individual frequently wakes up briefly in order to breathe

e. Associated with difficulty in falling asleep and/or frequently wakening during the night

f. Is associated with low-amplitude brain waves; individuals wakens easily

g. Occurs when delta waves predominate; it is difficult to wake an individual

h. According to Freud, the true meaning of a dream

i. Consists of four stages of sleep

Answer Key   1. f   2. g   3. b   4. i   5. h   6. c   7. a   8. d

          9. e

Meditation | Hypnosis

Concepts

_c_ 1. hypnosis **(172)**   _b_ 4. relaxation response **(170)**

_d_ 2. age regression **(172)**   _e_ 5. neodissociation theory **(174)**

_a_ 3. meditation **(169)**

Descriptions

a. A deliberate attempt to achieve a state of tranquillity, relaxation, and inner peace

b. Results in many of the physiological effects associated with description a

c. Is characterized by a state of relaxation and heightened suggestibility

d. Evidence suggests that individuals are role playing as opposed to reliving

e. Is associated with the "hidden observer"

Answer Key   1. c   2. d   3. a   4. b   5. e

Drugs

Concepts

_f._ 1. psychoactive drugs **(175)**
_d_ 2. physiological dependence **(175)**
_c_ 3. psychological dependence **(175)**
_a_ 4. depressants **(176)**

_e_ 5. stimulants **(180)**
_h_ 6. sedatives **(176)**
_b_ 7. hallucinogens **(183)**
_g_ 8. narcotics **(176)**

Descriptions

a. Includes sedatives, opiates, and alcohol
b. Result in changes in sensory perceptions, emotions, and thinking processes
c. Associated with when an individual perceives a drug as pleasurable and helpful
d. Associated with withdrawal symptoms
e. Increases the transmission of nerve impulses in the CNS
f. Alters perceptions and behavior by changing conscious awareness
g. Consists of morphine, codeine, and heroin
h. Includes tranquilizers and barbiturates

Answer Key 1. f 2. d 3. c 4. a 5. e 6. h 7. b 8. g

PART IV. TRUE-FALSE STATEMENTS

Fill in the blank before each statement with either a T (true) or an F (false). Check your answers against the Answer Key. Then go back to the items that are false and make the necessary change(s) to the statements to convert the items into true statements.

The Nature of Consciousness

_____ 1. Information in your preconscious is more easily brought to your consciousness than information in your unconscious.

_____ 2. Sleeping is considered a "normal" state of consciousness.

_____ 3. Alternative and altered states of consciousness are primarily quantitatively different from the "normal" state of consciousness.

Sleep and Dreaming

_____ 4. During REM sleep there is more muscular activity than there is during NREM sleep.

_____

_____

_____ 5. After being deprived of REM sleep, people then spend increased time in REM sleep, which is referred to as REM rebound.

_____

_____

_____ 6. Freud believed that people dream in order to solve problems.

_____

_____

_____ 7. Nightmares occur during REM sleep; night terrors occur during stage 4 sleep.

_____

_____

Meditation and Hypnosis

_____ 8. Meditation has been successfully used to reduce anxiety, decrease blood pressure, and reduce chronic pain.

_____

_____

_____ 9. Although the idea of hypnotized people acting out posthypnotic suggestions is commonly accepted, it has not been scientifically demonstrated.

_____

_____

_____ 10. There is disagreement over whether or not hypnosis is a special state of consciousness.

_____

_____

Drugs That Alter Consciousness

_____ 11. Drugs that only induce psychological dependence are less harmful than drugs that produce physiological dependence.

_____

_____

_____ 12. In addition to increasing alertness, amphetamines are appetite supressants.

_____

_____

_____ 13. Marijuana may have a sedative effect, stimulant effect, or hallucinogenic effect.

_____

_____

Answer Key	1. T **(152)**	6. F **(164)**	11. F **(175)**
	2. F **(153)**	7. T **(169)**	12. T **(181)**
	3. F **(153)**	8. T **(170)**	13. T **(185)**
	4. F **(158)**	9. F **(173)**	
	5. T **(161)**	10. T **(175)**	

PART V. MULTIPLE-CHOICE QUESTIONS

Choose the best answer to each question. Circle your choice. Check your answers against the Answer Key. Questions marked with an asterisk (*) include annotated answers.

The Nature of Consciousness

1. Before you read the following, the memory of what you had for dinner last night was probably in your

  a. conscious.
  b. preconscious.
  c. unconscious.
  d. nonconscious.

2. Which of the following is most likely to be in your unconscious?

  a. Your current blood pressure
  b. The name of your psychology professor
  c. The words printed on this page
  d. Your memory of witnessing a fight between your parents when you were 5 years old

3. Which of the following is considered an alternative state of consciousness?

  a. Meditation
  b. Dreaming
  c. A drug "high"
  d. Hypnosis

4. Which of the following is *not* a distinction between the "normal" state of consciousness and alternative or altered states of consciousness?

  a. A change in body awareness
  b. An altered sense of time
  c. A change in the response of sensory systems
  d. A change in the ability to concentrate

5. Altered States of consciousness result from deliberate efforts to change our state of consciousness; alternative states of consciousness

  a. are associated with the functioning of the preconscious.
  b. occur in response to the behavior or suggestions of other people.
  c. are associated with some form of damage to or malfunction of the CNS.
  d. are natural states of consciousness.

Sleep and Dreaming

*6. A natural recurring state of rest characterized by reduced activity, diminished responsiveness to stimuli, and distinctive brain wave patterns describes

   a. sleep
   b. meditation.
   c. hypnosis.
   d. dreaming.

7. The primary distinction between stage 3 and stage 4 sleep concerns

   a. the proportion of rapid eye movements to nonrapid eye movements.
   b. the relative proportion of delta waves to other brain waves.
   c. the amount of muscular activity.
   d. whether or not the person is experiencing a dream.

8. If you normally sleep eight hours each night, you probably experience complete sleep cycle(s) each night.

   a. one
   b. three
   c. five
   d. eight

9. Generally speaking, we tend to have our longest dream period during the _Last_ part of the night.

   a. first
   b. middle
   c. last
   d. quietest

10. Which of the following bodily functions are reduced during REM sleep?

   a. Muscular activity
   b. Brain wave activity
   c. Heart rate
   d. Breathing

11. The atonia produced during REM sleep

   a. is a result of a loss of sleep.
   b. causes nightmares.
   c. causes increased muscle activity.
   d. keeps one from physically acting out their dreams.

12. Compared to adults, babies sleep

   a. the same amount of time but their sleep is differently distributed throughout the day.
   b. much longer, but spend the same amount of time in REM sleep.
   c. much longer, and spend a smaller percentage of time in REM sleep.
   d. much longer, and spend a greater percentage in REM sleep.

13. Which of the following theories of why we need to sleep would be more applicable to a person barely surviving in a Third World country in the midst of a famine than to a typical American?

    a. To restore depleted resources
    b. To conserve energy
    c. To prevent boredom
    d. To clear the mind

14. Crick and Mitchison theorized that

    a. changes in electrical activity in the brain during sleep result in useless information being discarded.
    b. dreaming is helpful in that it allows people to solve problems.
    c. the brain "invents" dreams to explain or account for the changes in electrical activity during sleep.
    d. sleep is necessary to restore depleted resources, such as neurotransmitters.

15. When people deprived of REM sleep for a number of days are allowed uninterrupted sleep, they

    a. experience sleep apnea.
    b. show sleep cycles that are identical to people not deprived of REM sleep.
    c. spend a greater percentage of time in REM sleep than they would normally spend.
    d. sleep about 50 percent longer than they would normally sleep.

*16. Which theory, explaining why we dream, appears to be the best explanation for the observation that newborn babies spend more time in REM sleep than people of other ages?

    a. Mental reprogramming
    b. To conserve energy
    c. Explanation of stimuli
    d. Dealing with problems

17. A serious sleep disorder in which a person stops breathing and frequently must waken briefly in order to breathe describes

    a. lucid sleeping.
    b. narcolepsy.
    c. sleep apnea.
    d. night terrors.

18. A sleep disorder whereby a person falls asleep suddenly and uncontrollably is called

    a. night terrors.
    b. somnambulism.
    c. narcolepsy.
    d. apnea.

19. A person who is sleepwalking is

    a. acting out a dream.
    b. in REM sleep.
    c. experiencing night terrors.
    d. in stage 3 or stage 4 sleep.

*20. A person experiencing a high amount of stress or conflict in their life would be *least* likely to experience

    a. night terrors.
    b. insomnia.
    c. sleepwalking.
    d. nightmares.

Meditation | Hypnosis

21. Concentrative and opening-up are two techniques of

    a. hypnosis.
    b. meditation.
    c. the relaxation response.
    d. treating insomnia.

22. A person in a state of meditation shows all of the following physiological changes except a(n)

    a. decrease in heart rate.
    b. decrease in respiration.
    c. increase in beta waves.
    d. increase in alpha waves.

23. Herbert Benson's (1977) "relaxation response" is an alternative to

    a. hypnosis.
    b. meditation.
    c. drug therapy.
    d. lucid sleeping.

*24. Which of the following statements does *not* describe a hypnotized person?

    a. He or she is highly suggestible to the hypnotist's instructions
    b. He or she is passive
    c. He or she has few if any independent thoughts
    d. He or she is not alert

25. Although hypnosis has been shown to be helpful in a number of medical applications, it has been least effective in

    a. treating self-initiated behaviors such as smoking, alcoholism, and overeating.
    b. treating stress-related illnesses such as asthma and ulcers.
    c. reducing pain.
    d. treating skin ailments such as warts and psoriasis.

26. That people can selectively focus attention on one thing (hypnotic suggestion) and still perceive other things "subconsciously" is Hilgard's ___neo dissociation___ theory.

    a. psychoanalytic
    b. neodissociation
    c. role-playing
    d. meditation

Drugs That Alter Consciousness

27. The three major types of psychoactive drugs are

    a. sedatives, opiates, and hallucinogens.

    b. depressants, amphetamines, and cocaine.

    c. depressants, stimulants, and hallucinogens.

    d. alcohol, opiates, and hallucinogens.

28. Taking a drug to maintain adequate levels in order to avoid withdrawal symptoms is referred to as

    a. physiological dependence.

    b. psychological dependence.

    c. tolerance.

    d. prolonged dependence.

29. Repeated usage of opiates or narcotics quickly results in

    a. a need for depressants as well.

    b. psychological but not physiological dependence.

    c. physiological but not psychological dependence.

    d. both physical and psychological dependence.

30. A 1973 study by Mark and Linda Sobell reported success with male alcoholics taught

    a. to only drink beer.

    b. to drink coffee instead of alcohol.

    c. total abstinence.

    d. controlled-drinking skills.

31. In American society, the most widely used stimulant is

    a. diet pills.

    b. caffeine.

    c. cocaine.

    d. nicotine.

32. Amphetamines can dramatically increase alertness and promote feelings of euphoria and well-being by

    a. enhancing dopamine and norepinephrine activity.

    b. suppressing dopamine and norepinephrine activity.

    c. keeping dopamine and norepinephrine levels constant.

    d. None of the above.

*33. The effects of cocaine are similar to the effects of

    a. heroin.

    b. PCP.

    c. amphetamines.

    d. barbiturates.

34. Which of the following is *not* classified as a hallucinogen?

    a. Marijuana
    b. MDMA (or ecstasy)
    c. PCP
    d. LSD

35. A person, admitted to a hospital following a drug overdose, suddenly and violently attacked a fire hydrant because it was staring at him. Most likely he took which one of the following drugs?

    a. Seconal
    b. Heroin
    c. PCP
    d. Cocaine

Answer Key

1. b	(152)	8. c	(157)	15. c	(161)	22. c	(170)	29. d	(176)
2. d	(152)	9. c	(157)	*16. a	(163)	23. b	(170)	30. d	(179)
3. b	(153)	10. a	(158)	17. c	(168)	*24. d	(171)	31. b	(180)
4. c	(153)	11. d	(158)	18. c	(168)	25. a	(172)	32. a	(181)
5. d	(153)	12. d	(158)	19. d	(169)	26. b	(174)	*33. c	(182)
*6. a	(154)	13. b	(160)	*20. a	(169)	27. c	(175)	34. b	(183)
7. b	(155)	14. a	(160)	21. b	(170)	28. a	(175)	35. c	(184)

Annotated Answers

    6. The correct choice is a. It is the definition of sleep presented in the text.
        b. First, meditation is not a naturally occurring state; and, second, one technique of meditation (opening up) is characterized by increasing awareness to all forms of sensations.
        c. First, hypnosis is not a naturally occurring state; and, second, it is not characterized by distinctive brain wave patterns. Additionally, while responsiveness to most stimuli is reduced, an individual is very responsive to a hypnotist's suggestions.
        d. During dreaming or REM sleep, brain wave patterns are similar to those of wakefulness and the person is still responsive to many stimuli.

    16. The correct choice is a. The text states that "mental reprogramming" explains the observation that the elderly spend less time in REM sleep—presumably because they encounter few new experiences during the wakeful state. Similar logic would explain newborn babies requiring more REM sleep because they encounter a vast amount of new information each day.
        b. Although the "to conserve energy" theory may be a useful explanation of the length of time infants sleep, it would not explain the observation that infants spend increased time in REM sleep.
        c. "Explanation of stimuli" would be no more appropriate to infants than to individuals of other ages.
        d. "Dealing with problems" refers to a low-stress way of dealing with problems that typically contain a cognitive component. It does not seem appropriate to view a newborn as capable of these thought processes.

20. The correct choice is a. Night terrors appear to be associated with being suddenly wakened from a deep sleep and not an indication of an underlying psychological problem or stress; b, c, and d are all believed to be associated with or to increase during periods of high stress or conflict.

24. The correct choice is d. Even though the term *hypnosis* comes from the name of the Greek god of sleep, a hypnotized person is not drowsy but very alert.
   a. One of the characteristics of hypnosis, allowing it to be helpful in a variety of situations, is that the individual is highly responsive to the hypnotist's instructions.
   b. Hypnotized individuals are passive in that they do not independently initiate activities.
   c. Similar to b the hypnotized person does not tend to have independent thoughts.

33. The correct choice is c. Both cocaine and amphetamines are classified as stimulants.
   a. Heroin is classified as a depressant.
   b. PCP is classified as a hallucinogen.
   d. Barbiturates are classified as depressants.

PART VI. SUMMARY TABLES

To test your understanding of the material discussed in this chapter complete the following tables. Check your answers with those supplied in PART IX.

Stages of the Sleep Cycle

Stage	Brain Wave Patterns	Eye Movements	Muscular Activity	Other
1	Theta waves low amplitude - low frequency	Slow	Relaxed	Easily awakened
2	Burst of sleep spindles	minimal	decreases	—
3	Delta waves 20-50% of time High amplit, Low freq.	Virtually None	movement, may sleep walk	—
4	Delta waves over 50% of time	Virtually None	movement, may sleep walk	Difficult to awaken
Stage 1 REM	Beta waves low amplitude high frequency	Rapid (REM)	no movement muscular inhibition	Dreaming Easily awakened

Types of Psychoactive Drugs

Class	Effect	Neurotransmitters Affected by at Least Some Drugs of this Class
Depressants	decreases action in CNS	GABA
Stimulants	increases activity in CNS	Dopamine + Norepinephrine
Hallucinogens	Changes in sensory perception, thinking processes, + emotions	Serotonin

Specific Drugs

Drug	Class (Depressant, Stimulant, Hallucinogen)	Examples (If Appropriate)	Physiological or Psychological Dependence
Alcohol			
Amphetamines			
Caffeine			
Cocaine			
LSD			
Marijuana			
Nicotine			
Opiates			
PCP			
Sedatives			

PART VII. THOUGHT QUESTIONS/CRITICAL THINKING

Prepare answers to the following discussion questions.

1. With the amount of research being conducted in all areas of psychology, do you think it is "just a matter of time" before sleep researchers have definitive information concerning the effects of long-term sleep (or REM sleep) deprivation on humans? Explain your answer.

2. You get home from class and are tired and decide to take a nap before dinner. Based on your knowledge of the sleep cycle, what would be the ideal length of time for a nap? Explain. What would be one example of the worst length of time for a nap? Explain.

3. Which theory of why we sleep, or why we dream would best explain each of the following observations? Explain your choices.
   a. Why we sleep more when we are sick
   b. Why babies sleep more than adults
   c. Why babies have more REM sleep than adults
   d. Why a person might spend more time in REM sleep after attending a beneficial two-day workshop related to the performance of their job
   e. Why a person might sleep more after attending a useless two-day workshop related to the performance of their job
   f. Why pregnant women sleep more than they did before they were pregnant
   g. Why a student might dream more while working on a lengthy term paper

4. Obviously brain activity and dreaming are related. Which do you think comes first? Do you think brain activity causes dreams to develop, or does the dream result in changes in brain wave patterns? Explain your answers.

5. Many people take psychoactive drugs because they desire a specific consciousness-altering effect: to relax, to reduce stress or anxiety, to reduce boredom, to heighten sensory experiences, to obtain pain relief, to alter their thinking, to increase their physical arousal or energy level, or to gain personal insight. Many of these effects may also be obtained without the use of psychoactive drugs. For each of the following activities suggest which drug(s) would be appropriate substitutes. Explain your choices
   a. Jogging or some other physical exercise
   b. Taking a long, warm bath
   c. Hypnosis
   d. Sky diving
   e. Reading a good book
   f. Meditation
   g. Playing an intellectually stimulating computer game
   h. Taking a "nature walk"

PART VIII. APPLICATIONS

1. Chapter 5 describes a number of theories as to why we sleep and dream. This chapter also presents information that supports some of the theories. (Two examples: people sleep longer after vigorous exercise; people spend more time in REM sleep after activities requiring unusual mental efforts.) For the next week to 10 days keep a diary of your daily activities and the number of hours you sleep. Note the time you go to sleep each night and the time you wake up. Note whether or not you were wakened by an alarm clock or if you "just woke-up." If you wake up during the night, note the time. If you recall any dreams, write down what each dream was about. After you have completed your diary, examine it to answer the following:

a. Is there evidence to support any of the theories as to why we sleep?

b. Is there evidence to support any of the theories as to why we dream?

c. Was the content of your dreams similar to the list of college students' common dreams listed in Table 5.1 in the text?

d. Was the length of time you slept each night (or length of time you slept before wakening in the "middle of the night") consistent with a 90-minute sleep cycle?

2. In Chapter 2 in the text (The Methods of Psychology) it was noted that relatively similar experiments do not always yield similar results. From the information presented in the text on pages 161–162 concerning the effect of REM-sleep deprivation on rats there appears to be conflicting results. The first study (Morden et al., 1967) found that REM-deprived rats did not show any significant behavioral or emotional difficulties. While in the second study (Kushida et al., 1989) all the REM-deprived rats died. Prepare a list of questions you would like to see answered concerning these two studies that would help you decide how to reconcile these seemingly conflicting results. The discussion of the two studies in the text was necessarily brief, and your questions might be answered by reading the original reports of the experiments published in scientific journals. The references for the two experiments are listed in the bibliography of the text. If your college library subscribes to these journals, read the articles and decide if the conflicting results and conclusions can be reconciled by a difference in the procedures employed in the two studies or if additional research is needed to reach a conclusion concerning the effects of REM deprivation on rats.

PART IX. SUMMARY TABLE SOLUTIONS

Stages of the Sleep Cycle

Stage	Brain Wave Patterns	Eye Movements	Muscular Activity	Other

1	Theta waves
	Low amplitude–
	  low frequency
	  (3–7 cps)
		Slow	Relaxed	Easily wakened

2	Burst of sleep spindles (12–14 cps)	Minimal	Decreases	—

3	Delta waves 20–50
	  percent of the time
	High amplitude–
	  low frequency
	  (0.5–2 cps)
		Virtually none	Movement,
			May sleepwalk
				—

4	Delta waves over 50 percent of the time	Virtually none	Movement, May sleepwalk	Difficult to waken
Stage 1 REM	Beta waves Low amplitude– high frequency	Rapid (REM)	No movement Muscular inhibition	Dreaming Easily wakened

Types of Psychoactive Drugs

Class	Effect	Neurotransmitters Affected by at Least Some Drugs of this Class
Depressants	Decreases action in the CNS	GABA
Stimulants	Increases activity in the CNS	Dopamine and norepinephrine
Hallucinogens	Changes in sensory perception, thinking processes, and emotions	Serotonin

Specific Drugs

Drug	Class (Depressant, Stimulant, Hallucinogen)	Examples (If Appropriate)	Physiological or Psychological Dependence
Alcohol	Depressant	—	Physiological
Amphetamines	Stimulant	Benzedrine, dexedrine, methedrine, MDMA	Psychological and perhaps physiological
Caffeine	Stimulant	—	Psychological
Cocaine	Stimulant	—	Psychological and perhaps physiological
LSD	Hallucinogen	—	—
Marijuana	Hallucinogen	—	—
Nicotine	Stimulant	—	Physiological
Opiates	Depressant	Morphine, codeine, heroin	Physiological and psychological
PCP	Hallucinogen	—	Perhaps psychological
Sedatives	Depressant	Tranquilizers, barbiturates, nonbarbiturates	Physiological

CHAPTER **6**

Learning

PART I. LEARNING OBJECTIVES

When you finish studying this chapter you should be able to:

Learning Defined

1. Define learning and be able to discuss the three elements of the definition. **(193)**

2. Define associative learning and briefly discuss the two forms of associative learning. **(194)**

Classical Conditioning

3. Describe classical conditioning and explain, by using the appropriate terms, how a response is learned through classical conditioning. **(196)**

4. Define extinction and discuss how spontaneous recovery is related to extinction. **(201)**

5. Define generalization and discrimination and explain how the two processes differ. **(201-202)**

6. Describe higher order conditioning. **(202)**

Operant Conditioning

7. Describe the approaches used by Thorndike and Skinner to study operant conditioning. **(203-205)**

8. Define reinforcement and differentiate between positive reinforcement, negative reinforcement, and punishment. **(205-206)**

9. Discriminate between primary and secondary reinforcers, and explain how the latter acquire reinforcing properties. **(207-208)**

10. Explain the difference between continuous and partial reinforcement. **(208-209)**

11. Compare and contrast the four schedules of partial reinforcement. **(209)**

12. Describe five techniques that may be used to "speed-up" the obtainment of the initial operant response. **(212-213)**

13. Explain two important differences between classical and operant conditioning. **(213-214)**

14. Describe how two-process learning combines elements of classical and operant conditioning. **(214-216)**

Punishment: Is It Effective?

15. Discuss some of the problems or limitations associated with the use of punishment. **(216)**

16. Discuss some ways to make punishment more effective. **(217-219)**

17. Explain how extinction can sometimes be used in place of punishment. **(219)**

Cognitive Influences on Learning

18. Explain how the cognitive learning perspective differs from the associative learning perspective. **(220)**

19. Explain and give an example of insight learning. **(220-221)**

20. Describe Tolman's contributions involving latent learning and cognitive maps. **(221-222)**

21. Explain how cognitive learning theorists interpret classical and operant conditioning by utilizing cognitive processes. **(222-223)**

22. Describe the major principles associated with observational learning. **(223-224)**

PART II: OVERVIEW

Learning refers to a relatively enduring change in potential behavior that results from experience. The chapter begins with a description of two types of associative learning.

Classical conditioning involves learning an association between two stimuli. Before classical conditioning training, one stimulus (the unconditioned stimulus or UCS) naturally causes a specific response (the unconditioned response or UCR). During acquisition of classical conditioning, another stimulus (the conditioned stimulus or CS) is associated or paired with the UCS. Eventually the CS will come to elicit a response (the conditioned response or CR) that is similar to the UCR. In other words, the CS becomes a signal associated with the UCS and the individual begins to respond to the CS the same way that he or she previously responded to the UCS.

Operant conditioning involves learning an association between a behavior and the consequences of that behavior. If the consequences of a behavior are good, the behavior is reinforced and the probability of that behavior occurring again increases. There are two main categories of reinforcers: positive reinforcers result in a pleasant event starting, negative reinforcers result in the termination or avoidance of an unpleasant event. If the consequences of a behavior are unpleasant, the behavior is punished and the probability of that behavior reoccurring, decreases.

This chapter discusses a number of processes such as extinction, spontaneous recovery, generalization, and discrimination that relate to or elaborate on the general features of classical and operant conditioning.

This chapter also describes cognitive learning that is different from associative learning. Cognitive learning takes into account complex mental processes such as perception, thinking, and memory. Cognitive learning involves the study of insight learning whereby an individual learns a solution to a complex problem as a result of a sudden recognition of the relationships involved in the problem. Cognitive learning is also concerned with latent learning in which learning occurs in the absence of reinforcement. Cognitive learning is also concerned with observational learning in which an individual learns through observing another's behavior and imitating or modeling that behavior.

Finally, the chapter emphasizes the classical conditioning, operant conditioning, and cognitive learning interact in a complex fashion.

PART III. KEY TERMS/MATCHING EXERCISES

Match the following concepts and/or individuals with the appropriate descriptions. Check your answers against the Answer Key.

Learning Overview

Concepts

_c_ . 1. learning (**193**)   _a_ . 4. operant conditioning (**203**)

_b_ . 2. associative learning (**194**)   _e_ . 5. two-process learning (**214**)

_f_ . 3. classical conditioning (**194**) _d_ . 6. cognitive learning (**220**)

Descriptions

a. The learning process by which behavior is influenced by its consequences

b. The learning process by which a connection is made between two events

c. A relatively enduring change in potential behavior that results from experience

d. Learning theory that takes into account mental processes such as perception, thinking, and memory

e. The learning process that combines both classical and operant conditioning

f. the learning process by which one stimulus becomes a signal associated with another stimulus

Answer Key   1. c   2. b   3. f   4. a   5. e   6. d

Individuals

_e_ • 1. Pavlov (**196**)

_a_ • 2. Thorndike (**203**)

_c_ • 3. Skinner (**205**)

_b_ • 4. Köhler (**220**)

_d_ • 5. Tolman (**221**)

_f_ • 6. Bandura (**223**)

Descriptions

a. Developed the law of effect

b. Studied insight learning and not associative learning

c. Associated with positive reinforcement, shaping, and cumulative recorders

d. Believed that animals could develop cognitive maps of their environment

e. Studied learning that involved the association of two stimuli

f. Emphasized learning through observation and imitation

Answer Key   1. e   2. a   3. c   4. b   5. d   6. f

Classical Conditioning

Concepts

_d_ • 1. unconditioned stimulus (UCS) (**197**)

_a_ • 2. unconditioned response (UCR) (**197**)

_c_ • 3. conditioned stimulus (CS) (**197**)

_b_ • 4. conditioned response (CR) (**197**)

Descriptions

a. A response to a stimulus that does not require learning

b. A response given to a previously neutral stimulus

c. An originally neutral stimulus that eventually elicits a response

d. A stimulus that elicits a response before classical conditioning training

Answer Key   1. d   2. a   3. c   4. b

Concepts

_a_ • 1. extinction (**200**)

_d_ • 2. spontaneous recovery (**200**)

_e_ • 3. generalization (**200**)

_b_ • 4. discrimination (**200**)

_c_ • 5. higher order conditioning (**202**)

Descriptions

a. Occurs if a CS is repeatedly presented without being followed by a UCS

b. The tendency to respond to some stimuli while not responding to other similar stimuli

c. Occurs when a second stimulus is associated with a CS

d. Occurs when a CS is presented following extinction and the passage of time

e. The tendency for a new stimulus to elicit the same response as the original CS

Answer Key   1. a   2. d   3. e   4. b   5. c

Operant Conditioning

Concepts

_e_ 1. law of effect (**203**)

_h_ 2. discriminative stimulus (**204**)

_b_ 3. cumulative recorder (**205**)

_c_ 4. postive reinforcer (**206**)

_f_ 5. negative reinforcer (**206**)

_g_ 6. punishment (**206**)

_a_ 7. escape conditioning (**206**)

_d_ 8. avoidance conditioning (**206**)

Descriptions

a. Involves the termination of an unpleasant stimulus following an appropriate response

b. May be used to visualize an individual's rate of response

c. A stimulus that is presented following a response that increases the probability of that response occuring again

d. If an appropriate response is made, an unpleasant stimulus does not occur

e. States that behavior followed by a satisfying consequence will be strengthened

f. A stimulus that terminates or avoids an unpleasant event and increases the probability of that response occurring again

g. A stimulus that is presented following a response that decreases the probability of that response occurring again

h. A stimulus that signifies the availability of reinforcement

Answer Key   1. e   2. h   3. b   4. c   5. f   6. g   7. a   8. d

Concepts

_d_ 1. primary reinforcement (**208**)

_b_ 2. secondary reinforcement (**208**)

_a_ 3. continous reinforcement (**209**)

_e_ 4. partial reinforcement (**209**)

_c_ 5. shaping (**212**)

Descriptions

a. Should be used during acquisition of an operantly conditioned response

b. A stimulus, such as money or praise, that acquires reinforcing qualities

c   Involves reinforcing behaviors that are closer and closer to the desired operant response

d. A stimulus, such as food or water, that satisifies a biological drive or need

e. If persistent responding is desired, this should be used after the behavior has been learned

Answer Key   1. d   2. b   3. a   4. e   5. c

Schedules of Partial Reinforcement

Concepts

__a__ 1. fixed ratio (FR) **(209)**   __c__ 3. fixed interval (FI) **(210)**

__d__ 2. variable ratio (VR) **(210)**   __b__ 4. variable interval (VI) **(211)**

Descriptions

a. Reinforcement occurs following every specified number of responses

b. Reinforcement occurs following the first response after an unpredictable or average amount of time

c. Reinforcement occurs following the first response after a specific amount of time

d. Reinforcement occurs following an unpredictable or average number of responses

Answer Key   1. a   2. d   3. c   4. b

Cognitive Learning

Concepts

__b__ 1. Insight **(220)**   __a__ 4. Observational learning **(223)**

__d__ 2. Latent learning **(221)**   __c__ 5. Social learning theory **(223)**

__e__ 3. Cognitive map **(221)**

Descriptions

a. Learning that occurs as a result of modeling without the individual being reinforced

b. A sudden recognition of relationships that lead to the solution of a complex problem

c. Emphasizes the role of observation and imitation in learning

d. Learning that occurs in the absence of reinforcement

e. A mental representation of the elements in the environment

Answer Key   1. b   2. d   3. e   4. a   5. c

PART IV. TRUE-FALSE STATEMENTS

Fill in the blank before each statement with either a T (true) or an F (false). Check your answers against the Answer Key. Then go back to the items that are false and make the necessary change(s) to the statements to convert the items into true statements.

Learning Defined

_____ 1. A new behavior that is acquired as a result of an individual's maturation is considered a learned behavior.

_____

_____

Classical Conditioning

_____ 2. Ideally for classical conditioning to take place the UCS must be presented before the CS.

_____ 3. When a CR that has been extinguished suddenly returns after an interval of rest, we say spontaneous recovery has occurred.

_____ 4. Generalization describes the situation when a CR is made to a stimulus that is different from the original CS.

Operant Conditioning

_____ 5. A positive reinforcer increases the probability of a response occurring again, whereas a negative reinforcer decreases the probability of a response occurring again.

_____ 6. Typically, a rat on a FR schedule of reinforcement has a higher rate of responding than a rat on a FI schedule of reinforcement.

_____ 7. Shaping involves the physical guidance of the subject to make the desired response.

Punishment

_____ 8. While punishment usually suppresses an unwanted behavior temporarily, it does not necessarily extinguish the behavior.

_____ 9. If you are using punishment in an appropriate manner, it is not important to also reward acceptable behaviors.

Cognitive Learning

_____ 10. Both Köhler and Thorndike support the cognitive learning perspective.

_____ 11. Cognitive learning suggests that cognitive factors, such as expectancy, provide the basis for the behavior changes observed in classical and operant conditioning.

_____

_____

_____ 12. Bandura's study involving children and a Bobo doll demonstrated modeling.

_____

_____

Answer Key

1. F **(193)**	5. F **(206)**	9. F **(218)**
2. F **(199)**	6. T **(210–211)**	10. F **(220)**
3. T **(200)**	7. F **(213)**	11. T **(222)**
4. T **(200)**	8. T **(216)**	12. T **(224)**

PART V. MULTIPLE-CHOICE QUESTIONS

Choose the best answer to each question. Circle your choice. Check your answers against the Answer Key. Questions marked with an asterisk (*) include annotated answers.

Learning Defined

1. Learning refers to

  a. a change in behavior that is demonstrated immediately.
  b. a change in behavior that results from disease or maturation.
  c. a relatively enduring change in potential behavior that results from experience.
  d. all changes in behavior.

2. Associative learning describes the process by which a connection or association is made between

  a. two stimuli.
  b. a behavior and the consequences of that behavior.
  c. a problem and the solution to that problem.
  d. Both a and b are correct.

3. After receiving a traffic ticket for not coming to a complete stop at a stop sign, you now very carefully stop at that intersection. According to learning theorists, you have experienced

  a. social learning.
  b. associative learning.
  c. motor-skill learning.
  d. defensive learning.

Classical Conditioning

4. If a dog salivates after hearing the sound of a bell, salivation would be a(n)

   a. conditioned stimulus (CS).
   b. conditioned response (CR).
   c. unconditioned stimulus (UCS).
   d. unconditioned response (UCR).

5. Young children frequently cry when their mothers leave them. Sometimes they start to cry as soon as a babysitter arrives. This occurs because the

   a. babysitter is UCS associated with the mother leaving.
   b. babysitter uses negative reinforcement.
   c. babysitter is a CS associated with the mother leaving.
   d. child dislikes the babysitter.

6. Which of the following statements best describes the relationship between UCR and CR?

   a. They are identical in all respects.
   b. The CR is generally more intense.
   c. The UCR is generally more intense.
   d. The CR only occurs following the presentation of the UCS.

7. Which of the following is *not* an important factor in the initial acquisition of a CR?

   a. The motivation of the individual to perform the CR
   b. The timing of the presentation of the CS and UCS
   c. That the CS is clearly different from other stimuli
   d. How frequently the CS and UCS have been paired

8. To extinguish a CR you should

   a. pair the CS with a higher order stimulus.
   b. repeatedly present the CS while not presenting the UCS.
   c. withhold the UCR.
   d. not present the CS for a period of several days.

9. Years ago, a young woman's boyfriend broke up with her while they were watching the movie, *Top Gun*, starring Tom Cruise. Today, when she sees a Tom Cruise movie or sees him on TV, she starts to cry. Her behavior illustrates

   a. generalization.
   b. neurosis.
   c. latent learning.
   d. discrimination.

10. When driving, I stop when the light turns red and go when the light turns green. My driving illustrates

   a. spontaneous recovery.
   b. generalization.
   c. discrimination.
   d. UCR.

11. Teaching an organism to respond to only one of a series of similar stimuli is called
   a. operant conditioning.
   b. generalization.
   c. extinction.
   d. discrimination training.

*12. To demonstrate higher order conditioning it is necessary to
   a. pair the CS with a new UCS.
   b. employ discrimination training.
   c. pair a new stimulus with the CS.
   d. repeatedly present the CS while not presenting the UCS.

Operant Conditioning

*13. The most commonly used measure of the strength of an operant response is
   a. the rate of response.
   b. the calculation from the Law of Effect.
   c. the variety of stimuli that elicit the response.
   d. how much generalization is shown.

14. "Any event that increases the probability that a response will occur" is the definition of
   a. primary reinforcers.
   b. operant conditioning.
   c. rewards.
   d. reinforcement.

15. A reinforcer that is reinforcing because it causes something unpleasant to end or not occur is called a
   a. reverse reinforcer.
   b. negative reinforcer.
   c. positive reinforcer.
   d. punishment.

16. Secondary reinforcers
   a. satisfy biological based drives, such as hunger and thirst.
   b. acquire reinforcing properties through association with primary reinforcers.
   c. are reinforced on partial or secondary schedules of reinforcement.
   d. are less important than primary reinforcers.

*17. Even after getting 20 doors in a row slammed in his face, a door-to-door salesman doesn't quit because his behavior has most likely been reinforced on a _variable_ schedule of reinforcement.
   a. continuous
   b. fixed
   c. variable
   d. gambler's

18. Immediately after being reinforced, a rat on which schedule of reinforcement would show the longest pause before its next bar press?

   a. FR
   b. VR
   c. FI
   d. VI

19. Which technique for obtaining an initial operant response would be most effective in teaching a rat to bar press?

   a. Shaping
   b. Modeling
   c. Physical guidance
   d. Verbal instruction

20. A mental hospital patient is rewarded for each step of the dressing process until he is able to completely dress himself. This behavioral technique is called

   a. variable ratio schedules.
   b. shaping.
   c. variable interval schedules.
   d. modeling.

21. Many human phobias are learned as a result of

   a. two-process learning.
   b. spontaneous recovery.
   c. punishment.
   d. operant conditioning.

Punishment

22. A child's punishment for raiding the cookie jar successfully suppresses the behavior until the grandparents babysit and the cookie feast begins. The child's cookie-eating behavior increased because

   a. punishment suppresses but does not eliminate the behavior in many cases.
   b. the child enjoys punishment.
   c. the grandparents were not looking.
   d. the punishment was not strong enough.

23. Which of the following is *not* a limitation or undesirable side effect of punishment?

   a. It may induce counteraggression against the punisher.
   b. Anxiety may interfere with performance.
   c. Positive reinforcers lose their reinforcing properties.
   d. The results are often temporary.

24. For punishment to be effective it should

   a. be administered every time the inappropriate behavior occurs.
   b. not be too severe.
   c. be administered immediately after the inappropriate behavior occurs.
   d. All of the above are correct.

25. Sometimes the most effective way to stop undesirable behavior is to simply withhold the rewards that are maintaining it. In this instance, which behavioral technique is being used?

    a. Generalization
    b. Discrimination
    c. Extinction
    d. Shaping

Cognitive Learning

*26. Which line of research demonstrates the distinction between learning and performance?

    a. Köhler's insight learning
    b. Tolman's latent learning
    c. Thorndike's puzzle-box learning
    d. Both a and b are correct.

27. In your high school algebra class, you couldn't understand how to solve quadratic equations until one day (luckily the day before the exam) when everything suddenly fell into place and made so much sense that you couldn't believe you had been having difficulty with the equations. What happened?

    a. Trial-and-error learning finally occurred
    b. Observational learning
    c. Doing your homework was helpful
    d. Insight learning

*28. A mother attempts to take her 5-year-old son to a birthday party at a bowling alley they have been to only once before. While the mother is frantically reading the directions, her son says, "You should have turned at the McDonald's and again at the church." He's correct. What most likely explains his behavior?

    a. Latent learning
    b. Classical conditioning
    c. Modeling
    d. Positive reinforcement

29. If you believe that classical conditioning develops because the CS provides information about the UCS, you agree with

    a. Köhler.
    b. the cognitive learning perspective.
    c. Pavlov.
    d. Skinner.

30. The basic premise of observational learning is that

    a. behavior learned through observational learning is never extinguished.
    b. insight into the model's motivation is gained.
    c. learning may occur without physical responses or reinforcement.
    d. all learning results from modeling.

31. According to Bandura, the fourth and final step involved in observational learning concerns

    a. performing the modeled response.

    b. having our attention drawn to a modeled behavior.

    c. the decision to perform the modeled response when we are able to do so.

    d. whether we are reinforced for performing the modeled response.

Answer Key

1. c	**(193)**	8. b	**(200)**	15. b	**(206)**	22. a	**(217)**	29. b	**(222)**
2. d	**(194-195)**	9. a	**(200)**	16. b	**(208)**	23. c	**(217)**	30. c	**(223)**
3. b	**(194)**	10. c	**(202)**	*17. c	**(211)**	24. d	**(218)**	31. d	**(224)**
4. b	**(197)**	11. d	**(200)**	18. c	**(211)**	25. c	**(219)**		
5. c	**(197)**	*12. c	**(202)**	19. a	**(213)**	*26. b	**(221)**		
6. c	**(197)**	*13. a	**(205)**	20. b	**(213)**	27. d	**(221)**		
7. a	**(199)**	14. d	**(205)**	21. a	**(214)**	*28. a	**(221)**		

Annotated Answers

12. The correct choice is c. An example of higher order conditioning is as follows: After a dog learns to salivate to the sound of a bell, you then present a light before sounding the bell. The light would become a CS (a higher order CS) for the original CS, the bell.

    a. This would result in the animal learning to give another CR to the original CS.

    b. Discrimination is not related to higher order conditioning.

    d. This would result in the extinction of the CR.

13. The correct choice is a. This measure quantifies to number of responses given in a specified amount of time allowing a relative measurement of how strong a behavior is (stronger behaviors would result in higher rates of responding).

    b. There is no calculation from the Law of Effect. It merely states that a behavior that is followed by a satisfying consequence will be strengthened.

    c. This alternative relates to generalization and the term *elicit* implies classical conditioning.

    d. Generalization is relevant to operant conditioning as well as to classical conditioning, but it would be difficult to quantify as a measure of the strength of a behavior. For example, if the operant response for my dog to sit when I say "Sit," generalization would relate to both how frequently my dog sits when I say some other word or how frequently my dog sits when someone else says "Sit."

17. The correct choice is c. Because the salesman was reinforced on a variable schedule he would continue to believe that he might make a sale at the next house and would persist in this behavior.

    a. If the salesman was reinforced on a continuous schedule he would make a sale at every house.

    b. If the salesman was reinforced on a fixed schedule he would make a sale after every specific number of houses (FR) or after every specific amount of time (FI).

    d. While gambling can be reinforced on a variable schedule, the term "gambler's schedule of reinforcement" does not exist.

26. The correct choice is b. In Tolman's maze study, the rats in the latent learning group learned a cognitive map of the maze, but did not "show" this by their performance until the situation was changed so that they were reinforced after reaching the end of the maze.

a. In insight learning, when the individual learns the appropriate behavior, he or she immediately performs that behavior.

c. In trial-and-error learning an increase in performance is equated with with acquisition of the learned behavior.

d. This answer is incorrect because alternative a is incorrect.

28. The correct choice is a. The child learned a cognitive map of the relevant landmarks to the bowling alley on his first visit there.

b. Even if you could justify the McDonald's as being a CS for the bowling alley, classical conditioning would not explain how the behavior was learned in one trial.

c. Modeling is not appropriate for this question.

d. This is similar to the logic involved for alternative b. A weak case could be made for the turn at McDonald's being reinforced, however, operant conditioning would not explain how the behavior was learned in one trial. Alternative a is clearly the best choice.

PART VI: SUMMARY TABLES

To test your understanding of the materials discussed in this chapter, complete the following tables. Check your answers with those supplied in PART IX.

Associative Learning Comparison of Classical and Operant Conditioning

	Which two elements are associated?	Is response elicited or emitted?	Does subject play an active or passive role?	Is presentation of UCS/reinforcement contingent on the subject's behavior?
Classical conditioning	two stimuli CS + UCS	elicited	passive	not contingent
Operant conditioning	behavior + consequence	emitted	active	contingent

Comparison of Positive Reinforcement, Negative Reinforcement; and Punishment

	Consequences of Behavior		Probability of Response	Example
	(Good/Bad)	What occurs?	(Increases/Decreases)	
Positive reinforcement	good	pleasant events start	increases	food
Negative reinforcement	good	unpleasant event stops or avoided	increases	terminates or avoids shocks
Punishment	Bad	unpleasant consequence	decreases	shock administ.

Schedules of Partial Reinforcement

	Rate of Response (High/Low)	Pause after Reinforcement (Yes/No)	Length of Pause after Reinforcement (Brief/Extended)
Fixed ratio			
Variable ratio			
Fixed interval			
Variable interval			

PART VII: THOUGHT QUESTIONS/CRITICAL THINKING

Prepare answers to the following discussion questions.

1. Based on the definition of learning presented in the text, is it appropriate to say a young baby learns to eat solid foods? Why or why not?

2. You want to teach your dog to fetch the remote control for your TV. Why should you first use continuous reinforcement and then switch to partial reinforcement?

3. How is classical conditioning involved in avoidance conditioning?

4. Extinction is commonly thought of as the unlearning or forgetting of a learned response. Which of the following statements concerning extinction is more appropriate? (a) All memory traces of the learned response is wiped out; (b) Some learning remains or "an elephant never forgets." Explain your answer.

5. Think of one behavior that you would like someone you know to perform (for example, picking up their clothes, speaking English more grammatically, being on time). Based on the information discussed in this chapter, which strategy would you use (classical conditioning, operant conditioning, punishment, cognitive learning) to "teach" that behavior? What specific steps would you use to accomplish your objective?

PART VIII. APPLICATIONS

1. The following situation (or one similar to it) is relatively common in homes with young children:

> It's 10 minutes before dinner and the child asks for a cookie. The mother says, "No, it will spoil your appetite. The child begins to plead, beg, scream, and cry for the cookie. Mom continues to say, "No, no, no," until the child wears her down and she says, "OK, but you'd better eat all your dinner." The child stops screaming and takes the cookie.

In operant conditioning terms, what exactly is happening here?

- **a.** Is the child being reinforced? If so, in what manner?
- **b.** Is the mother being reinforced? If so in what manner?
- **c.** What do you think will happen tomorrow 10 minutes before dinner?
- **d.** What should the mother do if she wants to eliminate this pre dinner cookie-eating behavior?
- **e.** Why would B.F. Skinner say, "If you have the slightest doubt that you will give in and give the child the cookie, give it to the child when they first ask for it"?

2. Read each of the following descriptions of a behavior that you would like an individual to learn.

- **a.** A parent would like his/her child to say "please" and "thank you."
- **b.** You would like to teach your dog to "speak" on command.
- **c.** A parent would like his/her child to stop leaving their room a mess and start to make their bed each morning.
- **d.** You would like your dog to stop begging for food from the table while you are eating.
- **e.** You just bought a telephone answering machine for your apartment. You want your roommate to learn how to operate it.

What would be the most effective way to teach each behavior (classical conditioning, extinction, modeling, punishment, shaping, verbal instruction)? Explain how you would teach each behavior. Would another method also be effective in teaching the behavior? If your answer is yes, justify your original decision.

PART IX: SUMMARY TABLES SOLUTIONS

Associative Learning Comparison of Classical and Operant Conditioning

	Which two elements are associated?	Is response elicited or emitted?	Does subject play an active or passive role?	Is presentation of UCS/reinforcement contingent on the subject's behavior?
Classical conditioning	two stimuli (CS & UCS)	elicited	passive	not contingent
Operant conditioning	behavior and consequence	emitted	active	contingent

Comparison of Positive Reinforcement, Negative Reinforcement; and Punishment

	Consequences of Behavior		Probability of Response	Example
	(Good/Bad)	What Occurs?	(Increases/Decreases)	
Positive reinforcement	good	pleasant event starts	increases	food
Negative reinforcement	good	unpleasant event stops or avoided	increases	terminates or avoids shock
Punishment	bad	unpleasant consequence	decreases	shock administered

Schedules of Partial Reinforcement

	Rate of Response (High/Low)	Pause after Reinforcement (Yes/No)	Length of Pause after Reinforcement (Brief/Extended)
Fixed ratio	high	yes	brief
Variable ratio	high	no	—
Fixed interval	low	yes	extended
Variable interval	low	no	—

CHAPTER **7**

Memory

PART I. LEARNING OBJECTIVES

When you finish studying this chapter you should be able to:

What Is Memory?

1. Define memory, and identify the dual meanings of the term. **(229)**

2. Describe the information-processing model of memory including the three processes of encoding, storage, and retrieval. **(230)**

A Three-System Model of Memory

3. Explain the function of sensory memory, and compare and contrast iconic and echoic memory. **(231-232)**

4. Explain the function and capacity of short-term memory (STM), and explain the importance of rehearsal for STM. **(235)**

5. Describe chunking, and explain how chunking increases the capacity of STM. **(235-236)**

6. Describe how information is coded or represented in STM. **(236)**

7. Describe the function and capacity of long-term memory (LTM), and identify two types of LTM. **(236)**

8. Describe six mnemonic devices that can be used to improve coding in LTM. **(238-240)**

9. Define association networks and explain how these influence retrieval from LTM. **(241-242)**

10. Describe three methods to measure long-term memory, and order the three methods from most sensitive to least sensitive. **(243-244)**

Some Factors That Influence What We Remember

11. Describe the serial position effect and explain why it occurs. **(244-245)**

12. Define state-dependent memory and describe both physiological and emotional states that influence state-dependent memory. **(245)**

13. Define flashbulb memory and cite several examples of events that have resulted in flashbulb memories. **(245-246)**

Memory as a Constructive Process

14. Explain why memory is a constructive process, and describe how schemas are associated with memory being constructive. **(246-249)**

15. Summarize the results of experiments on eyewitness testimony, and discuss why eyewitness reports may not be accurate. **(249-251)**

Why We Forget

16. Describe the decay explanation of forgetting and explain why this theory is nearly impossible to prove or disprove. **(252)**

17. Describe the interference explanation of forgetting, and describe both retroactive and proactive interference. **(252-253)**

18. Explain forgetting from the retrieval failure perspective, and indicate two reasons why information may not be retrieved. **(253)**

19. Describe the motivated forgetting explanation of forgetting, and relate it to Freud's concept of repression. **(253-254)**

20. Define and describe three types of organic amnesia. **(254)**

The Physical Bases of Memory

21. Describe Hebb's conception of how STMs and LTMs are stored, and summarize recent experimental evidence indicating structural changes within the nervous system associated with LTM. **(255)**

22. Summarize the evidence concerning where LTMs are stored and processed. **(257, 259-261)**

Strategies for Improving Academic Memory

23. Describe nine strategies for improving academic memory. **(261-264)**

PART II. OVERVIEW

According to the information-processing perspective, being able to remember a piece of information involves three processes: (1) the information has to be encoded or translated into a neural code or message that the nervous system can process; (2) the encoded information then has to be stored or retained by the nervous system; and (3) when one wishes to recall the information it must be retrieved from storage.

There are three different memory systems. Sensory memory briefly holds an accurate "copy" of the sensory information people are exposed to. Sensory memories are held for a maximum of two seconds. Information in sensory memory is only encoded at the level of the sensory systems. Short-term memory (STM), which is referred to as the working memory, is the bridge or transition for the flow of information from sensory memory to long-term memory and then back to awareness (STM). STM can retain information for only about 20 seconds unless the information is actively rehearsed. The capacity of STM is limited to about seven pieces of information, but its capacity can be effectively increased through the process of chunking (or making each "piece" of information larger). Typically STMs are encoded acoustically. Long-term memory (LTM) has an unlimited storage capacity and may retain information for extensive periods of time. Typically information is stored in LTM in a verbal form. The efficiency of LTM is increased if information is stored in LTM in an organized or systematic manner that facilitates the retrieval of the information at a later time. Because memory is a constructive process, LTMs may not be completely accurate accounts of the original event. We may omit or add information to "construct" a memory that seems more "correct" to us.

A number of explanations for why forgetting occurs have been proposed. Decay theory proposes that the memory trace fades with the passage of time. Decay theory is an appropriate explanation of forgetting from sensory memory and at times from STM. However, there is disagreement as to whether LTMs decay over time. The interference explanation states that information may not be recalled because of the presence of other information or memories that make it difficult to recall the intended information. Information may also seemingly be forgotten from LTM when the information is merely inaccessible due to poor original encoding or the absence of sufficient retrieval cues. The motivated forgetting explanation states that some information may be forgotten or inaccessible to conscious awareness due to its unpleasant or threatening nature. Forgetting may also occur as a result of physical illness or injuries that affect the brain.

STMs appear to be associated with activity within the nervous system, whereas the storage of LTMs is associated with physical changes in the nervous system. LTMs appear to be represented by large networks of neurons distributed over broad portions of the brain. From extensive study of individuals with specific types of brain damage and memory deficits it has been shown that brain structures such as the hippocampus, amygdala, and thalamus are involved in the processing or transferring of memories between STM and LTM.

PART III. KEY TERMS/MATCHING EXERCISES

Match the following concepts and/or individuals with the appropriate descriptions. Check your answers against the Answer Key.

What Is Memory?

Concepts

_b_ 1. short-term memory (STM) **(231)**

_h_ 2. long-term memory (LTM) **(231)**

_e_ 3. sensory memory **(231-232)**

_f_ 4. chunking **(235-236)**

_d_ 5. storage **(230-231)**

_i_ 6. retrieval **(231)**

_a_ 7. encode **(230)**

_g_ 8. declarative memory **(237)**

_c_ 9. procedural memory **(237)**

Descriptions

a. Process of perceiving a stimulus and establishing associations between the stimulus and other information

b. Information is retained for no more than 20 seconds, unless it's rehearsed

c. Contains memories for how-to-perform skills

d. Process of retaining information in the nervous system

e. Holds visual information for 0.3 seconds and auditory information for 2 seconds.

f. Effective in increasing the capacity of STM

g. Contains memories for specific facts

h. Unlimited storage capacity (i.e., never fills up)

i. Process of recalling (or remembering) information

Answer Key   1. b   2. h   3. e   4. f   5. d   6. i   7. a   8. g   9. c

Encoding in Long-Term Memory (LTM)

Concepts

_f._ 1. narrative story (**239-240**)
_b._ 2. clustering (**239**)
_a._ 3. acronyms (**240**)
_c._ 4. peg-word system (**240**)

_d._ 5. mnemonic devices (**238**)
_g._ 6. method of loci (**239**)
_e._ 7. acrostics (**240**)

Descriptions

a. Consists of a group of letters that are cues for specific material

b. Involves grouping items into categories

c. Involves associating items with a series of words that correspond to a sequence of numbers

d. Memory systems to improve meaningful organization of material

e. Consists of making up a sentence in which the first letter of each word is a cue for specific material

f. Involves organizing items into a story

g. Involves forming mental associations between items and locations along a familiar route

Answer Key   1. f   2. b   3. a   4. c   5. d   6. g   7. e

Some Factors That Influence What We Remember

Concepts

_c._ 1. recognition task (**243**)
_d._ 2. relearning (**243-244**)
_f._ 3. recall task (**243**)
_b._ 4. flashbulb memory (**245-246**)

_e._ 5. schemas (**247-248**)
_g._ 6. state-dependent memory (**245**)
_a._ 7. serial position effect (**244-245**)

Descriptions

a. Observation that items at the beginning and end of a list are more likely to be remembered than items in the middle

b. Relates to vivid memories for first learning about an emotional event

c. Individual must search for a match between stored information and new information

d. Perhaps the most sensitive measure of memory

e. Conceptual frameworks used to make the world seem more predictable

f. Individual must reproduce information in the absence of specific retrieval cues

g. Observation that one remembers information better when in a situation similar to that in which the information was first encoded

Answer Key   1. c   2. d   3. f   4. b   5. e   6. g   7. a

Why We Forget | The Physical Bases of Memory

Concepts

_f._ 1. proactive interference **(252-253)**

_i._ 2. retroactive interference **(252)**

_k._ 3. retrograde amnesia **(254)**

_e._ 4. anterograde amnesia **(254)**

_c._ 5. decay **(252)**

_g._ 6. motivated forgetting **(253-254)**

_a._ 7. retrieval failure **(253)**

_b._ 8. organic amnesia **(254)**

_h._ 9. consolidation **(255)**

_j._ 10. cell assembly **(255)**

_d._ 11. engram **(257, 258)**

Descriptions

a. May occur because information was poorly encoded or lack of appropriate cues

b. Memory deficits resulting from some form of brain damage

c. Proposes that the memory trace fades with the passage of time

d. Lashley's term for the place where memories are stored

e. Memory loss in which old LTMs are accessible but new information cannot be retained

f. Occurs when earlier learning disrupts memory for later learning

g. Related to Freud's concept of repression

h. Process in which LTMs are coded by physical changes in the nervous system

i. Occurs when a later event interferes with recall of earlier information

j. Hebb's conception of how STM is maintained

k. Loss of memory of events that preceded an accident

Answer Key 1. f 2. i 3. k 4. e 5. c 6. g 7. a 8. b 9. h 10. j 11. d

PART IV. TRUE-FALSE STATEMENTS

Fill in the blank before each statement with either a T (true) or an F (false). Check your answers against the Answer Key. Then go back to the items that are false and make the necessary change(s) to the statements to convert the items into true statements.

Memory Systems

_____ 1. The first step in the processing of a memory is the storage of the information in the nervous system.

_____ 2. The term iconic memory refers to sensory memories of visual information.

_____ 3. Long-term memory is often referred to as our working memory.

_____

_____

_____ 4. Information in declarative memory is typically established more quickly, but is more likely to be forgotten than information in procedural memory.

_____

_____

_____ 5. The peg-word mnemonic system involves pegging or hanging an item to be remembered onto a familiar location.

_____

_____

Remembering | Forgetting

_____ 6. The serial position effect describes the observation that beginning-list items are remembered better than middle-list items, which are remembered better than end-of-list items.

_____

_____

_____ 7. The observation that people tend to remember events and facts that are inaccurate is evidence for memory being a constructive process.

_____

_____

_____ 8. Interference, in which later learning makes it more difficult to recall previously learned information, is labeled "proactive interference."

_____

_____

_____ 9. It is a well-established fact that LTM traces decay or fade with the passage of time.

_____

_____

_____ 10. A person suffering from anterograde amnesia is unable to adequately remember information received after the onset of their amnesia.

_____

_____

The Physical Bases of Memory

_____ 11. Recently, substantial evidence has shown that STMs are stored or coded by structural or physical changes in the nervous system.

_____

_____

_____ 12. The hippocampus, amygdala, and thalamus are believed to be associated with the transferring of information from STM to LTM and/or in consolidation.

_____

_____

_____ 13. Electroconvulsive shock therapy (ECT) causes retrograde amnesia.

_____

_____

Answer Key	1. F **(230)**	6. F **(244)**	10. T **(254)**
	2. T **(232)**	7. T **(246-247)**	11. F **(255)**
	3. F **(235)**	8. F **(252)**	12. T **(261)**
	4. T **(237)**	9. F **(252)**	13. T **(260)**
	5. F **(240)**		

PART V. MULTIPLE-CHOICE QUESTIONS

Choose the best answer to each question. Circle your choice. Check your answers against the Answer Key. Questions marked with an asterisk (*) include annotated answers.

Memory and Memory Systems

1. The three processes involved in memory are

   a. encoding, rehearsal, and retrieval.
   b. memorizing, reciting, and recalling.
   c. encoding, storage, and retrieval.
   d. recall, recognition, and relearning.

2. Encoding involves translating incoming information into a neural code and

   a. organizing the information in a meaningful way.
   b. rehearsing the information.
   c. retaining the information for a period of time.
   d. sensation.

3. The process of locating and recovering an item from one's "memory bank" is termed

   a. mnemonic.
   b. recall.
   c. retrieval.
   d. a "hit."

4. Which memory system briefly holds a largely accurate reproduction of the original sensory input?

   a. Sensory memory
   b. Short-term memory
   c. Medium-term memory
   d. Long-term memory

5. Immediately after you are briefly exposed to 20 items in a visual display, you would probably recall

    a. all of the items that had been transferred to STM.
    b. any of the items you were instructed to recall.
    c. four of the items.
    d. none of the items.

6. Echoic memories last longer than iconic memories probably because

    a. unlike light, energy sound waves produce echos for us to refer to.
    b. we do not have a second chance to review auditory information whereas it is usually possible to refer back to visual information.
    c. visual information is continually being replaced but auditory information is not.
    d. it is easier to concentrate on visual information.

*7. The most effective way to keep information in STM is by

    a. overlearning it.
    b. using a mnemonic device.
    c. rehearsing it over and over.
    d. converting it into a visual image.

8. The capacity of STM is about _____ pieces of information if the information has been encoded according to how it sounds.

    a. 3
    b. 7
    c. 15
    d. The capacity is unlimited.

9. Information is coded in STM most commonly in _____ form.

    a. acoustic
    b. semantic
    c. procedural
    d. visual

10. If you were asked to recall the letters Q, E, T, 10 seconds after viewing the letters, the error you would most likely make would be to recall _____ instead of _____ .

    a. $O \mid Q$
    b. $F \mid E$
    c. $C \mid T$
    d. $S \mid T$

11. The memories you have of your first day of psychology class this semester are in your

    a. chronological memory.
    b. LTM.
    c. sensory memory.
    d. STM.

12. Which statement is *true* of long-term memory?

  a. Old information is "displaced" by new information
  b. It is limited to several hundred items
  c. Information is stored by rote only
  d. There is no evidence for any limit to the amount of information that can be stored in long-term memory.

13. Which of the following memory sets are *both* included in declarative memory?

  a. Short term and long term
  b. Semantic and procedural
  c. Semantic and episodic
  d. Procedural and episodic

14. The _semantic_ memory contains general, nonpersonal knowledge concerning the meaning of facts and concepts.

  a. episodic
  b. semantic
  c. procedural
  d. iconic

*15. Eidetic imagery is most similar to the "typical" memory in _iconic_ memory.

  a. iconic
  b. echoic
  c. short-term
  d. long-term

16. The mnemonic device for improving recall of information from LTM that is most directly related to improving recall of information from STM through chunking is

  a. method of loci.
  b. acronyms.
  c. peg-word system.
  d. clustering.

*17. If it is necessary for you to remember a list of items in a specific order, which mnemonic device would probably be *least* appropriate to use?

  a. Narrative story
  b. Method of loci
  c. Clustering
  d. Peg-word

18. Simply repeating words without any attempt to find meaning in them is known as

  a. maintenance rehearsal.
  b. elaborative rehearsal.
  c. mnemonic strategy.
  d. acrostics.

19. The network of association interpretation of how information is retrieved from LTM states that we retrieve facts through the process of

    a. association to higher concepts.
    b. spreading activation.
    c. serial position.
    d. triggering nodes.

20. A student who is not doing well in psychology class would most likely hope that the professor would use which of the following techniques to measure memory of the material?

    a. Short answer
    b. Recall
    c. Relearning
    d. Recognition

21. The technique Ebbinghaus used to study LTM was

    a. recall.
    b. recognition.
    c. relearning.
    d. overlearning.

Some Factors That Influence What We Remember

22. If you usually study after having a few beers, there is evidence that suggests you would probably do better if you also had a few beers before taking the exam. This phenomenon is called _____ memory.

    a. context
    b. state-dependent
    c. state-delayed
    d. dual-coded

23. You would most likely have a flashbulb memory of

    a. your first date with your current boyfriend/girlfriend.
    b. your tenth birthday party.
    c. last spring vacation.
    d. the San Francisco earthquake during the 1989 World Series.

24. Which of the following is *not* a way Bartlett's subjects reconstructed the story "The War of the Ghosts"?

    a. Assimilation
    b. Sharpening
    c. Leveling
    d. Schemas

25. When people try to remember information that is not consistent with their schemas, they tend to

    a. distort facts to fit their schemas.
    b. change their schemas to fit the facts.
    c. exert more effort to organize their schemas.
    d. focus on the inconsistencies.

26. To which of the following questions would people most likely estimate the tallest response?

    a. What is the height of your psychology professor?

    b. How short is your psychology professor?

    c. How tall is your psychology professor?

    d. People would give the same response to each question.

Why We Forget

27. There is a difference of opinion among psychologists concerning whether long-term memories are forgotten because of

    a. motivated forgetting.

    b. decay.

    c. retrieval failure.

    d. interference.

*28. You took two years of French in high school and then two years of German in college. What would account for the observation that you have more difficulty remembering French vocabulary words than German words?

    a. Anterograde interference

    b. Retrograde interference

    c. Retroactive interference

    d. Proactive interference

29. Which explanation of forgetting states that a "forgotten" memory is not really forgotten, but only inaccessible at the current time?

    a. Anterograde amnesia

    b. Decay

    c. Interference

    d. Retrieval failure

The Physical Bases of Memory

*30. A person who is struck by lightning is most likely to suffer

    a. retrograde amnesia.

    b. anterograde amnesia.

    c. consolidation amnesia.

    d. Korsakoff's syndrome.

31. The coding of LTM by physical changes in the nervous system is referred to as

    a. encoding.

    b. consolidation.

    c. an engram.

    d. cell assemblies.

32. Compared to rats reared in a regular laboratory environment, the brains of rats reared in enriched environments would show

   a. more terminal buttons.
   b. more dendritic spines and synapses.
   c. fewer but larger synapses.
   d. larger cerebrums.

33. From the case of HM (discussed in the text), it seems likely that the hippocampus and amygdala are

   a. where LTMs are stored.
   b. only involved in the functioning of sensory memory.
   c. involved in the transferring of information from STM to LTM.
   d. involved in procedural memories.

Strategies for Improving Academic Memory

34. When studying for an exam you should

   a. study two hours for every hour you spend in class.
   b. continue to study after you have mastered the material.
   c. study until you can accurately "recite before the fact."
   d. study until you can accurately "recite after the fact."

35. After you finish studying for an exam you should

   a. reward yourself with a study break.
   b. relax by watching TV or visiting with friends.
   c. read assignments for other classes.
   d. go to sleep.

Answer Key

1. c	(230)	8. b	(235)	*15. a	(238)	22. b	(245)	29. d	(235)
2. a	(230)	9. a	(236)	16. d	(239)	23. d	(246)	*30. a	(260)
3. c	(230)	10. c	(236)	*17. c	(239)	24. d	(247-248)	31. b	(255)
4. a	(231-232)	11. b	(231)	18. a	(240)	25. a	(248)	32. b	(255, 257)
5. b	(233)	12. d	(236)	19. b	(241-242)	26. c	(250)	33. c	(260)
6. b	(234-235)	13. c	(237-238)	20. d	(243)	27. b	(252)	34. b	(263)
*7. c	(235)	14. b	(237-238)	21. c	(244)	*28. c	(252)	35. d	(264)

Annotated Answers

7. The correct choice is c. Unless rehearsed, information fades from STM within about 20 seconds.

   a. Overlearning is a useful technique to increase retention of LTM.
   b. Mnemonic devices are techniques to improve encoding and storage of information in LTM.
   d. Encoding the information in visual form would not be helpful because the capacity of acoustically coded STMs is seven items and STM's capacity is only three items for visually coded information.

15. The correct choice is a. Both eidetic imagery and iconic memory consist of vivid (and accurate) visual memories. Although these two memories differ greatly in duration they are qualitatively similar.

    b. Echoic memories are sensory memories for auditory information.

    c. STMs typically are acoustically coded and last only about 20 seconds, whereas eidetic imagery is visual and the image lasts for several minutes.

    d. Eidetic imagery is a form of coding in LTM, but it is not the typical way LTM would be encoded by the majority of people.

17. The correct choice is c. Clustering involves grouping the items to be remembered into appropriate categories. In a typical example, the categories formed might not be consistent with the order in which the items need to be recalled.

    a. Narrative story would be an appropriate device as long as the items to be remembered are incorporated into the narrative story in the proper sequence.

    b. Method of loci would be appropriate if the items to be remembered are "placed" in locations along the path in the proper sequence.

    d. The peg-word system could well be the best method (of those listed) to remember the items in a specific order. This mnemonic device pegs items to words that have previously been associated with or linked to numbers.

28. The correct choice is c. Retroactive interference occurs when later learning (i.e., German) interferes with the recall of earlier learned information (i.e., French).

    a. Anterograde refers to a type of amnesia and not a type of interference.

    b. Retrograde refers to a type of amnesia and not a type of interference.

    d. Proactive interference would account for this situation if it was reversed with you showing more difficulty in remembering German words than French words. Proactive interference occurs when earlier learning interferes with the memory of later learning.

30. The correct choice is a. The effect of being struck by lightning can be compared to electroconvulsive shock therapy (ECT), which causes retrograde amnesia by disrupting memory for events occurring before the shock.

    b. Anterograde amnesia is commonly associated with permanent injury to specific areas of the brain. While you could argue that the lightning might cause irreversible damage to one of these critical areas of the brain, choice a is a simpler and better choice.

    c. Consolidation amnesia is not a form of amnesia.

    d. Korsakoff's syndrome is associated with chronic alcoholism and includes both retrograde and anterograde amnesia.

PART VI. SUMMARY TABLE

To test your understanding of the material discussed in this chapter complete the following table. Check your answers with those supplied in PART IX.

The Three-System Model of Memory

Memory	Amount Stored	Duration	How Stored	How Forgotten
Sensory memory				
Short-term memory				
Long-term memory				

PART VII. THOUGHT QUESTIONS/CRITICAL THINKING

Prepare answers to the following discussion questions.

1. Imagine that one week ago you moved into a new apartment and got a new phone number. If someone asks for your phone number you will probably have a hard time remembering it. Six months from now, on the other hand, you might have difficulty remembering your old phone number. Name and describe in detail the processes responsible for your failure to recall both the old and new phone numbers.

2. Eidetic imagery (or photographic memory) is more common in children than in adults. Many individuals who have eidetic imagery in childhood lose the ability as they grow older. The text states that the greater prevalence of eidetic imagery in childhood "may reflect the fact that children's memory storehouses are less cluttered with extraneous facts, thus allowing for clearer, less encumbered images" (p. 238). Referring to the dual-code model of memory, propose an alternative explanation for the frequency of eidetic imagery declining with age. (**Hint:** If children have an advantage in sensory coding, do adults have an advantage in the use of semantic coding?)

3. Explain the relationship between retrograde amnesia and consolidation.

4. In Chapter 6 (learning) the phenomenon of spontaneous recovery was described to illustrate that following extinction all memory of a previously learned conditioned response is not eliminated. Could any of the techniques described in this chapter concerning the testing of long-term memory be useful in the classical conditioning procedure? If yes, which technique? Describe how this technique would be utilized to measure how much original learning is retained after extinction.

5. Discuss how police interviews of eyewitnesses to a crime should be structured and when they should take place in order to minimize the possibility that witnesses would recall inaccurate information.

PART VIII. APPLICATIONS

1. Take a few minutes to make each of the following lists. Write down in order:

   a. All the phone numbers you have had in your life
   b. The names of all your teachers from first grade through high school
   (When you get to the grade in which you first started changing classes and having a number of different teachers you can either list just the homeroom teacher or all your teachers.)
   c. The names of all the presidents of the United States
   (**Hint:** George Bush is the 41st president)

Serial position effect curves (see Figure 7.9 in the text) are compiled from the results of a large number of people. Keeping in mind that the lists you wrote were from only one person, do you see evidence to support the serial position effect?

2. Take two minutes to write down the names of as many states as you can remember. Start now, before you read further.

   a. You were not given any specific instructions or strategy to help you with this recall task. There are a variety of strategies to use to approach this task (recall the states alphabetically, or geographically). The geographical strategy could take a number of approaches: start with the east cost (similar to clustering), west coast, the state you are in, the states you have lived in, tracing the states you used to drive through during family vacations (similar to the method of loci). Examine the order in which you listed the states. Did you use a strategy (or a succession of strategies)?
   b. You probably did not list all 50 states within the two-minute time limit. Obtain a map of the United States and look at it to see if you omitted groups or geographic clusters of states or isolated states. Is there a simple explanation for why you failed to remember certain states? For example, if you've spent your whole life on the east coast, it would make sense that with a limited time frame you would recall more eastern states than western states.
   c. If your friends at college come from different states, ask a few of them to do the same task—but remember to give them the same instructions you were given: "Take two minutes to write down the names of as many states as you can remember." Examine your friends' lists to see if people from different parts of the country approach this task from different perspectives.

PART IX. SUMMARY TABLE SOLUTION

The Three-System Model of Memory

Memory	Amount Stored	Duration	How Stored	How Forgotten
Sensory memory	All sensory messages being received at any time	0.3 sec (visual) 2 sec (auditory)	Accurate reproduction of sensory input	Decay
Short-term memory	Approximately 7 items if acoustically coded Approximately 3 items if visually or semantically coded	Up to 20 seconds, longer if actively rehearsed	Usually acoustically (by sound)	Forget if not coded or rehearsed Decay, interference
Long-term memory	Unlimited	Up to a lifetime	Typically verbally	Interference, retrieval failure, motivated forgetting, and possibly decay

Thinking and Language

PART I. LEARNING OBJECTIVES

When you finish studying this chapter you should be able to:

Thought

1. Define thought, and describe the two main components of thought (mental images and concepts). **(269-272)**

2. Describe concept hierarchies, and discuss what is meant by the basic level for each concept. **(272)**

3. Define formal and natural concepts, and discuss how these differ. **(272-273)**

4. Describe three different theories that attempt to explain how we form concepts. **(273-274)**

Problem Solving

5. Define problem, and list the three components of a problem. **(275-276)**

6. Explain the three stages involved in solving a problem. **(276-278)**

7. Describe the four different strategies for solving a problem. **(278-280)**

8. Describe the two common heuristic strategies of means–ends analysis and working backward. **(279-280)**

9. Discuss two characteristics of some problems that make them difficult to solve. **(280-281)**

10. Discuss three perceptual obstacles that make problem solving more difficult. **(281-282)**

Reasoning and Decision Making

11. Explain deductive and inductive reasoning, and differentiate between the two. **(283-284)**

12. Define a syllogism, and explain how syllogisms are used to study deductive reasoning. **(284-285)**

13. Describe three common causes of reasoning errors. **(285-286)**

14. Define decision making and describe a number of compensatory and noncompensatory models used in the decision-making process. **(287-289)**

15. Discuss the advantages and potential disadvantages of heuristic approaches to decision making. **(290-291)**

Language

16. Describe the four levels of structure and rules of language: phonemes, morphemes, syntax, and semantics. **(292-293)**

17. Describe two major theories of language acquisition, and discuss the strengths and weaknesses of each theory. **(293-295)**

18. Describe and give examples to illustrate the five stages in the universal sequence of language acquisition. **(295-299)**

19. List five primary criteria of all human languages, and use these criteria to describe and evaluate research designed to teach language to chimpanzees. **(299-303)**

Thinking and Language

20. Describe and evaluate two different perspectives concerning the interrelationship of thinking and language. **(304-306)**

PART II. OVERVIEW

Thinking (or thought) refers to internal processes intended to solve problems and make decisions. Two components of thought are mental images and concepts. Concepts allow us to simplify our understanding of objects and events by grouping items into general, cognitive categories. Concepts that have well-defined rules to determine inclusion in a category are formal concepts. Natural concepts, on the other hand, do not have specific rules to determine membership. Three theories concerning how concepts are learned are discussed. The exemplar theory proposes that we structure natural concepts around typical examples or prototypes.

A problem exists when there is a discrepancy between one's present state and goal state. Problem solving involves developing a strategy to bring about the goal state. There are a number of problem-solving strategies: trial and error, testing hypotheses, algorithm, and heuristics. Algorithms systematically try every possible solution and are commonly used in computer programming. Heuristics are rule-of-thumb strategies designed to result in quick solutions. Problems that are not well defined or are complex are difficult to solve. Mental sets, functional fixedness, and confirmation bias are all obstacles an individual brings to a situation that makes a problem difficult to solve.

There are two types of logical reasoning: Deductive reasoning describes a situation begun with general observations or assumptions and a conclusion is drawn concerning specific instances. Inductive reasoning involves generalizing from specific instances to reach a general conclusion.

Decision making occurs when one alternative is selected while other alternatives are rejected. There are a number of rational approaches to decision making. Compensatory models involve evaluating all features (both positive and negative) of each alternative. In noncompensatory models all features of the alternatives are not examined. Because it typically takes a considerable investment in time and energy to make a decision using either the compensatory or noncompensatory models, people frequently resort to short-cut or heuristic approaches to make many decisions. The heuristic approaches are often successful, but they are not as thorough as other approaches and can result in poor decisions.

There are four levels of analysis used to describe language. The most basic element is the individual sounds—or phonemes—that are used. The smallest unit in a language that has meaning is the morpheme. Syntax describes the rules (or grammar) that state how words are combined into meaningful phrases or sentences. The final level of analysis concerns semantics or the rules that determine the meaning of sentences and words.

Two theories concerning language acquisition are discussed. The learning perspective proposes that children learn language in a way similar to how they learn many other tasks—through selective reinforcement and imitation. The nativistic perspective, which proposes that language acquisition is controlled by an innate mechanism (the Language Acquisition Device), offers a more thorough accounting of the sequence of language acquisition. All over the world children progress from cooing, babbling, holophrases, and telegraphic speech to more complex sentences.

Chapter 8 discusses the interrelationship of thinking and language. Whorf's hypothesis that language rigidly structures or determines thought is not generally accepted. However, it is well accepted that some thoughts are easier to express in certain languages. There is also some evidence that thoughts influence the structure of an individual's language.

PART III. KEY TERMS/MATCHING EXERCISES

Match the following concepts and/or individuals with the appropriate descriptions. Check your answers against the Answer Key.

Thought

Concepts

_____ 1. association theory (**273**)

_____ 2. basic level of a concept (**272**)

_____ 3. concepts (**271**)

_____ 4. exemplar theory (**274**)

_____ 5. formal concepts (**272**)

_____ 6. hypothesis-testing theory (**273**)

_____ 7. natural concepts (**272**)

_____ 8. thought (**269**)

Descriptions

a. Represents general cognitive categories

b. Proposes that concepts are structured around prototypes

c. Do not have specific rules to designate inclusion in a category

d. Proposes that concepts are acquired through the learning of stimulus–response associations

e. Collection of internal processes directed toward solving a problem

f. Have logical, well-defined rules to designate inclusion in a category

g. Optimal level of a concept hierarchy that is naturally used when one thinks about an object or event

h. Proposes that concepts are acquired in a systematic or scientific fashion

Answer Key   1. d   2. g   3. a   4. b   5. f   6. h   7. c   8. e

Problem Solving

Concepts

_____ 1. trial and error **(278)**

_____ 2. testing hypotheses **(278)**

_____ 3. problem **(275)**

_____ 4. heuristics **(279)**

_____ 5. working backwards **(279)**

_____ 6. algorithm **(279)**

_____ 7. means-ends analysis **(279)**

_____ 8. functional fixedness **(282)**

_____ 9. confirmation bias **(283)**

_____ 10. mental set **(281)**

Descriptions

a. Problem-solving strategy often employed by computers to systematically test every possible solution

b. Problem-solving strategy that uses rule-of-thumb strategies leading to a quick solution

c. Tendency to be unable to perceive a novel way of using a given object to solve a problem

d. Problem-solving strategy that starts with a goal and progress in steps toward the original state or problem

e. Exists when there is a discrepancy between present status and desired goal

f. Problem-solving strategy that uses a series of subgoals to move systematically closer to a final solution

g. Tendency to avoid looking for evidence that would disprove the hypothesis

h. Problem-solving strategy that involves trying possible solutions, one at a time, to see which is correct

i. Problem-solving strategy that utilizes hypotheses to more efficiently and systematically search for the correct solution to a problem

j. Tendency to approach a problem in a predetermined way regardless of the requirements of the specific problem

Answer Key 1. h 2. i 3. e 4. b 5. d 6. a 7. f 8. c 9. g 10. j

Reasoning and Decision Making

Concepts

_____ 1. syllogism **(284)**

_____ 2. representative heuristic **(290)**

_____ 3. availability heuristic **(291)**

_____ 4. inductive reasoning **(284)**

_____ 5. belief-bias effect **(286)**

_____ 6. deductive reasoning **(283)**

_____ 7. decision making **(287)**

_____ 8. compensatory models **(287)**

_____ 9. noncompensatory models **(289)**

Descriptions

a. Form of reasoning that begins with general assumptions that serve as a basis for drawing conclusions

b. Form of reasoning in which a conclusion is reached by generalizing from specific instances

c. Consists of two premises and a conclusion

d. Tendency to accept or reject a specific conclusion regardless of how logical that conclusion is

e. Process that occurs whenever one is faced with an array of alternative choices and one option is chosen while rejecting others

f. Decision-making models (including additive and utility-probability models) that evaluate how desirable potential outcomes stack up against undesirable outcomes

g. Decision-making models (including maximax and minimax models) that do not consider all features of each alternative

h. Strategy in which the likelihood of something is judged by intuitively comparing it to preconceived notions about a few characteristics of a category

i. Strategy that bases decisions primarily on the degree to which information can be accessed from memory

Answer Key   1. c   2. h   3. i   4. b   5. d   6. a   7. e   8. f   9. g

Language | Thinking and Language

Concepts

_____ 1. linguistic-relativity hypothesis **(304)**

_____ 2. language-acquisition device (LAD) **(294)**

_____ 3. syntax **(293)**

_____ 4. morpheme **(293)**

_____ 5. semantics **(293)**

_____ 6. phonemes **(292)**

_____ 7. telegraphic speech **(298)**

_____ 8. holophrases **(298)**

Descriptions

a. First-sentence form used by children

b. Proposed "prewiring" of an infant's brain to learn language

c. Rules of grammar that govern how words can be combined to form meaningful phrases and sentences

d. Individual or basic sounds that comprise a language

e. Single-word utterances designed to express a complete thought

f. Smallest unit of meaning in a language

g. Study of meaning in language

h. Whorf's view that language determines thought

Answer Key   1. h   2. b   3. c   4. f   5. g   6. d   7. a   8. e

PART IV. TRUE-FALSE STATEMENTS

Fill in the blank before each statement with either a T (true) or an F (false). Check your answers against the Answer Key. Then go back to the items that are false and make the necessary change(s) to the statements to convert the items into true statements.

Thought

_____ 1. Watson's idea that thought involves subvocal or implicit speech is now well accepted.

_____

_____

_____ 2. Formal concepts are easier to define or explain than natural concepts.

_____

_____

_____ 3. Exemplar theory suggests that natural concepts are usually structured around prototypes.

_____

_____

Problem Solving

_____ 4. The first step in problem-solving behavior involves generating possible solutions.

_____

_____

_____ 5. A main difference between the problem-solving strategies of algorithms and trial and error is that algorithms are more systematic.

_____

_____

_____ 6. When an individual incorrectly approaches a problem by applying strategies that have previously been successful with similar problems, that person is showing confirmation bias.

_____

_____

Reasoning and Decision Making

_____ 7. The first step in solving a logical syllogism is to determine if each of the two premises are true statements.

_____

_____

_____ 8. The belief-bias effect would cause an individual to accept believable but logically invalid conclusions.

_____

_____

_____ 9. In making routine or everyday decisions heuristic approaches often work rather well.

_____

_____

Language | Thinking and Language

_____ 10. Language and communication are synonymous.

_____

_____

_____ 11. The specific language a child is exposed to greatly effects the form (syntax and semantics) of the child's first sentences.

_____

_____

_____ 12. Careful evaluation of the research designed to teach language to chimpanzees leads to the unequivocal conclusion that only humans possess language.

_____

_____

_____ 13. There is very little support for Whorf's linguistic-relativity hypothesis that language determines or structures thought.

_____

_____

Answer Key	1. F **(271)**	6. F **(281)**	10. F **(292)**
	2. T **(272)**	7. F **(284)**	11. F **(298)**
	3. T **(274)**	8. T **(286)**	12. F **(303)**
	4. F **(276)**	9. T **(290)**	13. T **(305)**
	5. T **(279)**		

PART V. MULTIPLE-CHOICE QUESTIONS

Choose the best answer to each question. Circle your choice. Check your answers against the Answer Key. Questions marked with an asterisk (*) include annotated answers.

Thought

1. When you mentally group objects or events into general cognitive categories you

　　a. solve a problem.
　　b. form a mental image.
　　c. form a concept.
　　d. make a decision.

2. You would most likely have the shortest reaction time to answer which of the following questions?

　　a. Is a grandmother a person?
　　b. Is a newborn infant a person?
　　c. Is a child a person?
　　d. Is a college student a person?

3. Which of the following do we typically learn as the result of experience?

　　a. Natural concepts
　　b. Formal concepts
　　c. Disjunctive concepts
　　d. Conjunctive concepts

4. The concept _____ is subordinate to the concept _____ .

　　a. dog | bulldog
　　b. animal | dog
　　c. teacher | person
　　d. animal | bird

5. Children probably use _____ level concepts first as they name and classify events and objects.

　　a. formal-
　　b. natural-
　　c. basic-
　　d. subordinate-

6. Which of the following is a prototype?

    a. Siamese cat

    b. house cat

    c. tomcat

    d. Persian cat

7. The _____ theory of forming concepts is frequently observed in laboratory experiments, though it may not be used extensively in everyday life.

    a. exemplar

    b. association

    c. heuristics

    d. hypothesis-testing

8. When we encounter a novel instance of a concept, such as an exotic bird we have never seen before, we correctly label it *bird* on the basis of stimulus generalization. What theory of concept formation supports this view?

    a. Association theory

    b. Hypothesis-testing theory

    c. Exemplar theory

    d. Prototype theory

Problem Solving

9. Problems consist of three components. Which of the following is *not* a component of a problem?

    a. The goal state

    b. Generating possible solutions

    c. The rules or restrictions that govern possible strategies

    d. The original state of the situation

10. Trial-and-error problem solving is most effective when

    a. there is a wide range of solutions.

    b. there is a narrow range of solutions.

    c. strategies are needed.

    d. there must be a "quick-fix."

11. When one is systematically moved through a series of subgoals coming closer to a final solution, one is using the problem-solving strategy of

    a. working backwards.

    b. testing hypotheses.

    c. algorithm.

    d. means-ends analysis.

*12. If the number of possible solutions to a problem is large and there is a limited amount of time available to solve the problem, which pair of problem-solving strategies should be least likely used?

    a. Algorithm and testing hypotheses

    b. Trial and error and algorithm

    c. Heuristics and algorithm

    d. Heuristics and trial and error

13. _____ , in contrast to _____ , do (does) not guarantee a correct solution to a problem, but when they work they tend to allow for more rapid solutions.

   a. incubation | heuristics
   b. heuristics | incubation
   c. algorithms | heuristics
   d. heuristics | algorithms

14. Which of the following makes it more difficult to solve a problem?

   a. The problem contains a syllogism
   b. The problem is deceptively simple
   c. The problem involves formal concepts
   d. The problem is ill-defined

15. When we are unable to think of a novel use for a given object, which would aid in solving a problem, we experience

   a. functional fixedness.
   b. mental set.
   c. dead-end thinking.
   d. confirmation bias.

16. As a result of confirmation bias, people might jump to the conclusion incorrectly in attempting to solve a problem because they

   a. tend to approach a problem in a predetermined way if the approach has been successful in the past.
   b. stop an algorithm prematurely.
   c. have a prototype of the correct solution.
   d. do not look for evidence that will disprove their hypothesis.

Reasoning and Decision Making

17. If you decide to vote for a candidate, you know little about, solely because he or she is a Republican (or a Democrat), you would be using _____ to guide your decision.

   a. deductive reasoning
   b. inductive reasoning
   c. productive reasoning
   d. confirmation bias

18. Reasoning in which we reach a general conclusion by beginning with specific instances is called

   a. deductive reasoning.
   b. inductive reasoning.
   c. syllogistic reasoning.
   d. functional fixedness.

19. With _____ you can never be absolutely certain that you have reached a correct conclusion.

    a. algorithms
    b. syllogisms
    c. deductive reasoning
    d. inductive reasoning

20. The discipline of formal logic uses _____ to study reasoning.

    a. syllogisms
    b. formal concepts
    c. representative heuristics
    d. belief bias

*21. A syllogism is judged to be true if

    a. both premises are true.
    b. the logically obtained conclusion is also consistent with everyday beliefs.
    c. the conclusion applies to every conceivable combination of all possible meanings of the premises.
    d. the converse of each premise is also true (for example if "all As are Bs" is the premise and "all Bs are As" is a true statement).

22. The process that occurs whenever one is faced with an array of alternative choices and one option is chosen while others rejected describes

    a. decision making.
    b. formal logic.
    c. problem solving.
    d. functional fixedness.

23. The model for rational decision making that involves assigning values to potential outcomes associated with each alternative and also considering the likelihood of each outcome occurring is the

    a. conjunctive-strategy model.
    b. utility-probability model.
    c. additive model.
    d. maximax-strategy model.

24. When we compare the weakest features of each option and select the one whose weakest feature is most highly rated, we are using the _____ strategy of decision making.

    a. elimination-by-aspects
    b. conjunctive
    c. maximax
    d. minimax

25. If a voter decides which one of a number of candidates to vote for by applying a "litmus test" thereby rejecting candidates who do not agree with the voter's position on abortion, then welfare, then environmental issues, etc., this voter would be using the _____ decision-making strategy.

    a. subtractive
    b. conjunctive
    c. elimination-by-aspects
    d. minimax

*26. You have just won two tickets to a Rolling Stones concert. Most likely you'll decide who to invite by using a

    a. trial-and-error model.
    b. heuristic approach.
    c. compensatory model.
    d. noncompensatory model.

27. Which of the following is a shortcoming or potential drawback of using heuristic approaches to decision making?

    a. These often do not lead you to a specific decision, but only help you to narrow your options.
    b. These are too time consuming.
    c. These are ill-defined.
    d. You might make a costly error in judgment.

Language

28. The smallest unit of language that has meaning in a given language is the

    a. word.
    b. morpheme.
    c. syllable.
    d. phoneme.

29. A course in grammer would be primarily concerned with _____ . A literature course would more likely be concerned with _____ .

    a. syntax | semantics
    b. semantics | syntax
    c. syntax | morphemes
    d. morphemes | semantics

*30. Which language-acquisition perspective could best account for a young child (whose parents speak English grammatically) saying, "I goed to the zoo yesterday"?

    a. Syntactical
    b. Whorfian
    c. Nativistic
    d. Learning

31. In nativistic theory, the "prewiring" of the brain, presumed to facilitate the child's learning of grammar, is known as the

    a. programmed-language generator.
    b. language-acquisition device.
    c. programmed-linguistic achiever.
    d. surface/deep structure.

32. Which of the following observations does *not* offer strong support for the nativistic or "prewired" perspective of language acquisition?

    a. Babies, whose parents reinforce their early attempts at meaningful sounds, vocalize more than institutionalized babies who receive less attention.
    b. Under highly variable conditions, language acquisition follows an invariable sequence among children all over the world.
    c. When infants begin babbling, they babble sounds that are both phonemes and not phonemes of their future language.
    d. The telegraphic speech in young children is similar all over the world.

33. By the age of _____ most children have learned the majority of the basic grammatical rules for combining nouns, adjectives, and verbs into meaningful sentences.

    a. two or three
    b. three or four
    c. four or five
    d. five or six

*34 A basic question that chimpanzee research has not conclusively answered is:

    a. Can chimps talk?
    b. Can chimps convey meaning through the use of symbols?
    c. Can chimps communicate?
    d. Can chimps learn language?

35. The chimpanzee Washoe was taught

    a. to speak.
    b. American Sign Language.
    c. Yerkish.
    d. to manipulate plastic symbols and combine them in an apparently meaningful fashion.

Thinking and Language

36. Whorf's hypothesis, that people think differently in different languages, is the

    a. linguistic-relativeity hypothesis.
    b. nativistic hypothesis.
    c. exemplar hypothesis.
    d. linguistic-acquisition-device hypothesis.

37. The experiment comparing memory for colors between American and Dani individuals found

    a. Americans more successful in selecting the correct hue.
    b. the Dani more successful in selecting the correct hue.
    c. both Americans and Dani found the task very easy and made few mistakes.
    d. the performance of the Americans and Dani did not significantly differ.

38. Which of the following statements is *false*?

    a. It is often easier to express a particular concept or idea in one language as opposed to another.

    b. Thoughts and/or perceptions are largely determined or structured by our language.

    c. Expanding language through education and reading enhances our thinking processes.

    d. It is often easier to make a distinction about certain features of the environment in one language as opposed to another.

39. The observation that young children do not talk about objects that are not present in their immediate environment until they have mastered object permanence supports the position that

    a. mental images are necessary for thought to occur.

    b. children have a limited vocabulary.

    c. thought has an impact on the structure of language.

    d. language determines thought.

Answer Key

1. c	**(271)**	9. b	**(275-276)**	17. a	**(283)**	25. c	**(289)**	33. c	**(299)**
2. c	**(272)**	10. b	**(278)**	18. b	**(284)**	*26. b	**(291)**	*34. d	**(303)**
3. a	**(272-273)**	11. d	**(279)**	19. d	**(284)**	27. d	**(291)**	35. b	**(300)**
4. c	**(272)**	*12. b	**(279)**	20. a	**(284)**	28. b	**(293)**	*36. a	**(304)**
5. c	**(272)**	13. d	**(279)**	*21. c	**(285)**	29. a	**(293)**	37. d	**(305)**
6. b	**(274)**	14. d	**(280)**	22. a	**(287)**	*30. c	**(294)**	38. b	**(305)**
7. d	**(273-274)**	15. a	**(282)**	23. b	**(288)**	31. b	**(294)**	39. c	**(306)**
8. a	**(273-274)**	16. d	**(283)**	24. d	**(289)**	32. a	**(295)**		

Annotated Answers

12. The correct choice is b. Algorithms will guarantee a correct solution, but they are time consuming. The trial-and-error strategy is most effective when there is a small number of possible solutions.

    a. Testing hypotheses would be an effective strategy to narrow the number of solutions to try.

    c. Heuristics would be an effective strategy to use because a quick solution is desired.

    d. See the note for c above.

21. The correct choice is c. This statement is one of the three requirements for judging a syllogism to be true.

    a. In a syllogism both premises are presumed to be true.

    b. This relates to the belief-bias effect. It is not necessary for a valid syllogism to be consistent with everyday beliefs.

    d. The converse of a premise does not need to be true.

26. The correct choice is b. You would probably use the availability heuristic and first call a friend that you knew liked the Rolling Stones and concerts. Perhaps you would invite a friend that you have previously gone to a concert with.

    a. If you used trial and error you would simply call friends (or acquaintances or strangers) at random until one said that they would like to go.

    c. The strategies in both c and d would work, but for this example they would probably take an unreasonable amount of time to implement.

    d. See c above.

30. The correct choice is c. The nativistic perspective states that when children learn the basic rules of grammar they tend to make mistakes of overgeneralization.

  a. The syntactical perspective does not exist.

  b. The Whorfian or linguistic-relativity hypothesis is not concerned with how language is acquired.

  d. The learning perspective would have difficulty explaining why the child said "goed" if he or she had never heard the word before and thus could not be imitating another's speech.

34. The correct choice is d. Depending on the interpretation of the results of the research and the definition of language utilized, different answers to the question "Can chimps learn language?" are possible.

  a. Talk refers to verbal language. Chimps do not have the vocal apparatus to communicate verbally.

  b. The behavior of Sarah and Lana indicate that chimps are capable of conveying meaning through the use of symbols.

  c. Chimps, like many species, can communicate.

PART VI. SUMMARY TABLES

To test your understanding of the material discussed in this chapter complete the following tables. Check your answers with those supplied in PART IX.

Theories of Concept Formation

Theory	Individual	Assumptions	Strengths	Weaknesses
Association				
Hypothesis testing				
Exemplar				

Problem-Solving Strategies

Strategy	Description	Advantages	Limitations
Trial and error			
Testing hypotheses			
Algorithms			
Heuristics			

Rational Approaches to Decision Making

Approach	Examples	General Description	Strengths or Weaknesses
Compensatory			
Noncompensatory			
Heuristics			

Theories of Language Acquisition

Theory	Individuals	Description	Supporting Evidence	Weaknesses
Learning				
Nativistic				

PART VII. THOUGHT QUESTIONS/CRITICAL THINKING

Prepare answers to the following discussion questions.

1. Discuss the relationship between problem solving and decision making.

2. Discuss how a police detective might use deductive reasoning to try to solve a crime. How might the detective use inductive reasoning to try to solve the same crime?

3. Heuristic problem-solving strategies are frequently considered helpful and use a "repertoire of 'quick-fix' methods for dealing with problems, based on both experience with strategies that have worked in the past and our own personal storehouse of accumulated knowledge" (text p. 279). Mental sets frequently cause problems to be more difficult to solve and are described as "a tendency to approach a problem in a set or predetermined way regardless of the requirements of the specific problem" (text p. 281). Could a heuristic also be a mental set? Could a mental set also be a heuristic? Explain your answers.

4. Whorf's idea that language determines thought is not generally accepted and was not supported by the color-memory experiment with American college students and Dani individuals. Do you think the results of the experiment might have been different if American and Dani children, first becoming aware of the concept of color (perhaps 3-or 4-year-olds), were the subjects in this experiment? Explain your answer. (You might want to consider both the ideas that language determines thought, and that thought structures language.)

PART VIII. APPLICATIONS

1. If you're like many college students you might like to watch game shows on TV. If so, this application should not be objectionable to you. If you don't normally watch game shows this application might turn you into a "couch potato." Choose a game show in which contestants compete against each other (e.g., "Wheel of Fortune," "Hollywood Squares," "The Price is Right"). Watch the show carefully for two or three days and record the "choices" of each contestant. Do your records suggest that contestants used some sort of strategies? If so, which strategies were most common? Were some strategies more successful than others? If you were the contestant on the show, what strategy would you have used? Did contestants fall victim to some of the obstacles to problem solving such as mental sets or confirmation bias?

2. You will probably have to make a decision in the near future concerning your schedule of classes for next semester. It is not the most important decision in the world, but it should be seriously considered. There are probably some courses you need to take, some courses you'd like to take, some professors you'd like to have, some professors you'd not like to have, certain hours you'd want to have class, and certain hours you'd not want to have class. When the schedule of courses is available prepare two or three tentative schedules. Then, after using at least two different rational approaches to decision making, decide on your schedule for next semester.

PART IX. SUMMARY TABLES SOLUTIONS

Theories of Concept Formation

Theory	Individual	Assumptions	Strengths	Weaknesses
Association	Hull	Learn stimulus–response associations between common elements (S)–concepts (R)	Explains how to generalize concepts	—
Hypothesis testing	Bruner	Generating and testing hypothesis concerning critical attributes of formal concepts. Retain hypothesis if supported, develop another hypothesis if inaccurate in identifying membership in category	Often used in experimental situations with formal concepts	Because many day-to-day concepts involve natural concepts not precisely defined, may not apply to real-life situations
Exemplar	Rosch	Natural concepts are structured around typical examples or prototypes. The better the match between the prototype and object the more readily the object is included in the concept	In experimental situation people have faster reaction times to "Is ___ a ___?" questions when using examples of concepts that are more typical than when using less typical examples	—

Problem-Solving Strategies

Strategy	Description	Advantages	Limitations
Trial and error	Try different solutions one at a time in random order until correct solution is found	Works satisfactorily if limited number of possible solutions	May not be the most efficient strategy if there is a large number of possible solutions
Testing hypotheses	Develops hypothesis to narrow the number of possible solutions and then tries those selected solutions first	More efficient than trial and error if large number of possible solutions	May need to come up with additional hypothesis if first does not lead to correct solution
Algorithms	The systematic exploration of every possible solution (used by computers)	Guarantees a correct solution if one is aware of all possible solutions	Requires a lot of time and effort For real-life problems one may not be aware of all possible solutions
Heuristics	Rule-of-thumb strategies that are based on both experience with strategies that have worked in the past and personal knowledge Two common heuristic strategies are means-ends analysis and working backwards	May lead to quick solutions	Are not guaranteed to produce a correct solution

Rational Approaches to Decision Making

Approach	Examples	General Description	Strengths or Weaknesses
Compensatory	Additive Utility-probability	Evaluate how desirable potential outcomes stack up against undesirable potential outcomes for each alternative	Utility-probability model is generally more accurate than additive model
Noncompensatory	Maximax, minimax Conjunctive Elimination by aspects	All features of each alternative are not considered and features do not compensate for one another	Must rate each alternative on a number of features even though may not all be considered
Heuristics	Representative Availability	Concentrate on only a few relevant facts and rule-of-thumb approaches	Often work well and are quick, but may result in costly errors in judgment

Theories of Language Acquisition

Theory	Individuals	Description	Supporting Evidence	Weaknesses
Learning	Skinner Bandura	Learn to shape sounds into words and words into sentences through selective reinforcement and imitation	Babies whose parents reinforce their early attempts at meaningful sounds vocalize more than institutionalized children who receive less attention	Many words a child says are not words they have heard and could not be imitating Children show the same sequence of language acquisition even though their experience varies widely
Nativistic	Chomsky	People are "prewired" by the innate language-acquisition device to recognize phonemes, morphemes, syntax, and semantics	Universal sequence of language acquisition Infants recognize virtually all consonant sounds	Needs to be combined with the learning perspective to account for the specific language and grammar acquired

CHAPTER 9

Motivation

PART I. LEARNING OBJECTIVES

When you finish studying this chapter you should be able to:

The Nature of Motivation

1. Define motivation, and list the three related ways motivation influences behavior. **(312)**

Explaining Motivation: Theoretical Perspectives

2. Describe the instinct theory, and explain its basic flaw. **(313)**

3. Describe the drive-reduction theory, and discuss three problems this theory has in attempting to explain motivation. **(314)**

4. Discuss Maslow's hierarchy-of-needs perspective, and list the five levels of human needs. **(315)**

5. Describe the cognitive perspective of motivation. **(316)**

The Range of Human Motivation

6. Describe the four categories of human motives. **(316-317)**

Hunger and Eating

7. Describe the role of the stomach in regards to feelings of hunger and satiety. **(317)**

8. Discuss the dual hypothalamic control theory of hunger, and identify the two hypothalamic areas associated with hunger and satiety. **(318-319)**

9. Discuss the glucostatic theory of hunger and identify body structures associated with this theory. **(319)**

10. Describe the lipostatic theory and other mechanisms involved in long-term weight regulation. **(321)**

11. Define obesity and discuss four factors that are believed to be associated with obesity. **(322-324)**

12. Explain why weight is hard to keep off. **(324-325)**

13. Discuss two serious eating disorders, and describe the "typical" person who suffers from each disorder. **(325-327)**

Sensation-Seeking Motives

14. Define arousal, and explain the Yerkes-Dodson law concerning optimum levels of arousal for performing different types of tasks. **(328-329)**

15. Describe the relationship between level of arousal and how we feel, and discuss the idea that there are two preferred levels of arousal. **(329-331)**

16. Describe the effects of moderate and severe levels of sensory deprivation. **(331-332)**

Complex Psychosocial Motives: The Need for Achievement

17. Define need for achievement (nACH), and explain how hope of success and fear of failure interact to affect nACH. **(332-334)**

18. Evaluate the research findings concerning women and the fear of success. **(333)**

19. Describe how the way children are raised may influence their nACH. **(334-335)**

Sexual Motivation and Human Sexual Behavior

20. Describe the influence of hormones on male sexual motivation, and discuss research that links androgens with sexual activity. **(336-337)**

21. Discuss research findings concerning the influence of hormones on female sexual motivation. **(337)**

22. Describe the influence of psychosocial factors on human sexual motivation, and summarize cross-cultural evidence that indicates the effect of cultural mores on sexual expression **(337-340)**

23. List and describe four forms of sexual expression. **(340-342)**

24. Discuss AIDS, and describe a number of behaviors that increase the risk of being exposed to the AIDS virus. **(342-344)**

25. Define homosexuality, and describe the incidence of homosexuality. **(345, 347-348)**

26. Summarize the psychosocial and biological theories concerning the development of homosexuality. **(349-351)**

PART II. OVERVIEW

Motivation is defined as any condition that tends to energize and direct behavior. A number of theories have been proposed to explain motivation. The instinct theory postulated that motivated behaviors were under the control of innate behavior patterns or instincts. The instinct theory was largely unsuccessful in explaining behavior. The drive-reduction theory proposes that we are motivated into action in order to reduce unpleasant internal conditions associated with needs. Drive-reduction theory can fairly well account for some motivated behaviors related to biological needs, but has difficulty in explaining other examples of motivated behavior. Maslow's hierarchy-of-needs theory conceptualizes human needs as existing on five levels (biological, safety, love and belongingness, esteem, and self-actualization). Lower-level needs must be satisfied before an individual can address higher-level needs. The cognitive perspective of motivation emphasizes the role of mental processes in directing behavior. Human motives include biological, sensation-seeking, complex psychosocial, and multifactor motives.

Although hunger is a very basic type of motive, the control of eating behavior is very complex and not entirely understood. The stomach, hypothalamus, liver, and duodenum are all involved in the control of eating. The control of eating involves the bodily monitoring of the level of sugar in the blood. Long-term regulation of weight involves the bodily monitoring of the level of fat in the body.

The concept of arousal is introduced to explain sensation-seeking motives. There is an optimum level of arousal (which may vary from time to time and/or task to task) that results in most efficient performance. Sensory-deprivation studies indicate that people have a strong need for sensory stimulation.

The need for achievement (nACH) is discussed as an example of a complex psychosocial motive. An individual's nACH results from the interrelationship of two components (hope of success, and fear of failure). Individuals with varying levels of nACH approach tasks in different ways.

Sexual motivation is discussed as an example of a multifactor motive. There is well-documented evidence indicating the role of hormones on male sexual interest and activity. The relationship of hormones and female sexual expression is still unclear. While biological factors exert an influence on human sexual expression, psychological and cultural conditions play a larger role. This chapter concludes with a description of a number of sexual behavior patterns (masturbation, erotic fantasy, oral-genital stimulation, and coitus), AIDS, and a discussion of homosexuality. Two theories related to the development of homosexuality (psychosocial and biological) are described and it is concluded that there is no simple, universal explanation of homosexuality. Sexual orientation (heterosexual, homosexual, or bisexual) is influenced by a variety of psychosocial and biological factors unique to each individual.

PART III.   KEY TERMS/MATCHING EXERCISES

Match the following concepts and/or individuals with the appropriate descriptions. Check your answers against the Answer Key.

Motivation (Overview)

Concepts

_d._ 1.   motivation (**312**)

_j._ 2.   drive (**316-317**)

_h._ 3.   incentives (**314**)

_l._ 4.   instincts (**313**)

_e._ 5.   cognitive perspective (**316**)

_g._ 6.   complex psychosocial motives (**317**)

_a._ 7.   biologically based motives (**316**)

_k._ 8.   hierarchy of needs (**315**)

_f._ 9.   drive-reduction theory (**314**)

_c._ 10.   instinct theory (**313**)

_b._ 11.   sensation-seeking motives (**327-328**)

_i._ 12.   multifactor motives (**317**)

Descriptions

a.   Include(s) the need for food, water, air, sleep, temperature regulation, and the avoidance of pain

b.   Include(s) the need to manipulate and explore the environment for sensory stimulation

c.   Motivation theory that is flawed because it does not explain behavior but simply relabels it

d.   Any condition that energizes and directs an organism's actions

e.   Propose(s) that expectations are important motivators

f.   Propose(s) that organisms engage in behavior to reduce aversive conditions

g.   Determined by learning and are (is) aroused and satisfied by psychological and social events

h.   External stimuli that can energize and direct behavior even when no internal drive state exists

i.   Based on a combination of biological, psychological, and cultural factors

j.   Motives, such as hunger and thirst, that are based on internal biological needs

k.   Proposed by Maslow and states that human needs exist on five levels

l.   Innate patterns of behavior that occur under a certain set of conditions

Answer Key   1. d   2. j   3. h   4. l   5. e   6. g   7. a   8. k   9. f   10. c   11. b   12. i

Hunger and Eating

Concepts

_c_ 1. set point (**321**)
_h_ 2. obese (**322**)
_a_ 3. glucostatic theory (**319**)
_i_ 4. lateral hypothalamus (LH) (**319**)
_b_ 5. lipostatic theory (**321**)

_g_ 6. anorexia nervosa (**325**)
_e_ 7. ventromedial hypothalamus (VMH) (**318-319**)
_f_ 8. dual hypothalamic control theory (**318-319**)
_d_ 9. bulimia (**325**)

Descriptions

a. Suggests that hunger is triggered when glucose is not available for use by cells

b. Suggests that the amount of stored fat in the body regulates food intake

c. Physiologically preferred level of body weight for an individual

d. Characterized by episodes of binge- and purge-eating behavior

e. "Satiety center"

f. Suggests that eating behavior is controlled by the electrical activity of the satiety and feeding centers

g. Characterized by a prolonged refusal to eat adequate amounts of food

h. Describes an individual weighing at least 20 percent more than their desirable weight

i. "Feeding center"

Answer Key   1. c   2. h   3. a   4. i   5. b   6. g   7. e   8. f   9. d

Sensation-Seeking Motives | Complex Psychosocial Motives

Concepts

_c_ 1. fear of success (**333**)
_b_ 2. optimum level of arousal (**328**)
_e_ 3. sensory deprivation studies (**331**)

_d_ 4. Yerkes-Dodson law (**329**)
_a_ 5. need for achievement (nACH) (**332**)
_f_ 6. arousal (**329**)

Descriptions

a. Related to hope of success and fear of failure

b. Level at which performance would be most efficient

c. Associated with individuals who perceive negative consequences accompanying success

d. Describes the relationship between arousal and performance

e. Suggest(s) that individuals have a strong need for sensory stimulation

f. Affects performance and how one feels

Answer Key   1. c   2. b   3. e   4. d   5. a   6. f

Sexual Motivation and Human Sexual Behavior

Concepts

_a._ 1. acquired immunodeficiency syndrome (AIDS) **(342)**

_c._ 2. estrogens **(337)**

_e._ 3. homosexual **(345)**

_d._ 4. androgens **(336)**

_b._ 5. sexual orientation **(344)**

Descriptions

a. Causes an individual to be vulnerable to a variety of cancers and opportunistic infections

b. Refers to the sex to which an individual is attracted

c. Role of these in sexual motivation is far from clear

d. Produced by the testes and adrenal glands

e. Primary erotic, psychological, emotional, and social interest is directed at a member of the same sex, even though that interest may not be overtly expressed

Answer Key   1. a   2. c   3. e   4. d   5. b

PART IV. TRUE-FALSE STATEMENTS

Fill in the blank before each statement with either a T (true) or an F (false). Check your answers against the Answer Key. Then go back to the items that are false and make the necessary change(s) to the statements to convert the items into true statements.

Motivation (Overview)

_____ 1. The concept of motivation incorporates both physiological factors and cognitive conditions that influence behavior.

_____ 2. Drive-reduction theory proposes that we engage in activities to obtain incentives.

_____ 3. According to Maslow's hierarchy of needs, the highest level of human needs are esteem needs.

Hunger and Eating

_____ 4. The Cannon-Washburn hypothesis that the hunger motive is caused by stomach contractions has been well supported by a variety of research methods.

_____ 5. Research suggests that both the liver and duodenum contain glucoreceptors.

_____

_____

_____ 6. Once established, an organism's set point does not change.

_____

_____

_____ 7. Obese individuals have the same number of fat cells as normal-weight individuals but these obese individuals' fat cells are 50–100 percent larger.

_____

_____

Sensation-Seeking Motives

_____ 8. The Yerkes-Dodson law states that for most tasks as arousal increases so does performance.

_____

_____

_____ 9. Unlike severe sensory deprivation, mild forms of sensory restriction may be associated with positive outcomes.

_____

_____

Complex Psychosocial Motives: The Need for Achievement

_____ 10. A person with a low need for achievement, as a result of a high fear of failure, would be likely to attempt tasks that are either very easy or very difficult.

_____

_____

_____ 11. It is well established that women typically have more fear of success than men.

_____

_____

Sexual Motivation and Human Sexual Behavior

_____ 12. There is evidence to link androgens with sexual activity and motivation in both males and females.

_____

_____

_____ 13. Almost all human societies view homosexuality negatively.

_____

_____

_____ 14. Evidence from a variety of lines of research supports the psychosocial perspective concerning the development of homosexuality.

Answer Key

1. T (**312**)	6. F (**322**)	11. F (**334**)
2. F (**314-315**)	7. F (**323**)	12. T (**337**)
3. F (**315**)	8. F (**329**)	13. F (**348**)
4. F (**318**)	9. T (**332**)	14. F (**348**)
5. T (**320**)	10. T (**333**)	

PART V. MULTIPLE-CHOICE QUESTIONS

Choose the best answer to each question. Circle your choice. Check your answers against the Answer Key. Questions marked with an asterisk (*) include annotated answers.

Motivation (Overview)

1. Which of the following is *not* an affect motivation has on our actions?

  a. It directs or defines the direction of the resulting behavior
  b. It has an impact on how vigorous or intense a behavior is
  c. It controls instinctive behaviors
  d. It energizes or activates one to behave in a certain way

2. The instinct theory of motivation

  a. explains the observation that there appears to be more than one optimal level of arousal.
  b. shows the influence of Darwin's theory of evolution.
  c. shows the influence of behaviorism.
  d. explains the observation that organisms learn to perform specific behaviors.

3. Drive-reduction theory operates at which level of Maslow's hierarchy of needs?

  a. Biological only
  b. Biological and safety
  c. All levels
  d. None of the levels

***4.** Which of the following behaviors can be most easily explained by the drive-reduction theory of motivation?

  a. Some people like to climb mountains and ride roller-coasters
  b. A mother animal takes care of her babies
  c. Hungry rats in a Skinner box will press a bar in order to get food
  d. Hungry rats in a Skinner box will press a bar in order to get saccharin.

5. An external stimulus that can motivate behavior even when no internal drive state exists is a(n)

  a. instinct.
  b. need.
  c. motive.
  d. incentive.

6. The correct order of Maslow's hierarchy of needs, from lowest to highest is

  a. safety, biological, esteem, love and belongingness, self-actualization.
  b. self-actualization, esteem, love and belongingness, safety, biological.
  c. biological, esteem, love and belongingness, safety, self-actualization.
  d. biological, safety, love and belongingness, esteem, self-actualization.

7. According to Maslow, seeking approval, recognition, prestige, and status is an attempt to satisfy _esteem_ needs.

  a. biological
  b. belongingness
  c. self-actualization
  d. esteem

8. Which two theories of motivation can be criticized for failing to provide operational definitions and/or merely renaming as opposed to explaining behavior?

  a. Maslow's and drive-reduction
  b. Instinct and cognitive
  c. Maslow's and instinct
  d. Drive-reduction and arousal

9. The need for social approval is a _complex psychosocial_ motive.

  a. self-actualization
  b. biological
  c. sensation-seeking
  d. complex psychosocial

Hunger and Eating

10. There is evidence that the stomach contains

  a. caloric receptors.
  b. glucoreceptors.
  c. liporeceptors.
  d. pressure detectors.

11. If, after brain damage in an auto accident, a person gained 100 pounds in two months you would suspect damage to the

  a. ventromedial hypothalamus.
  b. dorsal hypothalamus.
  c. lateral hypothalamus.
  d. thyroid gland.

12. According to the dual-hypothalamic control theory, the _satiety center_ is normally active a vast majority of the time.

  a. set-point center
  b. satiety center
  c. feeding center
  d. lateral hypothalamic center

13. The _glucostatic_ theory states that hunger results when special receptors detect a lack of availability of blood sugar, because blood sugar or insulin levels are low.

    a. homeostatic
    b. lipostatic
    c. hypogonadic
    d. glucostatic

*14. Which one of the following does *not* stimulate hunger and eating behavior?

    a. Stomach contractions
    b. Reduced blood-sugar levels
    c. Increased levels of glycerol in the bloodstream
    d. Stimulation of the lateral hypothalamus

15. According to the _lipostatic_ theory, our bodies monitor the amount of fat contained and use this as a barometer to regulate food intake.

    a. obesity
    b. glucostatic
    c. lipostatic
    d. set-point

16. Which of the following statements is *true*?

    a. Not all obese people eat more than people of average weight.
    b. Average-weight people have more, but smaller, fat cells than obese individuals.
    c. Obese people have lower set points than average-weight people.
    d. Obese children are no more likely than average-weight children to have weight problems as adults.

17. Following dramatic weight loss as a result of a very low calorie diet (a starvation diet), people frequently regain much of the "lost" weight because

    a. they "fall off the wagon" and engage in binge eating.
    b. their bodies need to restock stored fat.
    c. their resting metabolic rate had increased during the diet and following the diet it is reduced.
    d. their resting metabolic rate was reduced during the diet and stays at the reduced level following the diet.

18. _Anorexia_ is characterized by a refusal to eat adequate amounts of food. _Bulimia_ is associated with episodes of binge-eating followed by purging.

    a. Anorexia nervosa | Bulimia
    b. Bulimia | Anorexia nervosa
    c. Starvation diets | Apnea
    d. Bulimia | Obesity

Sensation-Seeking Motives

19. If you could operantly condition a rat to turn on a TV set in order to watch Micky Mouse cartoons, it would illustrate that rats have _____ motives.

    a. complex psychosocial
    b. multifactor
    c. sensation-seeking
    d. biologically based

*20. According to the Yerkes-Dodson law, a college basketball player should complete a higher percentage of free throws

    a. in a regular season conference game.
    b. in a team scrimmage.
    c. when practicing alone.
    d. He should make the same percentage of free throws in all situations.

21. Sometimes on Saturday nights you like to go to parties and dance and socialize until 2 o'clock in the morning and on other Saturday nights you like to relax alone in your dorm room. Your behavior supports the idea that

    a. Maslow's hierarchy of needs change in response to certain situations.
    b. there are two preferred levels of arousal.
    c. some people are sensation seekers and others are sensation avoiders.
    d. arousal influences both performance and how we feel.

22. The results of experiments in sensory deprivation suggest that

    a. people prefer peace and quiet to activity.
    b. people need sensory stimulation.
    c. sensory deprivation leads to permanent changes in behavior.
    d. participants enjoyed the time spent in sensory deprivation.

Complex Psychosocial Motives: The Need for Achievement

23. Which of the following is *not* considered to be a complex psychosocial motive?

    a. Need for love and belongingness
    b. Need for achievement
    c. Need for safety
    d. Need for competence

24. Which of the following has *not* been related to the need for achievement (nACH)?

    a. Hope of failure
    b. Hope of success
    c. Fear of failure
    d. Fear of success

25. Joe is more motivated by his fear of failure than by his hope for success. If given a choice during a game of horseshoes he would probably stand _____ from the horseshoe pit.

    a. "close" to an "average" distance away
    b. an "average" distance to "far" away
    c. either "close" or "far" away
    d. the same distance as everyone else

26. Regarding Horner's 1969 study concerning women and fear of success, more recent evidence suggests that

    a. as a result of the women's movement, women have less fear of success today than they did in the late 1960s.

    b. subjects were responding in relation to gender-role stereotypes and not really indicating that they had a fear of success.

    c. the situation has changed so that today men have more fear of success than women.

    d. Horner was correct: women in 1969 and today do have more fear of success than men.

*27. In Horner's 1969 study concerning fear of success, who would have been more likely to finish the story, "After first-term finals, Anne (John) finds herself (himself) at the top of her (his) medical school class" by saying, "and went on to become an outstanding, successful, and well-respected doctor"?

    a. A female writing about John

    b. A male writing about John

    c. A female writing about Anne

    d. A male writing about Anne

Sexual Motivation and Human Sexual Behavior

*28. Which of the following statements is *true*?

    a. Androgen-blocking drugs such as Depo Provera may be effective in reducing sexual interest and activity in human males.

    b. Following castration (removal of the testes) human males always report a dramatic decrease in sexual desire and behavior.

    c. Estrogens play a significant role in the sexual interest and activity in human females.

    d. There is no systematic relationship between blood-androgen levels and strength of sexual motivation in young men.

29. Perhaps the strongest evidence for the importance of psychosocial factors in human sexual motivation and expression is that

    a. people engage in sexual behaviors that are not related to procreation.

    b. following menopause, most women do not experience a change in their level of sexual arousal.

    c. the cultural mores of most societies do not regulate sexuality.

    d. the only species to have highly localized patterns of sexual behavior is man.

30. Which society most actively encourages (encouraged) sexual activity?

    a. Colonial American

    b. Mangaia (in the Polynesian Islands)

    c. Dani (of New Guinea)

    d. Inis Beag (on an Irish island)

31. Which form of sexual behavior was widely condemned in the mid eighteenth century and labeled "self-abuse"?

    a. Coitus

    b. Bondage

    c. Masturbation

    d. Oral-genital stimulation

32. In the Judeo–Christian heritage, which one of the following has *not* been labeled an immoral act?

a. Coitus
b. Oral-genital stimulation
c. Homosexuality
d. Masturbation

33. The best hope for curtailing the epidemic spread of AIDS is

a. through a widespread immunization program.
b. careful screening of blood prior to using it for transfusions.
c. through education and behavior change.
d. castration of infected males (both homosexual and heterosexual).

34. Jane's attraction to other women is referred to as

a. heterosexuality.
b. her sexual orientation.
c. fantasy.
d. erotic attraction.

35. According to the text's definition of homosexuality,

a. only men can be homosexual, women with a "homosexual orientation" are lesbians.
b. homosexuals have a gender identity disorder.
c. a homosexual cannot engage in heterosexual activities.
d. it is not necessary to overtly express homosexual behavior to be a homosexual.

36. Which of the following statements is *true*?

a. Most homosexuals report that when they were young they were seduced by older homosexuals.
b. Homosexual and heterosexual people had dated (heterosexually) about equally in high school.
c. Most research studies, which have examined androgen levels in heterosexual and homosexual males, have found homosexuals to have lower androgen levels.
d. An overly seductive mother is associated with the development of homosexuality in male children.

Answer Key

1. c	**(312)**	9. d	**(317)**	16. a	**(324)**	23. c	**(332)**	30. b **(339)**
2. b	**(313)**	10. d	**(318)**	17. d	**(325)**	24. a **(332-333)**		31. c **(340)**
3. a	**(315)**	11. a **(318-319)**		18. a	**(325)**	25. c	**(333)**	32. a **(342)**
*4. c	**(314)**	12. b	**(319)**	19. c **(327-328)**		26. b	**(334)**	33. c **(343-344)**
5. d	**(314)**	13. d	**(319)**	*20. a	**(329)**	*27. b	**(334)**	34. b **(344)**
6. d	**(315)**	*14. c	**(321)**	21. b **(330-331)**		*28. a	**(336)**	35. d **(347)**
7. d	**(315)**	15. c	**(321)**	22. b	**(331)**	29. d	**(338)**	36. b **(349)**
8. c	**(313, 315)**							

Annotated Answers

4. The correct choice is c. Drive-reduction theory is best suited for primary drives that are induced by internal biological needs. Hunger is an unpleasant state of tension that is reduced by eating. A hungry rat would bar press in order to receive food.

a. Drive-reduction theory would have difficulty explaining mountain climbing and roller-coaster riding because it seems unreasonable to postulate a need or drive associated with those behaviors. Those behaviors would best be explained by the arousal theory.

b. The first theory to come to mind to explain maternal behavior would be instinct theory (which, as you have learned, would not provide a very insightful explanation). Although an argument could be made for maternal behavior reducing a drive associated with the hormonal stage of the mother, alternative c is a better choice.

d. Because saccharin, unlike food, does not satisfy hunger (or any other biological need), the drive-reduction theory has difficulty in explaining this behavior.

14. The correct choice is c. Increased levels of glycerol have the effect of reducing consumption of food.

  a. The Cannon-Bard study found a close relationship between stomach contractions and reports of hunger.

  b. According to the glucostatic theory, reduced levels of blood-sugar (detected by glucoreceptors) stimulate the feeding center of the lateral hypothalamus.

  d. Stimulation of the lateral hypothalamus (the feeding center) causes feeding behavior to occur.

20. We will assume that making free throws is a relatively easy task for a college basketball player, therefore the correct choice is a. A regular-season basketball game would result in the player experiencing a higher level of arousal than in the other situations described. Because the Yerkes-Dodson law states that performance is better for simple tasks with a high level of arousal, performance should be better in this situation.

  b. The situations in b and c would result in lower levels of arousal and performance should be reduced.

  c. See b above.

  d. The Yerkes-Dodson law states that the situation strongly affects performance, therefore this choice is incorrect.

27. The correct choice is b. Because females were more likely to complete the story with a negative (or fear of success) theme, it follows that males were more likely to complete the story with "successful" themes.

  a. In Horner's study, females did not complete the "John" version of the story.

  c. Females were more likely than males to complete the story with a negative (or fear of success) theme.

  d. In Horner's study, males did not complete the "Anne" version of the story.

28. The correct choice is a. While not guaranteed, a number of studies have shown that androgen-blocking drugs may be effective in reducing sexual interest and activity.

  b. Castration often significantly reduces sexual interest and activity, but it does not always do so. This indicates that sexual behavior is not entirely under the control of hormones.

  c. Postmenopausal women studies, examining the effect of estrogens on female sexual interest and activity, have contradictory findings. Some studies suggest that estrogen increases sexual interest and activity; other studies do not indicate such a result.

  d. Research has shown a strong positive correlation between blood-androgen levels and strength of sexual motivation as reflected by frequency of orgasm in young men.

PART VI. SUMMARY TABLES

To test your understanding of the material discussed in this chapter complete the following tables. Check your answers with those supplied in PART IX.

Theories of Hunger, Eating, and Weight Maintenance

Theory	Description	Supporting Evidence	Weaknesses
The stomach			
Dual hypothalamic control			
Glucostatic			
Lipostatic			

PART VI. SUMMARY TABLE

To test your understanding of the material discussed in this chapter complete the following table. Check your answers with those supplied in PART IX.

Theories of Motivation and Arousal

Theory	Individuals	Description	Strengths	Weaknesses
Instinct	William James	Darwin Theory		
Drive reduction	Clark Hull	Believed in Behaviorilism (need for food reduces hunger)		
Hierarchy of needs	Maslow	Humanistic psychology perspective biological, safety, love + belong, esteem, + self-actualization		

| Cognitive perspective | Rotter | cognitions, (thoughts + beliefs) motivate behavior | |
| Arousal | HEBB | Arousal optimum level of arousal results in most effici. performance | Yerkes-Dodson LAW |

PART VII. THOUGHT QUESTIONS/CRITICAL THINKING

Prepare answers to the following discussion questions.

1. Which theory of motivation and/or arousal (instinct, drive-reduction, Maslow's hierarchy of needs, cognitive perspective) would best explain why a male rat in a Skinner box would bar press in each of the following situations?

    a. To turn off an electric shock
    b. To turn on a colorful slide show
    c. To turn off a colorful slide show
    d. To get access to a sexually receptive female rat
    e. To get access to food
    f. To get access to a rat "playground"
    g. To receive intracranial self-stimulation (described in Chapter 3)
    h. To get access to saccharin

    Explain your choices.

2. A weight-reduction procedure for obese individuals that has received a lot of publicity in recent years is liposuction. Liposuction involves removing fat from an individual's body through a medical procedure. Obviously the immediate consequence of the procedure is substantial weight loss. Evaluate the procedure by referring to the lipostatic theory of long-term weight regulation. Do you think the individual would establish a new set point at the liposuction-induced body weight? Why or why not? Who would probably be more successful in maintaining a reduced body weight, a person who dieted and lost 50 pounds or a person who lost 50 pounds through liposuction? Explain your answer.

3. Refer back to Chapter 5 (States of Consciousness) and reread the section on meditation (pp. 169–170). Discuss the similarities between meditation and mild forms of sensory restriction as regards (a) the physical state (or experiences) of the individual, and (b) the benefits of the experience for the individual.

4. Determine the level of needs that each of the following individuals would be operating at according to Maslow's hierarchy of needs.

    a. An individual whose house was recently destroyed by a tornado
    b. A congressman who is more concerned with the amount of TV exposure he receives than in promoting the general welfare of the country
    c. A 14-year-old adolescent who recently moved and started attending a new school in the middle of the school year
    d. A successful businessman who volunteers his time to tutor disadvantaged children.
    e. An individual living in a Third World country that is in the midst of famine
    f. A college student who wants to do well enough in class to make the Dean's List this semester
    g. An abused child who has recently been placed in a foster home
    h. An individual whose car broke down on a deserted road in the middle of a snowstorm

PART VIII. APPLICATIONS

1. Hunger is a biological motive. However, at least for humans, eating behavior can be considered a multifactor motive partially controlled by biological, psychological, and cultural factors. We eat at specific times for a variety of reasons: we're hungry, it's mealtime, our friends invite us out for pizza, and perhaps at times when we're bored. Our choice of food is not always tied solely to our biological state of hunger: sometimes we eat a standard American meat-and-potatoes meal, other times we might prefer a spicy Mexican or Chinese meal, or we might just want a candy bar.

Keep a food diary for one week, recording everything you eat. Record the time you eat, what you eat, what if anything you did while eating, whether or not you felt hungry before you ate, and whether or not you felt hungry when you stopped eating. Also, record the physical activities you had each day. At the conclusion of the week examine your food diary and try to explain your eating behavior by referring to the theories of motivation discussed in this chapter. Next, examine your food diary to determine how the different hypotheses concerning the mechanisms that control eating and weight maintenance explain your eating behavior. For example, did you typically wait until you experienced stomach pangs before stopping your activities in order to eat? Did you experience symptoms of low blood-sugar (irritable, fatigued, anxious) before stopping to eat?

2. The text described the sexual behavior and customs of three societies (Mangaian, Inis Beag, and Dani) from an anthropological perspective. The three societies widely differed in their sexual expression. Because our American society consists of a number of varied subcultures it would be difficult to conduct a definitive study concerning the sexual behaviors and customs that would apply to all subgroups and regions of the United States. Your knowledge of the sexual behavior and attitudes of Americans is limited primarily to your personal experience and environment (family, community, and information from the media). Imagine that you are an anthropologist studying the patterns of sexual expression in the community in which you were raised. Describe the sexual behaviors and customs of the culture. Compare and contrast your culture to those described in the text. Which society described in the text is most similar to the culture in which you were raised? Which society is most different?

PART IX. SUMMARY TABLES SOLUTIONS

The following table solution corresponds to the table on pages 174–175.

Theories of Motivation and Arousal

Theory	Individuals	Description	Strengths	Weaknesses
Instinct	William James	Influenced by Darwin's theory of evolution. Proposed that instincts (innate patterns of behavior that occur under certain conditions) control behavior	Today, see only remnants of theory with the study of inborn or genetic influences on behavior	Contains basic flaw of merely supplying another name to a behavior and not explaining it (e.g., maternal behavior accounted for by maternal instinct)
Drive reduction	Clark Hull	Influenced by behaviorism. Motivated behavior results in the reduction of an aversive condition associated with a need (e.g., food reduces hunger)	Explains primary drives (related to internal biological needs) more effectively than secondary or acquired drives	Doesn't explain why many events influence behavior that are not associated with a drive, and not all behaviors decrease after they occur as would be expected if the behavior reduced a drive
Hierarchy of needs	Maslow	Humanistic psychology perspective. Human needs exist on five levels (biological, safety, love and belongingness, esteem, and self-actualization). Must take care of lower needs before higher needs can be met	Has intuitive appeal in explaining a variety of human behaviors	Lack of operational definitions make it difficult to test. Needs may not be as precisely or rigidly ordered as suggested by the theory

Cognitive perspective	Rotter	Cognitions (thoughts, beliefs, expectations, etc.) serve to influence or motivate behavior	Because behavior depends both on expectations of the behavior producing a desired goal and the value of the goal, can account for why motivated behavior does not always occur	Does not seem necessary to account for basic types of motivated behavior such as feeding
Arousal	Hebb	A minimal level of arousal (a mental and physical state) is necessary in order to engage in goal-directed or motivated behavior. An optimum level of arousal results in most efficient performance	Yerkes-Dodson law describing relationship between arousal and performance is generally supported. Subsequently, has been proposed that two optimal levels of arousal can explain why we sometimes seek and other times avoid sensation	More related to sensation-seeking motives as opposed to biological motives

The following solution corresponds to the table on page 173.

Theories of Hunger, Eating, and Weight Maintenance

Theory	Description	Supporting Evidence	Weaknesses
The stomach	Proposed by Cannon and Washburn: the stomach plays a major role in triggering hunger	Relationship between stomach contractions and reports of hunger Also, stomach apparently contains pressure detectors that signal satiety	People without stomachs experience normal hunger If nerves from stomach to brain are severed hunger still experienced
Dual hypothalamic control	The combined actions of the ventromedial hypothalamus (VMH) or satiety center and lateral hypothalamus (LH) or feeding center control feeding behavior	Stimulation of LH and/or destruction of VMH encourages feeding Stimulation of VMH and/or destruction of LH discourages feeding	Needs to explain what turns VMH and LH on off
Glucostatic	Proposed by Mayer and Russek Glucoreceptors monitor availability of glucose in bloodstream When unavailable triggers hunger and eating by influencing hypothalamus	Liver and duodenum apparently contain glucoreceptors	Needs to be combined with dual hypothalamic control theory
Lipostatic	Concerned with long-term weight regulation Body monitors and tries to maintain a certain amount (or set point) of body fat (or lipids) to maintain weight	Fat levels may be signaled by glyceral level in the blood Increase in glyceral results in reduced food consumption	Hypothalamus and nerve tracts through hypothalamus also involved in long-term weight maintenance

CHAPTER 10

Emotion and Stress

PART I. LEARNING OBJECTIVES

When you finish studying this chapter you should be able to:

Emotions (Overview)

1. Define emotion, and describe its four components. **(357)**

2. Describe Plutchik's conceptualization of the range of emotions (the emotion wheel). **(358)**

Emotions: Theories and Controversies

3. Describe the James-Lange theory of emotion, and discuss its strengths and weaknesses. **(359)**

4. Describe the Cannon-Bard theory of emotion, and discuss its strengths and weaknesses. **(362)**

5. Describe the Schachter-Singer theory of emotion, and discuss its strengths and weaknesses. **(362-363)**

6. Describe Tomkins' facial feedback theory of emotions, and discuss research supporting the view that facial expression is associated with emotion. **(364-365)**

7. Describe Solomon and Corbit's opponent-process theory of emotion, and discuss what the theory proposes happens with repeated exposure to an intense emotion-arousing stimulus. **(367-368)**

Stress (Responses to Stress)

8. Define stress, including its physiological and psychological components. **(368)**

9. Discuss Selye's general adaptation syndrome (GAS) regarding the body's physiological response to stress, and describe its three phases. **(370-372)**

10. Discuss cognitive responses to stress, and describe the processes of primary and secondary appraisal. **(372-373)**

11. Discuss emotional and behavioral responses to stress. **(373-374)**

Stress (Stressors)

12. List and describe three factors that contribute to an event or situation being perceived as stressful. **(374)**

13. Describe and evaluate the Social Readjustment Rating Scale (SRRS). **(379)**

Stress (and Illness)

14. Discuss the relationship between stress and coronary heart disease (CHD), and describe Type A and Type B personalities. **(381-382)**

15. Discuss the relationship between stress and hypertension (high blood pressure). **(382-382)**

16. Discuss the relationship between stress and the functioning of the immune system. **(383-384)**

17. Discuss the relationship between stress and cancer. **(384)**

18. Discuss the research related to a possible cancer-prone personality. **(384-385)**

PART II. OVERVIEW

Emotions are closely connected with motivation (the topic of Chapter 9). Emotion refers to subjective feelings and moods. In addition to subjective feelings, major components of emotion include cognitive processes, physiological arousal, and behavioral responses. A number of conflicting theories to explain emotion have been proposed. The James-Lange theory states that in an emotion-arousing situation, one first experiences physiological and muscular responses and only after this is an emotion experienced. The Cannon-Bard theory states that an emotional state, physiological arousal, and muscular response are experienced simultaneously. The Schachter-Singer theory proposes that although physiological changes occur first, the key to what emotion is experienced involves how one cognitively assesses their physical response and the situation. Tomkins' facial-feedback theory states that knowledge of one's facial expression (which has been shown to be cross-culturally similar) influences emotional state. Finally, Solomon and Corbit's opponent-process theory proposes that emotions exist in pairs. When one emotion is strongly aroused eventually the opponent (or opposite) emotion will be activated to restore emotional equilibrium.

Stress is often a by-product of disruptive unpleasant emotions. A number of factors that are related to an event being perceived as stressful are lack of control, suddenness, and ambiguity. Selye's general adaptation syndrome (GAS) describes the physiological response to stress as consisting of three phases. Initially the alarm phase occurs and the sympathetic nervous system is activated to confront the stress. If the stress continues, in the second phase (resistance), the parasympathetic nervous system is activated to limit the body's energy expenditures while continuing to deal with the stress. If the stress continues the exhaustion phase is eventually reached in which the body shows wear and tear and the individual becomes more susceptible to illness. In addition to physiological responses, there are also distinct psychological responses to stress. Cognitive responses include reduced concentration, impaired performance on cognitive tasks, and disruptive thoughts. Emotional responses include anxiety, anger, and depression. Behavioral responses include either dealing with the situation (fight) or avoiding the situation (flight).

Stress is a factor in many illnesses. Certain personality characteristics are related to the tendency to develop specific illnesses. Individuals who show Type A behaviors (ambitious, competitive, easily angered) are prone to develop coronary heart disease (CHD). Type A individuals and people who suppress anger are prone to develop high blood pressure. Because increased levels of stress tend to decrease the functioning of the immune system individuals who are under stress are more likely to contract a variety of infectious illnesses. Some evidence exists linking stress and personality characteristics to cancer. The proposed cancer-prone personality is an individual who is inhibited, conforming, inclined to depression, and tends to suppress his or her emotions.

PART III.   KEY TERMS/MATCHING EXERCISES

Match the following concepts and/or individuals with the appropriate descriptions. Check your answers against the Answer Key.

Emotions: Theories and Controversies

Concepts

_g_ 1. Canon-Bard theory **(362)**

_e_ 2. Tomkins' facial feedback theory **(365)**

_b_ 3. Plutchik's emotion wheel **(358)**

_a_ 4. Schachter-Singer theory **(363)**

_f_ 5. emotion **(357)**

_d_ 6. James-Lange theory **(360)**

_c_ 7. Solomon and Corbit's opponent-process theory **(367)**

Descriptions

a. Proposes that cognitive processes of interpreting both the emotion-causing event and bodily changes are central to the emotion experienced

b. Describes primary human emotions as consisting of four pairs of opposites (e.g., sadness and joy)

c. Proposes that following an emotional response the opposite emotional response occurs to restore emotional equilibrium

d. Proposes that bodily changes and behavioral reactions precede emotions

e. Proposes that knowledge of facial expression determines emotions

f. Subjective feelings and moods that often motivate actions

g. Proposes that bodily changes, behavioral responses, and emotions occur simultaneously

Answer Key   1. g   2. e   3. b   4. a   5. f   6. d   7. c

Stress

Concepts

_b._ 1. cancer-prone personality (**384**)

_c._ 2. stressors (**374**)

_f._ 3. general adaptation syndrome (**370**)

_a._ 4. stress (**369**)

_h._ 5. exhaustion (**371-372**)

_j._ 6. Social Readjustment Rating Scale (SRRS) (**379**)

_e._ 7. resistance (**371**)

_g._ 8. Type B personality (**381**)

_i._ 9. alarm (**370**)

_d._ 10. Type A personality (**381**)

Descriptions

a. Process of appraising events (as harmful, threatening, or challenging), of assessing potential responses, and of responding

b. Describes inhibited, compliant, conforming individuals who tend to suppress their emotions

c. Situations or events that produce stress

d. Describes ambitious, demanding, and easily angered individuals who are prone to heart disease

e. Second phase of the body's reaction to a stressful event that involves activation of the parasympathetic nervous system

f. Physiological response to stress originally proposed by Selye

g. Describes relaxed, easy-going individuals who are not easily angered

h. Third phase of the body's reaction to a stressful event that results in increased susceptibility to disease

i. Body's initial reaction to a stressful event that involves activation of the sympathetic nervous system

j. Assesses the amount of stress a person has experienced in the past year

Answer Key   1. b   2. c   3. f   4. a   5. h   6. j   7. e   8. g   9. i   10. d

PART IV. TRUE-FALSE STATEMENTS

Fill in the blank before each statement with either a T (true) or an F (false). Check your answers against the Answer Key. Then go back to the items that are false and make the necessary change(s) to the statements to convert the items into true statements.

Emotions (Overview)

_____ 1. Subjective feelings of emotions include both a general state and a specific feeling tone.

_____

_____

_____ 2. According to Plutchik's emotion wheel there are only eight human emotions.

_____

_____

Emotions: Theories and Controversies

_____ 3. According to the Cannon-Bard theory of emotion one first experiences physiological and muscular changes, then experiences an emotion.

_____ 4. The facial feedback theory of emotion is consistent with the results of cross-cultural studies concerning the ability of individuals to consistently label the emotional state of other people.

_____ 5. Schachter and Singer's theory of emotion agrees with the James-Lange theory in that emotions follow physiological and behavioral changes.

Stress (Responses to Stress)

_____ 6. Selye's general adaptation syndrome (GAS) emphasizes psychological factors associated with an individual's response to a stressful situation.

_____ 7. Psychological responses to stress include cognitive, emotional, and behavioral responses.

Stress (Stressors)

_____ 8. By definition, stress is always associated with negative events or situations.

_____ 9. Situations that an individual does not have control over and are sudden and ambiguous are likely to be perceived as stressful.

Stress (and Illness)

_____ 10. In the original long-term study of personality type and coronary heart disease, Type A men were three times as likely as Type B men to suffer heart attacks.

_____ 11. Stressful events decrease the functioning of the body's immune system.

_____

_____

Answer Key	1. T **(358)**	5. T **(362-363)**	9. T **(374)**
	2. F **(358)**	6. F **(370)**	10. F **(382)**
	3. F **(362)**	7. T **(372)**	11. T **(383)**
	4. T **(365)**	8. F **(379)**	

PART V. MULTIPLE-CHOICE QUESTIONS

Choose the best answer to each question. Circle your choice. Check your answers against the Answer Key. Questions marked with an asterisk (*) include annotated answers.

Emotions (Overview)

1. The four integral components of human emotions are

    a. cognitive processes, subjective feelings, behavioral reactions, and facial expressions.

    b. primary appraisal, secondary appraisal, behavioral reactions, and physiological arousal.

    c. cognitive processes, subjective feelings, physiological arousal, and behavioral reactions.

    d. cognitive processes, stressors, physiological arousal, and subjective feelings.

2. The physiological component of emotion is closely associated to the

    a. autonomic nervous system.

    b. central nervous system.

    c. skeletal or somatic nervous system.

    d. brain stem functions.

3. During an emotional state, which of the following would indicate physiological arousal?

    a. A sense of fear

    b. Perception of the event as dangerous

    c. Screaming

    d. An increase in blood pressure

4. According to Plutchik's emotion wheel, emotions that are directly across from each other

    a. are opponent processes.

    b. have the most in common.

    c. are oppoosites.

    d. are secondary emotions.

Emotions: Theories and Controversies

*5. Imagine you are driving and a small child runs out in front of your car. You slam on the brakes to avoid hitting the child. It is only as you drive away and notice your heart pounding that you say to yourself, "Boy, that was scary!" For which theory of emotion does this situation give support?

    a. James-Lange only
    b. Cannon-Bard only
    c. Schachter-Singer only
    d. Both James Lange and Schachter-Singer

6. The James-Lange theory is supported by evidence that indicates that

    a. the hypothalamus is involved in emotional expression.
    b. people report less-intense emotional feelings after suffering a spinal cord injury.
    c. following a fear response, people experience elation.
    d. individuals tend to cognitively look for an appropriate emotional label for physiological changes.

7. The Cannon-Bard theory states that

    a. emotional experiences and physical changes occur simultaneously.
    b. physical changes are necessary for emotional experiences.
    c. emotional experiences precede physical changes.
    d. emotional experiences follow physical changes.

8. The Schachter-Singer theory agrees with the _____ theory in that emotions follow physical and behavioral changes, and agrees with the _____ theory in that cognitive processes are central to emotional experiences.

    a. James-Lange | Solomon Corbit
    b. James-Lange | Cannon-Bard
    c. Solomon and Corbit | Cannon-Bard
    d. Cannon-Bard | James-Lange

*9. In Schachter and Singer's experiment, subjects who were uninformed or misinformed concerning the side-effects of "Suproxin" and waited with a confederate who acted happy or euphoric, tended to

    a. provide no emotional label to their arousal.
    b. label their arousal as happy also.
    c. label their arousal as anger directed at the "silly" confederate.
    d. report no changes in their physical state.

10. The idea that facial expressions of many human emotions are similar in all human cultures was originally proposed by

    a. William James.
    b. Charles Darwin.
    c. Paul Ekman.
    d. Sylvan Tomkins.

11. When actors were coached to assume a specific facial expression corresponding to a negative emotion (anger, fear, disgust, and sadness), they
    a. exhibited parasympathetic nervous system arousal.
    b. exhibited the same physiological response to all four emotions.
    c. exhibited distinct physiological responses to each of the four emotions.
    d. could not tell what emotion they were modeling.

12. Ekman's research in which subjects were instructed to merely move their facial muscles in specific ways that automatically produced emotional reactions lends support to the _____ theory.
    a. James-Lange
    b. Cannon-Bard
    c. Schachter-Singer
    d. Solomon-Corbit

13. Solomon and Corbit's opponent-process theory proposes that, with repeated exposure to a situation that produces an intense emotion, the initial emotional reaction will _weaken_ , while the opponent emotional reaction will _grow stronger_ .
    a. weaken | remain constant
    b. remain constant | grow stronger
    c. weaken | grow stronger
    d. grow stronger | weaken

14. Which theory (theories) of emotion fail(s) to adequately recognize that emotions are more than automatic reactions to stimuli?
    a. Both the James-Lange and the Cannon-Bard theories
    b. The Schachter-Singer theory
    c. The James-Lange theory
    d. The Solomon-Corbit theory

Stress (Responses to Stress)

15. The process of appraising events (as harmful, threatening, or challenging), of assessing potential responses, and of responding to those events defines
    a. the general adaptation syndrome.
    b. stressors.
    c. stress.
    d. facial feedback theory.

*16. The headline in *The National Busybody* reads "97 Pound Mom Lifts Minivan Off Toddler." Which phase of the general adaptation syndrome was "Mom" in at the time?
    a. Exhaustion
    b. Resistance
    c. Peak
    d. Alarm

17. The correct order of the phases of Selye's general adaptation syndrome (GAS) is

    a. alarm, exhaustion, and resistance.
    b. peak, exhaustion, and resistance.
    c. alarm, resistance, and exhaustion.
    d. resistance, alarm, and exhaustion.

18. At which stage of GAS does the body begin to show signs of wear and tear and exhibit increased susceptibility to disease?

    a. Final
    b. Exhaustion
    c. Resistance
    d. Immunocompetence

19. According to Lazarus and Folkman, when in a potentially stressful situation we first engage in _____ to determine if the event is positive, neutral, or negative and if it is negative we then engage in _____ to determine if we have sufficient resources and coping abilities to successfully deal with the situation.

    a. initial analysis | final analysis
    b. emotional appraisal | cognitive appraisal
    c. primary appraisal | secondary appraisal
    d. alarm reaction | resistance reaction

20. According to Lazarus and Folkman, if we perceive harm and threat in a situation to be high, we are likely to experience _____ ; however, if we feel we can cope, we will likely experience _____ .

    a. low stress | lower stress
    b. high stress | higher stress
    c. minimal stress | higher stress
    d. a high degree of stress | lower stress

*21. Which of the following is *not* a common cognitive response to a stressful situation?

    a. Disruptive thoughts
    b. Higher than normal levels of distraction
    c. Feelings of anxiety
    d. Impaired performance on cognitive tasks

22. The term "fight or flight" suggests which of the following psychological response to stress?

    a. Behavioral
    b. Physiological
    c. Emotional
    d. Cognitive

Stress (Stressors)

*23. Which of the following events should be *least* stressful?

    a. Having your parents tell you they are divorcing
    b. Having your roommate tell you to move out
    c. Having your partner initiate the break up of a long-term relationship
    d. Initiating the break up of a long-term relationship

24. Which of the following characteristics is *not* associated with increasing the likelihood that an event will be perceived as stressful?

    a. Ambiguity
    b. Context
    c. Suddenness
    d. Lack of control

25. The main reason why ambiguous situations may cause stress is that one

    a. may not be able to determine an appropriate course of action.
    b. needs time to mobilize a defense.
    c. may feel out of control.
    d. may not be able to plan ahead.

26. One of the primary problems with the Social Readjustment Rating Scale (SRRS) is that

    a. it is difficult to test the predictions associated with the scale.
    b. total life-change units can vary widely from person to person.
    c. positive events may also be stressful.
    d. it does not take into consideration the fact that people experiencing the same life-change event may react very differently.

Stress (and Illness)

27. The evidence linking stress to _____ is less conclusive and more controversial than for the other illnesses listed.

    a. malfunctioning of the immune system
    b. coronary heart disease
    c. cancer
    d. hypertension

28. Which of the following has *not* been explored as a possible explanation for the link between Type A behavior and coronary heart disease?

    a. Type A behavior may be a coping response to a naturally more reactive nervous system
    b. Type A behavior decreases the functioning of the immune system
    c. Type A individuals are more physiologically reactive to stress than Type B individuals
    d. Type A individuals engage in more high-risk behaviors for developing coronary heart disease

29. Stress effects the immune system by

    a. reducing immunocompetence.
    b. enhancing immunocompetence.
    c. activating the immune system.
    d. destroying the immune system.

30. There are some indications of the existence of a cancer-prone personality characterized by the tendency to be

    a. hard driving, ambitious and competitive.

    b. angry, combative, and driven to achieve perfection.

    c. inhibited, compliant, and depressed.

    d. anxious, irritable, and easily embarrassed.

31. One probable variable linking stress and cancer is

    a. absence of stressful life changes.

    b. a Type B personality.

    c. hypertension.

    d. an impaired immune system.

Answer Key

1. c	**(357)**	8. b **(362-363)**	14. a	**(362)**	20. d	**(373)**	26. d	**(384)**		
2. a	**(358)**	*9. b	**(364)**	15. c	**(369)**	*21. c	**(373)**	27. c	**(384)**	
3. d	**(358)**	10. b **(364-365)**	*16. d	**(370)**	22. a	**(373)**	28. b	**(382)**		
4. c	**(358)**	11. c	**(366)**	17. c	**(370)**	*23. d	**(374)**	29. a	**(383)**	
*5. d	**(362-363)**	12. a	**(366)**	18. b	**(372)**	24. b	**(374)**	30. c	**(384)**	
6. b	**(360)**	13. c	**(367)**	19. c	**(373)**	25. a	**(379)**	31. d	**(385)**	
7. a	**(362)**									

Annotated Answers

    5. The correct choice is d. First, the James-Lange theory proposes that physiological and muscular responses precede emotional states (I'm scared because my heart is pounding). Second, the Schachter-Singer theory proposes that emotions arise after one cognitively evaluates both the emotion-causing event and the body's physiological state.

        a. This choice is incorrect because it does not include the Schachter-Singer theory.

        b. The Cannon-Bard theory proposed that one would feel scared at the same time as the heart rate increased.

        c. This choice is incorrect because it does not include the James-Lange theory.

    9. The correct choice is b. Subjects who were uninformed and misinformed tended to use the confederate's behavior as a relevant cue for identifying and labeling their unexplained arousal.

        a. The informed subjects who correctly anticipated the side effects of the injection tended not to supply an emotional label to their arousal.

        c. The uninformed and misinformed subjects "adopted" the emotion of the confederate and did not respond to or evaluate it.

        d. All subjects (except for the control group) experienced physiological changes and would have reported so.

    16. The correct choice is d. During the initial alarm phase, the sympathetic nervous system is activated and the body's resources are mobilized. During the alarm phase people can perform seemingly "superhuman" feats.

        a. The exhaustion phase only occurs after prolonged or repeated stress.

        b. During the reistance phase the parasympathetic nervous system is active and the person would not have the extra energy available to perform a superhuman feat.

        c. There is no peak phase in GAS.

21. The correct choice is c. Even though anxiety contains a cognitive element, feelings of anxiety (or any other feeling) are emotional and not cognitive responses. The choices in a, b, and d are common cognitive responses to stress.

23. The correct choice is d. First, because you are initiating the break up you have control over the situation. Second, you would probably not experience the situation as sudden because you most likely would have been thinking about breaking up for a period of time.

- **a.** Your parents telling you of their impending divorce is something you would lack control over, increasing the situation's stressfulness. The news of the divorce might also have been sudden, which would also increase its stressfulness.
- **b.** Your roommate telling you to move out could be sudden and you would not have control. It would also have a high measure of ambiguity (Where will I live?), which would further increase the stress of the situation.
- **c.** Unlike the situation in which you initiated the break up, in this case you have less control and would probably perceive the situation as sudden.

PART VI. SUMMARY TABLE

To test your understanding of the material discussed in this chapter complete the following table. Check your answers with those supplied in PART IX.

Theories of Emotion

Theory	Description	Supporting Evidence	Weaknesses
James-Lange			
Cannon-Bard		—	
Schachter-Singer			
Tomkins			—
Solomon-Corbit			—

PART VII. THOUGHT QUESTIONS/CRITICAL THINKING

Prepare answers to the following discussion questions.

1. Imagine that over Christmas vacation you've been separated from your boyfriend/ girlfriend for three weeks. You've just arrived at the airport to meet your friend's plane. The plane is due to land any minute and you are hurrying to get to the waiting area before the plane lands. While passing through the mandatory metal detector, you set off the alarm. The guard looks at you suspiciously and sternly demands that you empty your pockets. You are offended and annoyed but empty your pockets until the problem is resolved and you are no longer suspected of being a terrorist. Your friend gets off the plane just as you arrive. When you see your friend's face, which instead of the warm smile you expect, has a completely foreign expression (due to a very rough landing) you become concerned that your reunion may not be as happy as you expected. When you friend reaches you he or she says, "What's wrong, you look upset?" What emotions would the different theories of emotion predict that you would be experiencing? How would these theories explain the reason for your experiencing a particular emotion?

2. In Chapter 9 (Motivation) you learned that there may be two optimum levels of arousal (one high and one low) that may switch back and forth. Which theory of emotion (James-Lange, Cannon-Bard, Schachter-Singer, Tomkins, or Solomon-Corbit) is most consistent with this view of arousal? Explain your answer.

3. Using terminology from Chapter 8 (Thinking and Language) explain why ambiguous situations are more likely to be stressful than situations which are more clear-cut.

4. The link between stress and some illnesses (coronary heart disease, hypertension, malfunctioning of the immune system, and perhaps cancer) is becoming well established. It also appears that people who possess certain personality characteristics are more likely to develop specific illnesses. The Health Psychology section sidebar in this chapter suggests a number of stress-management strategies. Choose two or three of the strategies that would be most beneficial for an individual with Type A personality to use, and explain why these strategies would be important to use. Choose two or three of the strategies that would be most beneficial for an individual with a cancer-prone personality to use, and explain why these strategies would be important to use.

PART VIII. APPLICATIONS

1. Tomkins' facial feedback theory proposes that different facial expressions are associated with different emotional states. Cross-cultural research by Ekman found that people had 80 percent accuracy in identifying the correct emotion when viewing photographs illustrating happiness, sadness, surprise, anger, fear, and disgust. The figure (right) illustrates Plutchik's emotion wheel with the eight primary human emotions and the adjacent emotions listed.

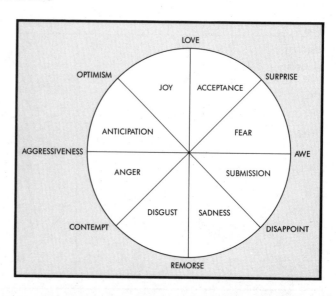

Do you think it would be possible to link these two conceptualizations? (Do not as yet refer to Figure 10.4 on page 365 in the text which shows photographs of the six emotional expressions.) Do you think that emotions close to each other on the emotion wheel would be represented by similar facial expressions? Do you think that emotions opposite each other on the emotion wheel would be represented by dissimilar facial expressions? According to the emotion wheel, does it make sense that in the Ekman study fear and surprise were most commonly confused?

Now examine Figure 10.4 to see if it provides evidence to support your answers to the questions in the preceding paragraph.

2. Holmes and Rahe's Social Readjustment Rating Scale for measuring the amount of stress a person has experienced in the last year contains questions that are relevant to people of all ages. However, as a college student many of the typical stressors you experience (term papers, final exams, dorm living, etc.) are not listed. Develop a stress scale for college students. Identify at least 15–20 stressors commonly encountered by college students and decide on a life-change unit score for each stressor. What do you think would be a typical number of stress points (life-change units) for a college student to receive in a semester? What do you think would be a value associated with a high (and low) level of stress? Add up your points for the past semester and determine if your point total level (low, average, high) corresponds to the amount of stress you intuitively felt over the semester. If you have friends in psychology class who also did this application, compare your stress scales and look for similarities and differences in both the items included on the sale and the number of life-change units assigned to the stressors.

PART IX. SUMMARY TABLE SOLUTIONS

Theories of Emotion

Theory	Description	Supporting Evidence	Weaknesses
James-Lange	Environmental stimuli trigger physiological and muscular responses, which then activate emotional states. Different physiological responses result in different emotions	After spinal-cord injuries, people report less-intense emotions. Negative emotions show specific physiological "fingerprints"	General physiological reactions associated with a variety of emotions are similar (for example, increased heart rate). Completely ignores the role of cognitive processes
Cannon-Bard	Subjective experiences and physiological and muscular responses occur simultaneously and are triggered by the thalamus	—	Perceives emotions as automatic reactions and does not discuss the role of cognition in evaluating emotions
Schachter-Singer	Physiological and behavioral response occur first, then one cognitively evaluates the situation and messages from the body to interpret or label the emotion	Results of study with subjects who received epinephrine injections and were informed, uninformed, and misinformed	Some sudden emotional experiences seem to happen faster than would be predicted if it is necessary to evaluate the situation and physiological response
Tomkins	Facial muscles respond to a variety of situations automatically, and feedback from facial muscles determine emotional experiences	Cross-cultural similarities exist in facial expression. If face "posed" into a negative expression, individual shows physiological response characteristic of the emotion	—
Solomon-Corbit	Emotions exist in opponent-process fashion. After one strong emotion is experienced the opposite emotion is activated to restore emotional balance. With repeated activation of one emotion, the intensity of the original emotion weakens and the intensity of the opponent emotion grows stronger	Accounts for "addictive" behaviors, such as mountain climbing, and also accounts for addictions to drugs, such as heroin	—

CHAPTER 11

Development from Conception to the End of Childhood

PART I. LEARNING OBJECTIVES

When you finish studying this chapter you should be able to:

Some Development Issues

1. Describe the two sides of the nature–nurture controversy, and discuss the current perspective psychologists have concerning the controversy. **(392)**

2. Discuss the opposing views regarding whether development is characterized by continuity (with quantitative changes) or discontinuity (with qualitative changes). **(392)**

3. Define and give an example of a critical period, and summarize research on whether there are critical periods in human development. **(393)**

How Development Is Studied

4. Describe three different research designs used to study development, and explain the strengths and weaknesses of each design. **(395-396)**

The Beginnings of Life

5. Define chromosomes, genes, and DNA, and discuss how the three terms are interrelated. **(396)**

6. Explain how monozygotic and dizygotic twins differ, and explain why psychologists are interested in studying these two types of twins. **(398)**

7. Discriminate between genotypes and phenotypes, and explain how dominant, recessive, and sex-linked games influence the phenotype. **(398)**

8. Describe the symptoms of a number of genetic disorders, and discuss the genetic causes of each. **(399)**

9. Discuss procedures utilized in genetic counseling, and discuss the potential of genetic engineering. **(403)**

Prenatal Development

10. Name and describe the three stages of prenatal development. **(405)**

Physical Development from Birth to the End of Childhood

11. Describe the development of the brain from birth to the end of childhood. **(406)**

12. Describe physical growth from birth to the end of childhood, and explain the cephalocaudal and proximodistal patterns of growth. **(409)**

13. Describe motor development from birth to the end of childhood, and discuss hereditary and environmental influences on motor development. **(409-410)**

Cognitive Development from Birth to the End of Childhood

14. Define Piaget's basic concepts: schemas, assimilation, and accommodation, and discuss how these are interrelated. **(412-413)**

15. Name and list the ages associated with Piaget's four stages of cognitive development, and summarize the major changes that take place in each stage. **(413-419)**

16. Describe the proposed gender differences in cognitive abilities. **(419-420)**

Psychosocial Development from Infancy to the End of Childhood

17. Define attachment, and describe the three stages of child–caretaker attachment. **(422-423)**

18. Describe the effects of attachment deprivation in monkeys and humans, and summarize research concerning whether these effects can be reversed. **(423-425)**

19. Describe infants who show secure and insecure attachment, and discuss factors that influence the type of attachment an infant will display. **(425)**

20. Describe father–child attachment. **(425-426)**

21. Describe three styles of parenting, and indicate the influence that each may have on the personality of a child. **(426-427)**

22. List the ages associated with Erikson's eight stages of psychosocial development, and explain the crisis faced in each stage. **(427-429)**

The Formation of Gender Identity and Gender Roles

23. Define gender identity, and outline six levels of biological factors that influence gender identity. **(429)**

24. Describe three conditions resulting in abnormal prenatal differentiation and discuss how these conditions relate to gender identity. **(431-434)**

25. Discuss social-learning factors in gender identity, and explain why the interactional model is commonly used to account for gender identity. **(434-436)**

26. Define gender roles, and describe four important agents that influence the socialization of gender roles. **(436-438)**

PART II. OVERVIEW

This chapter begins with a discussion of a number of historical issues related to the study of development. The central issue is the nature–nurture controversy. Individuals who emphasize the role of learning and experience in controlling development support the nurture view and visualize development as exhibiting continuity and being characterized by quantitative changes. Individuals who support the nature view emphasize the role of maturation and genetics in development and view development as a process that unfolds in a predetermined fashion characterized by discontinuity and qualitative changes. Another issue concerns critical periods. Although critical periods (a specific time frame during which an aspect of behavior is easily acquired) exist in some animals, most contemporary psychologists do not support the idea of critical periods in regard to many aspects of human development.

The basic mechanisms of heredity and genetics are described. A number of genetic disorders (Huntington's disease, PKU, and Down's syndrome) are described and the mechanism of transmission of the disorders are explained.

Prenatal development is composed of three stages. The first two weeks are the germinal (or zygote) stage. The embryonic stage (third to eighth week) is a period of rapid growth and differentiation of a number of body systems. During the fetal stage (third month to birth) bone and muscle tissue form and organs and body systems continue to develop. At birth, the infant's brain contains most—if not all—of the neurons he or she will ever have. For the first several years of life neural networks continue to develop and may be influenced by environmental stimulation. Physical and motor development of the child follows two distinct patterns: cephalocaudal (from head to foot) and proximodistal (from inner to outer) patterns.

Piaget's stage theory proposes that cognitive development is governed by the processes of assimilation and accommodation, which serve to maintain (assimilation) and revise (accommodation) our schemas or mental structures, for understanding the world around us. Piaget's theory contains four stages of cognitive development, each having qualitatively different types of thinking and limitations. The sensorimotor infant learns through sensing and doing and acquires object permanence or the realization that objects continue to exist even when they are not within view. Preoperational children (age 2–7) are capable of symbolic thought or language but their thought process is severely limited by intuitive thought and the immediate appearance of objects. Children in the concrete operations stage (age 7–12) are capable of logical thought and can apply rules (mental operations) to situations that are concrete but not to abstract or hypothetical situations. Children in the formal operations stage (age 12+) are capable of abstract thought and are more systematic in their problem-solving approach.

How the attachment is formed between an infant and the primary caretaker is described. Harlow's research with monkeys that experienced early social deprivation is described and related to human experiences. Erikson's stage theory of psychosocial development divides the life cycle into eight stages of development. At each stage the individual is concerned with a specific issue or crisis that must be resolved in order for development to proceed in a healthy fashion.

Chapter 11 concludes with a discussion of gender identity (one's subjective sense of being male or female) and gender roles (societal standards of behavior appropriate for each sex). A number of biological factors combine to influence the development of a male or female body type and thus a male or female gender identity. In general, psychosocial factors also influence gender identity, and socialization greatly influences the development of gender roles.

PART III. KEY TERMS/MATCHING EXERCISES

Match the following concepts and/or individuals with the appropriate descriptions. Check your answers against the Answer Key.

Development Issues | How Development Is Studied

Concepts

_____ 1. nurture **(391)**   _____ 4. longitudinal design **(395)**

_____ 2. critical periods **(393)**   _____ 5. cross-sequential design **(396)**

_____ 3. nature **(392)**   _____ 6. cross-sectional design **(395)**

Descriptions

a. Simultaneously evaluates subjects of different ages in order to study development

b. View that development unfolds in a genetically determined fashion

c. Time interval in which proper experience greatly facilitates an aspect of development

d. Evaluates a group of subjects at several different times in order to study development

e. View that development is determined by experiences

f. Evaluates subjects of different ages at more than one time in order to study development

Answer Key   1. e   2. c   3. b   4. d   5. f   6. a

The Beginnings of Life (Mechanisms of Heredity)

Concepts

_____ 1. concordant **(398)**

_____ 2. heterozygous **(398)**

_____ 3. homozygous **(398)**

_____ 4. genes **(398)**

_____ 5. dizygotic twins **(398)**

_____ 6. monozygotic twins **(398)**

_____ 7. dominant gene **(398)**

_____ 8. sex-linked inheritance **(399)**

_____ 9. recessive gene **(398)**

Descriptions

a. Identical twins that develop from a single egg and therefore have the same genetic material

b. When an individual has two similar genes for a specific trait and the same genotype and phenotype

c. Gene that is only expressed in the phenotype when an individual has two similar or only one gene for the trait

d. Fraternal twins that develop from separate eggs and thereby not having the same genetic material

e. When an individual has two dissimilar genes for a specific trait and does not have the same genotype as phenotype

f. Composed of DNA and determines or influences physical and behavioral traits

g. Explains why males are more likely than females to exhibit a number of recessive genetic traits

h. Describes the degree to which twins share a particular trait

i. Gene that is always expressed in the phenotype

Answer Key   1. h   2. e   3. b   4. f   5. d   6. a   7. i   8. g   9. c

The Beginnings of Life (Problems in Inheritance) (Genetic Counseling and Genetic Engineering)

Concepts

_____ 1. phenylketonuria (PKU) **(402)**

_____ 2. genetic engineering **(404)**

_____ 3. amniocentesis **(403)**

_____ 4. Huntington's disease **(400)**

_____ 5. Down syndrome **(402)**

_____ 6. genetic counseling **(403)**

Descriptions

a. Along with chorionic villi sampling, provides two methods to detect birth defects *in utero*

b. Results from an extra 21st chromosome and is characterized by distinctive appearance and mental retardation

c. Incurable disorder caused by a dominant gene that is not apparent until age 35–45

d. Genetic condition that, if undiagnosed and treated, can cause mental retardation

e. Uses family histories and medical examinations to inform couples of the probability of having children with certain genetic disorders

f. Involves using recombinant DNA techniques to identify and correct a defective genetic code

Answer Key   1. d   2. f   3. a   4. c   5. b   6. e

Prenatal Development | Physical Development

Concepts

_____ 1. proximodistal **(409)**

_____ 2. cephalocaudal **(409)**

_____ 3. embryonic stage **(405)**

_____ 4. fetal stage **(405)**

_____ 5. germinal (zygote) stage **(405)**

Descriptions

a. Lasts from the third through the eighth week of prenatal development when the embryo is extremely vulnerable to negative environmental events

b. Pattern of development that proceeds from head to foot

c. Pattern of development that proceeds from inner (or close to the body) to outer (or farther away from the body)

d. Extends from the third month of development until birth

e. Refers to the first two weeks of development during which time the amniotic sac, umbilical cord, and placenta are established

Answer Key   1. c   2. b   3. a   4. d   5. e

Cognitive Development

Concepts

_____ 1. concrete-operations stage **(418)**   _____ 5. accommodation **(412-413)**

_____ 2. sensorimotor stage **(414)**   _____ 6. assimilation **(412)**

_____ 3. formal-operations stage **(419)**   _____ 7. schemas **(412)**

_____ 4. preoperational stage **(415)**

Descriptions

a. Involves restructuring existing knowledge to account for new information

b. Stage of cognitive development when object permanence is developed

c. Mental structures for organizing information

d. Stage of cognitive development in which the child is first capable of decentration and can use mental operations

e. Involves interpreting new information in accordance with one's existing knowledge

f. Stage of cognitive development characterized by abstract thought and the systematic testing of hypothetical solutions

g. Stage of cognitive development characterized by centration and egocentrism

Answer Key   1. d   2. b   3. f   4. g   5. a   6. e   7. c

Psychosocial Development | Gender Identity and Gender Roles

Concepts

_____ 1. socialization **(436)**   _____ 5. authoritative **(426)**

_____ 2. attachment **(422-424)**   _____ 6. permissive **(426)**

_____ 3. gender roles **(436)**   _____ 7. gender identity **(429)**

_____ 4. authoritarian **(426)**

Descriptions

a. Develops in sequence from indiscriminate to specific to separate

b. Parental style characterized by strictly enforced rules; typically, minimal warmth is expressed

c. Parental style characterized by open discussion and rule-making in an atmosphere of warmth

d. Parental style characterized by few demands; reluctance to punish inappropriate behavior

e. Societal standards of behavior that are considered normal and appropriate for each sex

f. Process whereby society conveys behavioral expectations to the individual

g. Individual's subjective sense of being male or female that is influenced by biological and social-learning factors

Answer Key   1. f   2. a   3. e   4. b   5. c   6. d   7. g

PART IV. TRUE-FALSE STATEMENTS

Fill in the blank before each statement with either a T (true) or an F (false). Check your answers against the Answer Key. Then go back to the items that are false and make the necessary change(s) to the statements to convert the items into true statements.

Some Development Issues | How Development Is Studied

_____ 1. Developmental psychologists who emphasize maturation view development as occurring in stages that are qualitatively diffferent.

_____

_____

_____ 2. A major drawback of the cross-sectional design is that it takes an extended period of time to collect all the necessary information.

_____

_____

The Beginnings of Life

_____ 3. The terms *chromosome*, *gene*, and *DNA molecules* are arranged from largest to smallest independent unit.

_____

_____

_____ 4. Huntington's disease is a genetic condition that newborn infants are routinely screened for; if the condition is present, dietary changes can prevent the symptoms of the disease.

_____

_____

Prenatal Development | Physical Development

_____ 5. By the end of the eighth week of prenatal development almost all of an embryo's organs are formed and the heart is already functioning.

_____

_____

_____ 6. Results of experiments with rats suggest that early experience effects the anatomy and biochemistry of the brain.

_____

_____

Cognitive Development

_____ 7. The process of assimilation allows one to adapt and change schemas as new information is gained.

_____

_____

_____ 8. Children are first able to understand the principle of conservation in the preoperational stage of cognitive development.

_____

_____

Psychosocial Development

_____ 9. Harlow's research with infant monkeys raised in isolation with artificial mothers demonstrated the high level of importance the feeding situation has in establishing an attachment to the "mother."

_____

_____

_____ 10. According to Erikson's theory of psychosocial development the major conflict of adolescence is identity versus role confusion.

_____

_____

Gender Identity and Gender Roles

_____ 11. Chromosomal make-up (XX or XY) determines gender identity.

_____

_____

_____ 12. Assimilation refers to the process whereby society conveys behavioral expectations to the individual.

_____

_____

Answer Key

1. T **(392)**	5. T **(405)**	9. F **(423–424)**
2. F **(395)**	6. T **(407–408)**	10. T **(428)**
3. T **(396)**	7. F **(412–413)**	11. F **(429)**
4. F **(402)**	8. F **(415)**	12. F **(436–437)**

PART V. MULTIPLE-CHOICE QUESTIONS

Choose the best answer to each question. Circle your choice. Check your answers against the Answer Key. Questions marked with an asterisk (*) include annotated answers.

Some Development Issues | How Development Is Studied

1. Individuals who believe that learning and experience largely determine development

  a. view maturation as an important process.
  b. support the nurture side of the nature–nurture controversy.
  c. support the nature side of the nature–nurture controversy.
  d. see development as being comprised of qualitatively distinct stages.

2. In the nature–nurture controversy, the majority of contemporary psychologists

  a. tend to support the nurture side.
  b. tend to support the nature side.
  c. are interested in how nature and nurture interact to influence development.
  d. are interested in identifying specific behaviors that can be explained by referring only to nature or only to nurture.

3. Unlike psychologists who emphasize the role of learning, psychologists who emphasize maturation view development as a _____ process that results in _____ changes.

  a. continuous | qualitative
  b. continuous | quantitative
  c. discontinuous | qualitative
  d. discontinuous | quantitative

4. If you believe that certain experiences must occur during a specific window of time in our lives in order for development to proceed normally, you would support the view that

  a. critical periods exist.
  b. critical periods can be indefinitely extended.
  c. imprinting is responsible for much of human development and behavior.
  d. critical periods do not exist.

*5. A parent who measures his or her child each year by putting a mark on the wall to note how tall that child is, would basically be using a _____ design.

  a. correlational
  b. cross-sequential
  c. cross-sectional
  d. longitudinal

6. Lewis Terman's classic long-term study of gifted children is of which research design?

  a. Cross-sectional design
  b. Longitudinal design
  c. Cross-sequential design
  d. Double-blind design

7. The research design used in developmental research that attempts to overcome some of the drawbacks associated with the other two designs is the _____ design.

    a. cross-longitudinal
    b. cross-sequential
    c. cross-sectional
    d. longitudinal

The Beginnings of Life

*8. If a woman gives birth to twins, and one of the twins is a boy and the other a girl, it can be concluded that the twins are _____ twins.

    a. monozygotic
    b. dizygotic
    c. identical
    d. You require more information before you can reach a conclusion.

9. If a woman gives birth to twins who are both boys, it can be concluded that the twins are _____ twins.

    a. monozygotic
    b. dizygotic
    c. identical
    d. You require more information before you can reach a conclusion.

10. If an individual is homozygous for a specific trait, his or her genotype and phenotype will

    a. be consistent.
    b. not be consistent.
    c. only be consistent if that person has at least one dominant gene.
    d. only be consistent if that person has at least one recessive gene.

*11. A person who is heterozygous for a sex-linked recessive trait (e.g., red-green color blindness)

    a. will not exhibit the recessive trait in their phenotype.
    b. is female.
    c. may have offspring who exhibit the recessive trait regardless of the genetic make up of the other parent.
    d. All of the above are correct.

12. Which of the following genetic abnormalities does *not* result from a defective gene?

    a. Sickle-cell anemia
    b. Phenylketonuria (PKU)
    c. Down's syndrome
    d. Huntington's disease

13. Examining information about a couple's genetic background to determine possible future genetic problems in their offspring is referred to as

    a. phenotyping.
    b. amniocentesis.
    c. genetic counseling.
    d. CVS.

Prenatal Development | Physical Development from Birth to the End of Childhood

14. In order, the three stages of prenatal development are:

  a. embryonic, fetal, prenatal.
  b. germinal, nonviable, viable.
  c. germinal, embryonic, fetal.
  d. embryonic, germinal, fetal.

15. The period from the third through the eighth week of prenatal development that is characterized by very fast growth and differentiation of many organs is called the

  a. embryonic stage.
  b. fetal stage.
  c. germinal stage.
  d. zygote stage.

16. A newborn's brain has

  a. only 25 percent of the neurons of an adult.
  b. 75 percent of all the neurons it will ever have.
  c. 50 percent of all the neurons it will ever have.
  d. most—if not all—the neurons it will ever have.

17. The physical growth of children is more rapid during the first _____ year(s) of life before growth stabilizes at about two or three inches a year until the adolescent growth spurt.

  a. one
  b. two
  c. three
  d. four

18. That babies have proportionally larger heads than adults, illustrates the _____ pattern of development.

  a. proximocaudal
  b. proximodistal
  c. cephalocaudal
  d. cephalodistal

19. Early experience or training _____ the rate at which children acquire motor skills such as standing, walking, and bladder control.

  a. does not significantly accelerate
  b. significantly accelerates
  c. significantly slows down
  d. This effects children in an unpredictable fashion.

Cognitive Development from Infancy to the End of Childhood

20. A mental structure that guides future behavior while providing a framework for making sense out of new information is called

    a. an operation.
    b. a schema.
    c. accommodation.
    d. assimilation.

21. A child sees a cow and says, "Look, Mommy, at the big doggie." According to Piaget he or she is using a mental process known as

    a. conservation.
    b. centration.
    c. assimilation.
    d. accommodation.

22. The process of _____ is used when it is necessary to modify or revise a schema to account for new information.

    a. restructuring
    b. accommodation
    c. assimilation
    d. either assimilation or accommodation

23. The correct order of Piaget's stages of cognitive development is:

    a. sensorimotor, concrete operations, preoperational, formal operations.
    b. preoperational, sensorimotor, concrete operations, formal operations.
    c. concrete operations, preoperational, sensorimotor, formal operations.
    d. sensorimotor, preoperational, concrete operations, formal operations.

24. A child is first capable of imitating the facial expression of another

    a. within a few days of birth.
    b. at about six months of age.
    c. in the latter part of the sensorimotor stage.
    d. in the early preoperational stage.

*25. If a child believes that a nickel is more desirable to have than a dime, that child is probably in the _____ stage of cognitive development.

    a. concrete operations
    b. preoperational
    c. formal operations
    d. sensorimotor

26. A child begins to use logic to solve problems during the _____ stage of cognitive development, and can first think abstractly in the _____ stage of cognitive development.

    a. formal operations | concrete operations
    b. preoperational | concrete operations
    c. concrete operations | formal operations
    d. preoperational | formal operations

27. Regarding gender differences in cognitive abilities, females surpass males in

    a. spatial skills.
    b. logical skills.
    c. mathematical skills.
    d. verbal skills.

Psychosocial Development

28. Harlow's study revealed that _____ was more important in attachment then being fed.

    a. the odor of the feeding mother
    b. the type of food being given
    c. contact comfort
    d. the taste of the milk

29. The effects of emotional and social deprivation in infancy

    a. have devastating and irreversible effects.
    b. can be overcome if the child later receives plenty of loving nurturance.
    c. can be overcome in humans but not in monkeys.
    d. can be overcome in monkeys but not in humans.

30. The "strange situation" is used to evaluate

    a. a child's stage of cognitive development.
    b. infant–mother attachment.
    c. mother–infant attachment.
    d. a child's stage of psychosocial development.

31. Infants in the process of forming a secure attachment to their primary caretaker would be in the _____ stage of Erikson's theory of psychosocial development.

    a. security versus insecurity
    b. trust versus mistrust
    c. belongingness versus rejection
    d. intimacy versus isolation

32. While in an unfamiliar environment, an infant who shows apprehension and tends not to leave his or her mother's side to explore, would be said to be _____ attached.

    a. overly
    b. securely
    c. insecurely
    d. permissively

33. The parent who establishes reasonable rules in an atmosphere of warmth and open dialogue would be a(n) _____ parent.

    a. authoritarian
    b. authoritative
    c. permissive
    d. autocratic

34. The stage of Erikson's theory of psychosocial development, characterized by an extensive reflection concerning past accomplishments and failures, concerns the _____ crisis.

  a. ego integrity versus despair
  b. initiative versus guilt
  c. generativity versus stagnation
  d. industry versus inferiority

Formation of Gender Identity and Gender Roles

*35. For every developing individual, during the first few weeks of prenatal development the gonads have the capacity to become

  a. either testes or ovaries.
  b. either a penis or a clitoris.
  c. Both of the above.
  d. Neither of the above.

36. Which of the following is *not* a biological factor that influences gender identity?

  a. Gonadal sex
  b. Sex of the internal reproductive structures
  c. Sex differentiation of the brain
  d. Androgeny

37. Pseudohermaphrodites

  a. possess sexually ambiguous external reproductive structures.
  b. have gonads that match their chromosomal sex.
  c. have both ovaries and testes.
  d. Both a and b are correct.

38. If your daughter developed breasts but, even after several years, did not begin menstruation, and all other causes had been ruled out, a medical doctor would most likely diagnose

  a. the presence of two Y chromosomes.
  b. androgen insensitivity syndrome.
  c. DHT deficient male syndrome.
  d. fetally androgenized female syndrome.

39. Concerning gender identity, most researchers support the

  a. perceptual model.
  b. overwhelming importance of psychosocial factors over biological factors.
  c. overwhelming importance of biological factors over psychosocial factors.
  d. interactional model.

40. Socialization is most directly associated with

  a. gender roles.
  b. gender reality.
  c. the timing of puberty.
  d. gender identity.

Answer Key

1. b	**(391)**	9. d	**(398)**	17. c	**(409)**	˙25. b	**(415)**	33. b	**(426)**
2. c	**(392)**	10. a	**(398)**	18. c	**(409)**	26. c	**(418, 419)**	34. a	**(429)**
3. c	**(392)**	˙11. d	**(399)**	19. a	**(409-410)**	27. d	**(419-420)**	˙35. a	**(430)**
4. a	**(393)**	12. c	**(402)**	20. b	**(412)**	28. c	**(423-424)**	36. d	**(429)**
˙5. d	**(395)**	13. c	**(403)**	21. c	**(412)**	29. b	**(424)**	37. d	**(431)**
6. b	**(395)**	14. c	**(405)**	22. b	**(412-413)**	30. b	**(425)**	38. b	**(432-433)**
7. b	**(396)**	15. a	**(405)**	23. d	**(414-420)**	31. b	**(428)**	39. d	**(436)**
8. b	**(398)**	16. d	**(406)**	24. a	**(414)**	32. c	**(425)**	40. a	**(436-437)**

Annotated Answers

5. The correct choice is d. The longitudinal design would require measuring the height of a child (or more accurately a number of children) at several different times.
   a. A correlational design would require measuring a number of children on two variables (e.g., height and age) to determine the relationship between the variables.
   b. A cross-sequential design would require measuring a number of children of different ages at more than one time.
   c. The cross-sectional design would require measuring a number of children of different ages (e.g., 6, 8, 10) at one specific time.

8. The correct choice is b. Dizygotic or fraternal twins do not have the same genetic make up. Because one twin is a girl having two X chromosomes, and the other twin a boy having one X and one Y chromosome, these twins must be dizygotic.
   a. Monozygotic twins have exactly the same genetic make up.
   c. Identical twins is another term for monozygotic twins.
   d. The fact that the sex of the twins differ is sufficient to allow you to draw a conclusion.

11. The correct choice is d. All of the alternatives are correct.
   a. Because an individual who is heterozygous for the trait has at least one dominant gene, he or she would not show the recessive trait.
   b. Because males only have one gene for sex-linked traits (their Y chromosome does not contain the gene), a heterozygous individual must be female.
   c. If a heterozygous female were to conceive a child with a male who did not have the recessive gene, there is a 50 percent probability that any sons they would have would receive the recessive gene from the mother and exhibit the recessive trait.

25. The correct choice is b. A preoperational child (say a 4-year-old) whose thinking is governed by appearances would interpret the larger nickel as bigger and more desirable than the smaller dime.
   a. A child in the concrete-operations stage, who is capable of decentration, would logically evaluate the nickel and dime according to their monetary worth and ignore the physical size of the coins.
   c. A child in the formal-operations stage would be able to approach the problem in the same manner as the concrete-operational child, and additionally might approach the problem from an abstract perspective.
   d. It would be unrealistic to view a sensorimotor child as thinking of either the nickel or dime as particularly desirable.

35. The correct choice is a. The term gonads relates to either the male testes or female ovaries. If H–Y antigen is prenatally present during the first few weeks, the gonadal tissue differentiates into testes. If H–Y antigen is not present the gonadal tissue differentiates into ovaries.

b. The penis and/or clitoris do not develop from the gonads. The development of both is determined after the gonads develop. If the gonadal tissue becomes testes they normally secrete suffcent levels of androgens to influence the development of the penis.

c. This choice is incorrect because b is incorrect.

d. This choice is incorrect because a is correct.

PART VI. SUMMARY TABLES

To test your understanding of the material discussed in this chapter complete the following tables. Check your answers with those supplied in PART IX.

Piaget's Theory of Cognitive Development

Stage	Ages	Characteristics	Limitations
Sensorimotor			
Preoperational			
Concrete operations			
Formal operations			

Biological Factors Influencing Gender Identity

Factor	Influence
Chromosomal sex	
Gonadal sex	
Hormonal sex	
Sex of internal organs	
Sex of external organs	
Sex differentiation of the brain	

PART VII. THOUGHT QUESTIONS/CRITICAL THINKING

Prepare answers to the following discussion questions.

1. Describe what Piaget's position would be regarding the nature–nurture controversy.

2. Genetic counseling allows couples to estimate the probability of conceiving a child with a specific genetic disorder. Imagine that you are a genetic counselor helping the following couples decide on whether or not to conceive. In each of the following examples determine the probability of conceiving a child who would exhibit the genetic disorder in their phenotype.

    a. For a trait in which the disorder is associated with a recessive gene (for example, PKU):

      (1) Both parents are homozygous for the dominant gene

      (2) Both parents are homozygous for the recessive gene

      (3) One parent is homozygous for the dominant gene and the other parent is heterozygous

      (4) One parent is homozygous for the recessive gene and the other parent is heterozygous

      (5) Both parents are heterozygous

      (6) One parent is homozygous for the dominant gene and the other parent is homozygous for the recessive gene

b. For a trait in which the disorder is associated with a dominant gene (for example, Huntington's disease):

(1) Both parents are homozygous for the dominant gene

(2) Both parents are homozygous for the recessive gene

(3) One parent is homozygous for the dominant gene and the other parent is heterozygous

(4) One parent is homozygous for the recessive gene and the other parent is heterozygous

(5) Both parents are heterozygous

(6) One parent is homozygous for the dominant gene and the other parent is homozygous for the recessive gene

3. What would you tell your brother and sister-in-law who are concerned about their four-year-old child who had previously grown at a steady and fairly rapid rate but has only grown two inches in the past year?

4. For each of the following examples determine at which stage of cognitive development the child is in. Explain your reasoning.

a. I have a vivid memory of sitting at the kitchen table while my two children were standing and twirling themselves around in circles. After spinning for a while they asked, "Are you dizzy yet, Mom?"

b. You place five toy dogs and three toy cats on a table and ask a child, "Are there more dogs or more animals?" Child #1 replies, "More dogs." Child #2 replies, "More animals."

5. As a result of genetic counseling, a couple decides not to conceive a child. They are considering adopting an eight-month-old infant who was recently placed in foster care after a history of abuse and neglect in the biological family. The couple is concerned whether or not adopting this child is a good idea or if they would be "asking for trouble" in the future. Based on the information in the text concerning the effects of early social deprivation and attachment, what advice would you give the couple?

6. Imagine that you and your spouse just had a baby who was born with sexually ambiguous external reproductive structures. In order to help you decide whether it would be best to raise your child as your son or as your daughter, what questions would you ask the doctor?

PART VIII. APPLICATIONS

1. Imagine that you are a developmental psychologist interested in studying how children of different ages respond and adjust to changing schools in the middle of a school year. Design three studies to evaluate the topic: a cross-sectional design, a longitudinal design, and a cross-sequential design. For each of the three designs: What age(s) of children you would study? When or how long after the school change you would evaluate the children? Discuss possible weaknesses or limitations associated with each design. Which design would give you the most complete information?

2. Problem: You are given six different-colored plastic tokens (red, orange, yellow, green, blue, and purple). List all the possible pairs of colors that can be made from these six colors. Write down your solution to the problem.

For the following three solutions to the problem decide at what stage of cognitive development an individual would be at who would give each solution.

a. It's easy, you could have R & O, Y & G, B & P.

b. R & O, Y & G, B & P, R & G, B & G, Y & P, B & R, Y & R, B & O, G & P, R & B.

c. R & O, R & Y, R & G, R & B, R & P, O & Y, O & G, O & B, O & P, Y & G, Y & B, Y & P, G & B, G & P, B & P.

Refer back to your solution. What stage of cognitive development does your solution suggest?

PART IX. SUMMARY TABLES SOLUTIONS

Piaget's Theory of Cognitive Development

Stage	Ages	Characteristics	Limitations
Sensorimotor	0–2	Learns through sensing and doing Acquires object permanence Can perform goal-directed behavior	Does not think, per se, just senses and does
Preoperational	2–7	Can think symbolically (language) Thoughts dependent on appearance or are intuitive Exhibits egocentrism	Incapable of conservation because shows centration
Concrete operations	7–12	Uses logical mental operations Masters conservation because shows decentration	Cannot yet think abstractly and hypothetically
Formal operations	12+	Abstract thought Systematically tests hypotheses to solve problems	Unlike other stages, a variety of situations may postpone or prevent individuals from entering this stage

Biological Factors Influencing Gender Identity

Factor	Influence
Chromosomal sex	Y chromosome necessary for complete development of internal and external male sex organs (normal male XY) If no Y chromosome, female external sex organs develop Two X chromosomes necessary for complete development of internal and external female sex organs (normal female XX)
Gonadal sex	During first few weeks of development, presence of Y chromosome causes gonads to become testes Without Y chromosome, gonads become ovaries
Hormonal sex	Male gonads (testes) secrete androgens that cause development of external male sex organs Without androgens (or too low a level of androgen), female structures develop
Sex of internal organs	Follows from gonadal sex (above)
Sex of external organs	Follows from hormonal sex (above)
Sex differentiation of the brain	During prenatal development, level of testosterone results in sex differences in the hypothalamus and cerebral hemispheres

CHAPTER **12**

Development from Adolescence to the End of Life

PART I. LEARNING OBJECTIVES

When you finish studying this chapter you should be able to:

Adolescence

1. Define adolescence, and discuss how adolescence differs in different societies. **(445-446)**

2. Summarize the physical changes of puberty, and describe secular growth trends. **(446)**

3. Compare the effects of early and late maturation on boys and girls. **(447)**

4. Describe the formal-operational thinking of the adolescent, and discuss factors that facilitate or hinder the development of formal-operational thought. **(448-449)**

5. Define morality, and summarize and evaluate Köhlberg's theory of moral development. **(449-452)**

6. Describe the adolescent's search for identity, and discuss the role parents and the peer group play in the process of establishing an identity. **(452)**

7. Discuss a number of factors that influence adolescent sexual behavior. **(455-456)**

Adulthood

8. List the ages commonly associated with the three periods of adulthood and discuss why these categories may not always be appropriate to use. **(457-458)**

9. Summarize the changes in physical capacities in early and middle adulthood **(458)**

10. Discuss hormonal changes for men and women during early and middle adulthood, and describe the double standard of aging. **(458-459)**

11. Summarize the evidence as to whether or not intelligence (in general and specific types of intelligence) changes during adulthood. **(459-460)**

12. Describe two conceptualizations concerning a fifth stage of cognitive development. **(460-461)**

13. Discuss how Erikson's developmental task of early adulthood—intimacy versus isolation—is related to the single, cohabitation, and married lifestyles. **(461, 463-465)**

14. Discuss how Erikson's developmental task of middle adulthood—generativity versus stagnation—is related to commitments to parenting and work. **(465)**

15. Compare younger adults and middle-aged adults in terms of job satisfaction, and discuss recent changes concerning the number of women in the work force. **(465-468)**

The Older Years

16. Describe changes in life expectancy since 1900, and discuss the phrase "the graying of America." **(468-469)**

17. Summarize the physical changes that occur in the latter (older) years, and discuss how some of these changes may be reduced or compensated for. **(469-470)**

18. Describe two theories concerning the physical process of aging, and discuss the implications of each. **(470-471)**

19. Describe the cognitive abilities of older adults, and discuss the symptoms and probable causes of senile dementia and Alzheimer's disease. **(471-473)**

20. Discuss factors related to "successful aging," and compare two theories concerning the psychosocial adjustment to aging. **(473-474)**

21. Define thanatology, and describe Kübler-Ross' five stages of dying. **(475-476)**

PART II. OVERVIEW

Adolescence (approximately age 12–20) or the transition from childhood to adulthood is characterized by a number of dramatic changes. The adolescent growth spurt results in a rapid physical growth that is markedly different from the slow and steady growth characteristic of middle and late childhood. Sexual maturity is reached shortly after completion of the adolescent growth spurt (typically two years in duration). Cognitively, the adolescent may enter Piaget's stage of formal operations and become capable of abstract and hypothetical thought—able to approach problems in a more systematic manner than younger children. The psychosocial development of adolescence is exemplified by the tendency to be strongly influenced by the peer group and a striving for independence from the parents. The adolescent is concerned with establishing a sense of identity and may experiment with many identities or roles before establishing a firm sense of identity.

Köhlberg's theory of moral development has three levels of moral reasoning. It proposes that individuals progress in their moral reasoning from a self-serving approach to morality, to an approach to morality governed by a desire to gain approval and maintain social order. In Köhlberg's third level of moral development (which is attained by only 25 percent of adults) the individual's moral reasoning affirms individual rights and ethical principles.

During adulthood (prior to age 65) an individual reaches his or her physical and reproductive peak and then begin to decline. Depending on what aspect of cognitive or intellectual functioning is being referred to, cognitive abilities may increase (crystallized intelligence), or reach a peak in early adulthood and then decline (fluid intelligence).

According to Erikson's theory of psychosocial development, during early adulthood the individual is concerned with establishing intimacy. Most commonly, marriage is viewed as the way to establish intimacy, but cohabitation and remaining single (if the individual has an appropriate network of friends) can alternatively fulfill intimacy needs. According to Erikson, middle adulthood is characterized by a desire to achieve continual productivity or generativity, which is associated with a commitment to raising children and/or employment (career).

There are many negative stereotypes associated with the older years (after age 65), however, most older adults continue to function very well. Many of the physical changes associated with the older years may be compensated for (e.g., hearing aids) or postponed if the individual regularly exercises. Although a small but significant number of elderly individuals do suffer from senile dementia, 90 percent or more of older adults show little cognitive deterioration. Alzheimer's disease is the most common form of senile dementia and is currently being extensively studied. Evidence links Alzheimer's disease to a genetic defect on chromosome 21, which is also the chromosome associated with Down's syndrome. Older individuals who have relatively good health, close ties to family and friends, and are financially secure tend to have the best psychosocial adjustment to aging. Older individuals frequently conduct life reviews examining their past successes and failures. Life reviews are consistent with Erikson's view that the main task of the older years is to achieve a sense of integrity that is associated with one's successes in earlier stages of psychosocial development.

Chapter 12 concludes with a brief description of the five stages of dying described by Kübler-Ross: denial, anger, bargaining, depression, and acceptance.

PART III. KEY TERMS/MATCHING EXERCISES

Match the following concepts and/or individuals with the appropriate descriptions. Check your answers against the Answer Key.

Adolescence

Concepts

_____ 1. secular growth trends (**446**)

_____ 2. puberty (**446**)

_____ 3. secondary sex characteristics (**446**)

_____ 4. adolescence (**445**)

_____ 5. formal-operational thinking (**448**)

_____ 6. adolescent growth spurt (**446**)

_____ 7. conventional morality (**450**)

_____ 8. postconventional morality (**450**)

_____ 9. preconventional morality (**450**)

Descriptions

a. Period of rapid physical growth that precedes sexual maturity

b. Characterized by the capacity to mentally manipulate objects and use deductive reasoning

c. Characterized by a desire to gain the approval of others or maintain social order

d. Period of development that lasts for several years; the transition between childhood and adulthood

e. Describe(s) difference(s) in the physical growth and age of sexual maturity that exist between generations or societies

f. Characterized by a desire to avoid punishment or obtain rewards

g. Characterized by a desire to affirm the values of society or to uphold universal ethical principles

h. Approximately two-year period of rapid physical change that culminates in sexual maturity

i. Result(s) from the release of increased levels of gonadtropins during puberty

Answer Key 1. e   2. h   3. i   4. d   5. b   6. a   7. c   8. g   9. f

Adulthood

Concepts

_____ 1. crystallized intelligence **(460)**

_____ 2. dialectic operations **(460)**

_____ 3. menopause **(458)**

_____ 4. generativity **(461)**

_____ 5. climacteric **(458)**

_____ 6. problem finding **(460)**

_____ 7. intimacy **(461)**

_____ 8. fluid intelligence **(460)**

Descriptions

a. According to Erikson's psychosocial theory, the primary developmental task of middle adulthood

b. Includes language skills and knowledge of how to reason, and tends to improve during one's lifetime

c. Proposed fifth stage of cognitive development in which an individual is concerned with posing new questions about the world and discovering novel solutions to old problems

d. Describe(s) the physiological changes associated with women's transition from fertility to infertility

e. Include(s) the ability to conceptualize abstract information and draw inferences; tends to decline steadily after age 30

f. According to Erikson's psychosocial theory, the primary developmental task of early adulthood

g. Proposed fifth stage of cognitive development in which an individual realizes and accepts that conflict and contradiction in many areas are natural consequences of living

h. Cessation of menstruation that commonly occurs between age 45–50

Answer Key   1. b   2. g   3. h   4. a   5. d   6. c   7. f   8. e

The Older Years

Concepts

_____ 1. activity theory **(473)**

_____ 2. accumulating damages theory **(470)**

_____ 3. genetic clock (programmed) theory **(470)**

_____ 4. disengagement theory **(473)**

_____ 5. thanatology **(475)**

_____ 6. organ reserve **(470)**

_____ 7. senile dementia **(471)**

_____ 8. the graying of America **(468-469)**

_____ 9. integrity **(474)**

_____ 10. hospices **(475)**

_____ 11. Alzheimer's disease **(471-472)**

_____ 12. life review **(474)**

Descriptions

a. Ability of the heart, lungs, and so forth to perform at levels above normal range that declines with age

b. Proposes that physical aging and duration of life is basically the result of the body wearing out

c. Study of death and dying

d. Proposes that older people tend to reminisce about past accomplishments and failures

e. Proposes that the duration of life is limited by the inability of cells to divide more than a predetermined number of times

f. Condition that affects cognitive abilities and may be associated with a genetic defect

g. Refers to the trend that the proportion of older people in our population has (and will continue to) increase dramatically

h. Proposes that older individuals are more likely to be happy if they reduce their level of activity by reducing social obligations and taking time to relax

i. Proposes that older individuals are more likely to be happy if they maintain a high level of involvement in activities

j. Facilities designed to care for the special needs of the dying: love and support, pain control, and maintaining a sense of dignity

k. Describes a variety of conditions characterized by cognitive symptoms, altered personalities, and interpersonal difficulties

l. According to Erikson's psychosocial theory, the primary developmental task of the older years

Answer Key   1. i   2. b   3. e   4. h   5. c   6. a   7. k   8. g   9. l   10. j   11. f   12. d

PART IV. TRUE-FALSE STATEMENTS

Fill in the blank before each statement with either a T (true) or an F (false). Check your answers against the Answer Key. Then go back to the items that are false and make the necessary change(s) to the statements to convert the items into true statements.

Adolescence

_____ 1. Adolescence refers to the approximately two-year period of rapid physical change that culminates in sexual maturity.

_____ 2. Secular growth trends refers to the observation that in recent times industrial societies' adolescents reach sexual maturity at a later age than previous generations.

_____ 3. Typically by late childhood or early adolescence an individual would be functioning at the level of conventional morality.

_____ 4. An important part of an adolescent's establishing an identity is gaining independence from parents.

Adulthood

_____ 5. The term *climacteric* refers to physiological changes associated with the transition from fertility to infertility for both men and women.

_____ 6. The results of longitudinal studies suggest that people retain their intellect well into middle age.

_____ 7. Young adults tend to report less job satisfaction than middle-aged and older workers.

The Older Years

_____ 8. Alzheimer's disease is the most common form of senile dementia.

_____   9. The activity theory proposes that the aging process is a consequence of wear and tear on one's body.

_____

_____

_____   10. The first stage of Kübler-Ross' stages of dying is anger.

_____

_____

Answer Key

1. F **(446)**	5. F **(458)**	8. T **(471)**
2. F **(446)**	6. T **(460)**	9. F **(473)**
3. T **(450)**	7. T **(467)**	10. F **(475)**
4. T **(453)**		

PART V. MULTIPLE-CHOICE QUESTIONS

Choose the best answer to each question. Circle your choice. Check your answers against the Answer Key. Questions marked with an asterisk (*) include annotated answers.

Adolescence

1. Which of the following would *not* be included in a definition of adolescence concerning youth in the United States today?

  a. It typically spans age 12–20
  b. It is marked by a rite of passage
  c. It is a time of social role development
  d. It is a time of dramatic physiological change

2. It would be appropriate for parents to be concerned if their _____ started to undergo the beginning of puberty.

  a. 8-year-old girl
  b. 8-year-old boy
  c. 14-year-old girl
  d. 16-year-old boy

*3. The adolescent growth spurt

  a. occurs at a younger age in boys than in girls.
  b. refers to a four-year time span of rapid physical growth in early adolescence.
  c. is completed before a child reaches sexual maturity.
  d. occurs after a child reaches sexual maturity.

*4. Which of the following is a secondary sex characteristic?

  a. Pubic hair
  b. A penis or vagina
  c. Adult height
  d. None of the above.

5. Advantages such as being poised, popular, and academically successful are associated with

   a. early-maturing girls.
   b. late-maturing girls.
   c. early-maturing boys.
   d. late-maturing boys.

6. When people have cognitively matured to the point where they can explore "what if" possibilities, Piaget would say that they are in the _____ stage.

   a. sensorimotor
   b. preoperational
   c. concrete-operations
   d. formal-operations

7. Approximately _____ of American college students would be considered to be in the formal-operations stage of cognitive development.

   a. 15 percent
   b. 50 percent
   c. 80 percent
   d. 95 percent

*8. Köhlberg was most interested in a person's _____ rather than in their _____ .

   a. moral behavior | moral reasoning
   b. yes or no answer to a moral dilemma | moral behavior
   c. yes or no answer to a moral dilemma | moral reasoning
   d. moral reasoning | yes or no answer to a moral dilemma

9. According to Köhlberg, a period in which moral judgments are derived from moral principles and personal values, and not from authority figures is the _____ stage.

   a. concrete-conventional
   b. postconventional
   c. preconventional
   d. conventional

10. In response to Köhlberg's moral dilemma concerning Heinz, a person answers, "He shouldn't have stolen the drug because it's against the law to steal." That person would be classified at the _____ stage of moral development.

    a. second
    b. third
    c. fourth
    d. fifth

11. The popular image of the teenage years as a time of rebellion, storm and stress is

    a. substantiated by studies.
    b. applicable only to early adolescent years.
    c. more myth than fact.
    d. true only in America.

12. An adolescent is most influenced by the peer group in matters concerning

    a. dress and hair styles.

    b. moral values.

    c. career choice.

    d. politics.

13. In response to greater awareness of AIDS, many studies have found that a large proportion of adolescents

    a. have adopted safer sex practices.

    b. have reduced their level of sexual activity.

    c. discuss the possibility of AIDS before engaging in sexual activity with a new partner.

    d. are not inclined to reduce their level of sexual activity or use safer sex practices.

Adulthood

14. Most people reach the peak of their reproductive capacities and enjoy the best health of any time in their lives during

    a. middle adulthood.

    b. early adulthood.

    c. later adulthood.

    d. late adolescence.

15. One problem with cross-sectional studies on intelligence is that the

    a. older group experienced less formal education.

    b. older group has less experience with standardized tests.

    c. groups have experienced varied cultural conditions.

    d. All of the above reasons are valid.

16. _____ intelligence results from accumulated knowledge and is closely linked to education and experience. _____ intelligence allows a person to conceptualize abstract information and is relatively independent of education.

    a. Crystallized | Fluid

    b. Fluid | Crystallized

    c. Problem-finding | Dialectic-operation

    d. Dialectic-operation | Problem-solving

17. Research indicates that crystallized intelligence

    a. peaks in early adulthood and remains at that level.

    b. peaks in early adulthood and then steadily declines.

    c. peaks in middle adulthood and then slowly declines.

    d. increases with age.

18. A fifth stage of cognitive development (after Piaget's fourth stage) proposed by Klaus Riegel, in which an individual realizes and accepts that conflict and contradiction are natural consequences of living is known as

    a. dialectic operations.

    b. concrete operations.

    c. formal operations.

    d. problem finding.

19. One study linked satisfaction with single life to

  a. avoiding the fear of divorce.
  b. the number and types of friendships.
  c. not needing sexual relations.
  d. having more money to spend.

*20. The text does *not* report research findings indicating that cohabitation

  a. is becoming more common today than it was in the early 1970s.
  b. has a positive effect on a subsequent marriage.
  c. has a negative effect on a subsequent marriage.
  d. has no effect on a subsequent marriage.

21. The nurturing of children is

  a. incompatible with a successful career.
  b. helpful in the expression of generativity.
  c. helpful in the expression of intimacy.
  d. helpful in the discovery of an identity.

The Older Years

22. Over the past few decades the proportion of Americans 65+ has

  a. stabilized after an increase in the early 1900s.
  b. grown at twice the rate of the rest of the population.
  c. grown at three times the rate of the rest of the population.
  d. slightly decreased.

23. People over age 65 are *less likely* than younger people to suffer from

  a. hypertension.
  b. hearing loss.
  c. digestive problems.
  d. arthritis.

24. The _____ theory of aging is supported by the observation that identical twins have very similar life spans.

  a. genetic clock or programmed
  b. climacteric
  c. accumulating damages
  d. activity

25. A possible explanation of why fluid intelligence declines in older years and crystallized intelligence remains the same is that

  a. fluid intelligence is genetic.
  b. fluid intelligence is learned.
  c. older people are not challenged to use their fluid intelligence.
  d. older people do not need fluid intelligence.

26. Research examining a genetic basis for Alzheimer's disease has implicated

    a. chromosome 21.
    b. chromosome 17.
    c. the X chromosome.
    d. the Y chromosome.

27. Of the population that is over 65, _____ show little or no cognitive deterioration.

    a. 10 percent
    b. 25 percent
    c. 60 percent
    d. 90 percent

28. Satisfaction with life in general, feelings of well-being, and marital satisfaction _____ among the aged than among younger adults.

    a. is similar
    b. tends to be higher
    c. tends to be slightly lower
    d. tends to be dramatically lower

*29. The _____ theory suggests that people will more likely experience happiness in their "golden years" if they cut back on the stresses associated with an active life.

    a. disassociation
    b. activity
    c. inactivity
    d. disengagement

30. Erikson's developmental task of the older years—ego integrity versus despair—is consistent with the idea that older people

    a. select a lifestyle that reflects their personality.
    b. are concerned with problem finding.
    c. conduct a life review.
    d. demonstrate postconventional thought.

31. Kübler-Ross developed her theory of dying by

    a. using naturalistic observation.
    b. interviewing doctors who treat terminal patients.
    c. interviewing patients who were dying.
    d. using a correlational approach.

32. Kübler-Ross' final stage of dying is

    a. acceptance.
    b. awareness.
    c. defeat.
    d. depression.

Answer Key

1. b	**(445-446)**	*8. d	**(449)**	15. d	**(459)**	21. b	**(465)**	27. d	**(472)**
2. b	**(446)**	9. b	**(450)**	16. a	**(460)**	22. b	**(468-469)**	28. b	**(473)**
*3. c	**(446)**	10. c	**(450)**	17. d	**(460)**	23. c	**(469-470)**	*29. d	**(473)**
*4. a	**(446)**	11. c	**(452)**	18. a	**(460-461)**	24. a	**(470-471)**	30. c	**(474)**
5. c	**(447)**	12. a	**(455)**	19. b	**(463)**	25. c	**(471)**	31. c	**(475)**
6. d	**(449)**	13. d	**(456-457)**	*20. b	**(464)**	26. a	**(472)**	32. a	**(475)**
7. b	**(449)**	14. b	**(458)**						

Annotated Answers

3. The correct choice is c. Sexual maturity is typically attained soon after the adolescent growth spurt is completed.
   a. Because girls typically enter and complete puberty two years before boys do, the adolescent growth spurt occurs at a younger age for girls than for boys.
   b. The adolescent growth spurt is two years in duration and not four years.
   d. The adolescent growth spurt occurs before sexual maturity is attained.

4. The correct choice is a. Secondary sex characteristics refer to physical changes of the body that occur during puberty and are controlled by gonadotropins and testosterone (in males) and estrogens (in females). Pubic hair is present in mature males and females and is not present in either sex prior to puberty.
   b. The penis and vagina are primary sex characteristics present from birth.
   c. Adult height is reached during puberty, but it is not a secondary sex characteristic. Secondary sex characteristics are related to gonadotropins and sex hormones whereas adult height is controlled by other growth hormones.
   d. This choice is incorrect because choice a is correct.

8. The correct choice is d. Köhlberg was interested in the thought process (moral reasoning) and not in the yes or no answer a person gave in response to a moral dilemma. People at very different stages of development could give the same yes or no answer. For example, "Yes, he should steal it because if he let his wife die he would get in trouble" (stage 1); and "Yes, if he had failed to act in this fashion to save his wife, he would not have lived up to his own standards of conscience" (stage 6).
   a. Köhlberg's theory is not concerned with an individual's actual actions (moral behavior). In fact, moral behavior and moral reasoning often do not go hand in hand.
   b. The person's yes or no answer was not what Köhlberg was most interested in. He was interested in the person's moral reasoning.
   c. This choice has the two correct components of Köhlberg's approach to studying moral development, but here the components are reversed.

20. The correct choice is b. The text does not mention any studies to indicate that cohabitation has a positive effect on subsequent marriages.
   a. The text reports that the number of couples cohabiting more than quadrupled between 1970 and 1988.
   c. The text reports, for example, that one study found more marriages fail within 10 years if the couple lived together before marriage than if the couple did not cohabitate.
   d. The text reports, for example, that another study found that cohabitation did not have any influence on subsequent marital happiness.

29. The correct choice is d. This theory proposes that, if older individuals cut back or disengaged themselves from stressors and took time to relax, more likely they would be happy or content.
   a. There is no disassociation theory related to successful aging.
   b. Unlike the disengagement theory, the activity theory proposes that the key to successful aging is to remain active and involved in activities.
   c. There is no inactivity theory related to successful aging.

PART VI. SUMMARY TABLE

To test your understanding of the material discussed in this chapter complete the following table. Check your answers with those supplied in PART IX.

Adolescence, Adulthood, and the Older Years

Type of Development	Adolescence	Adulthood	Older Years
Physical			
Cognitive			
Psychosocial			

PART VII. THOUGHT QUESTIONS/CRITICAL THINKING

Prepare answers to the following discussion questions.

1. In many families in which both father and son are athletically inclined it is a memorable occasion when the son first beats the father in a game of one-on-one basketball (or some other similar event). Assume that the father was 25 years old when the son was born. Predict how old each would be when the son first beats his father.

2. Discuss possible reasons why there are more advantages associated with being an early-maturing boy than are associated with being an early-maturing girl.

3. The influence of Piaget's theory of cognitive development is apparent in many aspects of development. Discuss each of the following examples from a Piagetian perspective.

   a. Erikson states that the primary developmental task of adolescence is establishing an identity. Why doesn't this crisis develop at a younger age?

   b. Köhlberg's theory of moral development is in many ways an outgrowth from Piaget's theory. At which level of cognitive development would an individual most likely be, whose moral reasoning would be at each of Köhlberg's levels of moral development? Explain.

   c. The text describes two different proposals concerning a fifth stage of cognitive development: Arlin's problem finding and Riegel's dialectic operations. Discuss which of these two approaches seems to be the most natural extension of Piaget's theory.

4. Explain why you believe or disbelieve that it is reasonable for women to go through a definite transition from fertility to infertility (menopause and the climacteric) usually between age 45–50, whereas men remain fertile for a much longer period of time and only gradually become infertile.

PART VIII. APPLICATIONS

1. The text describes Köhlberg's theory of moral development and Table 12.1 (p. 451) provides sample answers to the Heinz dilemma illustrating the six levels of moral development. This application involves evaluating the stage of moral reasoning of three or four individuals. Ideally, the individuals should range in age from junior high age through college or adulthood, however, if you do not have access to young individuals, using only college students is acceptable. Read the Heinz dilemma to each individual and ask them the following questions. Record their responses to each question.

   a. Should Heinz have stolen the drug? Why or why not?

   b. What's to be said for obeying the law in this situation? In general?

   c. If the husband doesn't love his wife, is he obligated to steal the drug for her? Why or why not?

   d. Would it be as moral to steal the drug for a stranger as for his wife? Why or why not?

   e. If Heinz steals the drug and is arrested, should the judge sentence him or let him go free? Explain.

Decide at which stage of moral development you believe each individual is functioning. Because an individual's answers may not be completely consistent, this may be a difficult task. Did you find that older individuals gave answers that were characteristic of higher levels of moral development?

2. How would knowledge of Kübler-Ross' five stages of dying (denial, anger, bargaining, depression, and acceptance) be beneficial for the family members of a terminal patient? Suggest specific behaviors or attitudes for family members to adopt that would be appropriate for comforting the patient at each of the five stages of dying. For example, how should family members react to outbursts from the patient who is in the anger stage? If the patient has reached the stage of acceptance, should family members continue to urge medical treatments? Why or why not?

PART IX. SUMMARY TABLE SOLUTIONS

Adolescence, Adulthood, and the Older Years

Type of Development	Adolescence	Adulthood	Older Years
Physical	Period of rapid growth (adolescent growth spurt) Sexual maturity (puberty) is attained	Physical abilities peak during early adulthood and then begin to gradually decline Reproductive abilities also peak in early adulthood and slowly decline in men, while women show a marked transition from fertility to infertility (the climacteric)	Although many bodily systems decline, most individuals maintain relatively good health
Cognitive	Formal-operations stage of cognitive development emerges: capable of abstract thought, deductive reasoning, and able to use strategies to approach problem solving	Crystallized intelligence (accumulated knowledge) continues to increase with age, while fluid intelligence (conceptualizing abstract information) peaks in early adulthood and then steadily declines	For most individuals, crystallized intelligence continues to improve or remain stable, while fluid intelligence continues to decline Small percentage of individuals experience severe reduction in mental functioning or senile dementia
Psychosocial	Concerned with identity formation or dealing with questions such as "Who am I?" and "Where am I headed?" Strives to gain independence from parents and is strongly influenced by the peer group	In early adulthood, concerned with finding intimacy In middle adulthood, concerned with generativity, which is associated with raising a family and employment (career)	Concerned with evaluating life and hopefully achieving a sense of integrity Feelings of satisfaction with life tends to be higher in older individuals than in young adults

Intelligence

PART I. LEARNING OBJECTIVES

When you finish studying this chapter you should be able to:

What Is Intelligence?

1. List and discuss two categories of behavior both psychologists and laypeople believe are characteristics of intelligent individuals, and describe a third category of behavior often included by laypeople. **(482)**

2. Compare and contrast the models of intelligence proposed by Spearman, Thurstone, and Guilford. **(483-484)**

3. Discuss Sternberg's information-processing approach to problem solving, and describe ways good problem solvers differ from other individuals. **(484)**

4. Describe Sternberg's triarchic theory of intelligence. **(486)**

5. Discuss Gardner's theory of multiple intelligences. **(486-487)**

6. Discuss the operational definition of intelligence that is generally used. **(487)**

Measuring Intelligence

7. Describe the approach Binet used to test intelligence, and discuss what intelligence quotient (IQ) refers to and how it is determined. **(489-490)**

8. Discuss how Terman adapted Binet's test for American children and developed the Stanford–Binet test. **(491)**

9. Explain why Wechsler developed the Wechsler Adult Intelligence Scale (WAIS), and describe its basic design. **(491)**

10. Describe a number of group intelligence tests, and compare the advantages and disadvantages of group and individual intelligence tests. **(491-492)**

11. Define aptitude test and achievement test, and discuss why the differences between these two types of tests is not as clear-cut as these definitions imply. **(493)**

Evaluating Intelligence Tests

12. List and describe the four steps in developing a standardized test. **(493-495)**

13. Define reliability and validity and describe several ways each is measured. **(495-496)**

14. Define cultural bias, and describe the influence cultural bias may have on the intelligence test scores of individuals. **(496-497)**

What Determines Intelligence?

15. Differentiate between the hereditarian and environmentalist views on intelligence **(498-499)**

16. Discuss the results of twin and adoption studies regarding the hereditarian and environmentalist view concerning intelligence. **(499-500)**

17. Describe and summarize the results of orphanage and environmental enrichment studies that have examined the effects of early stimulation on intelligence. **(501-502)**

18. Summarize the research concerning birth order and intelligence. **(502-503)**

19. Describe Tryon's research with maze-bright and maze-dull rats. **(505-506)**

20. Summarize the evidence concerning the relative effects of nature and nurture on intelligence, and discuss the heritability of intelligence. **(506-507)**

Racial Differences in Intelligence: Fact or Fiction?

21. Describe the difference in average IQ scores between whites and blacks, and discuss factors that contribute to this average difference. **(507-509)**

Intelligence and Creativity

22. Define creativity, and discuss the relationship between creativity and intelligence. **(508-509)**

PART II. OVERVIEW

Intelligence is a concept that all are familiar with but because it refers to an abstract quality it is difficult to precisely define. It is therefore difficult to determine how to measure intelligence. Perhaps the best operational definition of intelligence is that it is what is measured by intelligence tests.

Three models of intelligence that attempted to describe the structure of intelligence are discussed. Spearman believed that intelligence consisted of a general intelligence (g-factor) and also a number of specific abilities (s-factors). A person with a higher level of g-factor would tend to perform better on many tasks than a person with a lower level of g-factor. Thurstone believed that intelligence consisted of seven independent primary mental abilities. Guilford believed that intellectual tasks could be described as involving a number of operations (how we think) and contents (what we think about) that produce a number of different products. By calculating all the possible combinations of the above he proposed that there were 150 kinds of intelligence. More recently, two theorists have attempted to describe the process of intelligence or how people effectively solve problems and interact with their environment. Sterenberg's triarchic theory proposed that intelligence is composed of three separate abilities (componential, experiential, and contextual). An individual need not have similar intellectual levels concerning these three abilities. Gardner provided a view of intelligence that is much broader than the other approaches and describes intelligence as being composed of seven multiple intelligences that include musical, body, and interpersonal and intrapersonal intelligence.

In 1905, the first practical intelligence test was developed in France by Binet in order to predict children's future success in school (specifically, the test was designed to predict those children who would have difficulty in a regular classroom). The average IQ (100) is calculated by the following formula: mental age/chronological age $\times$ 100. An American version of Binet's test (the Stanford–Binet test) was developed by Terman. The Wechsler Adult Intelligence Scale (WAIS) was developed to determine the IQ of older adolescents and adults and provides more detailed information than the Stanford–Binet test.

There are four primary steps involved in developing a test (either an intelligence test or other type of psychological test): (1) developing a pool of test items, (2) evaluating the test items, (3) standardizing the test, and (4) establishing norms. Additionally, for a test to be worthwhile and allow a psychologist to trust its results, it must have reliability (give consistent results for an individual) and validity (accurately measure what it is intended to measure).

A number of types of studies (twin, adoption, orphanage, and enrichment) have been conducted to help determine the relative influence of heredity and environment on intelligence. Both factors exert an influence on an individual's IQ but most psychologists believe that heredity plays the more prominent role. Environmental factors exert a more obvious effect in situations where a disadvantaged environment tends to result in lower IQs than would develop in a more appropriate environment.

Racial differences in average IQ exist with American blacks scoring, on average, about 15 points lower than American whites. This result is due to blacks being more likely to come from disadvantaged environments than whites and a cultural bias in the IQ test items. Evidence exists, however, that this difference in average IQ scores between blacks and whites is decreasing.

Chapter 13 concludes with a discussion of intelligence and creativity. Creativity refers to the ability to produce an original or novel and useful or valuable outcome. Intelligence is only moderately correlated with creativity. Creative individuals tend to have above-average IQs. However, a high IQ does not guarantee creativity and creativity does not require a high IQ.

PART III. KEY TERMS/MATCHING EXERCISES

Match the following concepts and/or individuals with the appropriate descriptions. Check your answers against the Answer Key.

What Is Intelligence?

Concepts

_____ 1. triarchic theory of intelligence **(486)**

_____ 2. intelligence **(487)**

_____ 3. primary mental abilities **(483-484)**

_____ 4. g-factor **(483)**

_____ 5. s-factors **(483)**

Descriptions

a. Refer(s) to a group of specific intellectual abilities

b. Proposes that intelligence consists of componential, experiential, and contextual abilities

c. Refer(s) to the general component of intelligence

d. Include(s) verbal comprehension, numerical ability, spatial relations, perceptual speed, word fluency, memory, and inductive reasoning

e. Operationally defined as that which intelligence tests measure

Answer Key   1. b   2. e   3. d   4. c   5. a

Measuring Intelligence

Concepts

_____ 1. achievement tests **(493)**

_____ 2. intelligence quotient (IQ) **(409)**

_____ 3. Army Alpha and Army Beta tests **(493)**

_____ 4. Stanford–Binet test **(491)**

_____ 5. Wechsler Adult Intelligence Scale (WAIS) **(491)**

_____ 6. aptitude tests **(493)**

_____ 7. mental age **(490)**

_____ 8. chronological age **(490)**

_____ 9. Otis-Lennon School Ability Test (OLSAT) and Cognitive Abilities Test (CAT) **(492)**

Descriptions

a. Terman's American version of Binet's intelligence test

b. Designed to predict an individual's ability to learn new information or new skill

c. Mental age/chronological age $\times$ 100

d. Two of the first group-administered intelligence tests

e. Two group-intelligence tests commonly used today

f. Actual or calendar age of an individual

g. Designed to measure what an individual has already learned

h. Corresponds to the age of an average child who receives a similar test score on an IQ test

i. Provides an overall IQ as well as a verbal and performance IQ

Answer Key 1. g   2. c   3. d   4. a   5. i   6. b   7. h   8. f   9. e

Evaluating Intelligence Tests | What Determines Intelligence | Intelligence and Creativity

Concepts

_____ 1. reliability (**495**)

_____ 2. creativity (**509**)

_____ 3. standardization procedures (**494**)

_____ 4. cultural bias (**496**)

_____ 5. validity (**496**)

_____ 6. heritability (**506**)

_____ 7. norm (**494**)

Descriptions

a. Refer(s) to the fact that intelligence tests tend to favor some individuals while placing others at a disadvantage

b. Refer(s) to the ability to produce outcomes that are both novel and useful or valuable

c. Refer(s) to whether a test measures with dependable consistency

d. Reflect(s) the average test performance of a particular group of people

e. Provide(s) an estimate of the amount of variation in a trait that is due to genetic factors

f. Refer(s) to whether a test accurately measures what it is intended to measure

g. Refer(s) to uniform and consistent procedures for administering and scoring a test

Answer Key   1. c   2. b   3. g   4. a   5. f   6. e   7. d

Individuals

_____ 1. Spearman **(483)**   _____ 6. Thurstone **(484)**

_____ 2. Wechsler **(491)**   _____ 7. Terman **(491)**

_____ 3. Galton **(481)**   _____ 8. Sternberg **(484, 486)**

_____ 4. Binet **(489)**   _____ 9. Gardner **(486)**

_____ 5. Guilford **(484)**

Descriptions

a. Proposed that there are 150 kinds of intelligence

b. Developed an intelligence test for late adolescents and adults that calculates verbal and performance IQs as well as overall IQ

c. Proposed that intelligence is composed of general intelligence and specific intellectual abilities

d. Adapted Binet's test for American children

e. Proposed that intelligence includes a diversity of abilities, some of which (such as musical talent) are not typically included in definitions of intelligence

f. Developed an information-processing approach to problem solving and the triarchic theory of intelligence

g. Developed the first intelligence test, but it was not successful in measuring intelligence

h. Developed the first modern intelligence test

i. Proposed that intelligence is a composite of seven primary mental abilities

Answer Key   1. c   2. b   3. g   4. h   5. a   6. i   7. d   8. f   9. e

PART IV. TRUE-FALSE STATEMENTS

Fill in the blank before each statement with either a T (true) or an F (false). Check your answers against the Answer Key. Then go back to the items that are false and make the necessary change(s) to the statements to convert the items into true statements.

What Is Intelligence?

_____ 1. Both laypeople and psychologists tend to view intelligence as being composed of verbal ability, practical problem-solving ability, and social competence.

_____

_____

_____ 2. Sternberg and Gardner's models of intelligence seek to understand intelligence as a process.

_____

_____

_____ 3. A good operational definition of intelligence is "the ability to think abstractly."

_____

_____

Measuring Intelligence

_____ 4. Stanford adapted Binet's test for American children and developed the Stanford–Binet test.

_____

_____

_____ 5. The Stanford–Binet test allows for the calculation of overall IQ and also of the verbal and performance IQ.

_____

_____

Evaluating Intelligence Tests

_____ 6. The first step in developing a test is to standardize the test.

_____

_____

_____ 7. If a person took the same IQ test three times and received a similar score each time, it could be said that this test is reliable.

_____

_____

What Determines Intelligence? |
Racial Differences in Intelligence: Fact or Fiction?

_____ 8. The IQs of adopted children are more similar to their biological parents than to their adoptive parents.

_____

_____

_____ 9. Disadvantaged children who attend Head Start programs show short-term gains in IQ.

_____

_____

_____ 10. Genetic factors account for 60 percent of one's intelligence.

_____

_____

_____ 11. Most psychologists believe that differences in intelligence between racial groups are largely—if not exclusively—the result of environmental factors.

_____

_____

Intelligence and Creativity

_____ 12. Psychologists use tests of convergent thinking to measure creativity.

_____

_____

_____ 13. Creative people tend to have above-average IQs, but do not differ in level of intelligence from their less-creative peers.

_____

_____

Answer Key			
	1. F **(482)**	6. F **(494)**	10. F **(506–507)**
	2. T **(484)**	7. T **(495)**	11. T **(507)**
	3. F **(487)**	8. T **(500–501)**	12. F **(509)**
	4. F **(491)**	9. T **(501–502)**	13. T **(509)**
	5. F **(491)**		

PART V. MULTIPLE-CHOICE QUESTIONS

Choose the best answer to each question. Circle your choice. Check your answers against the Answer Key. Questions marked with an asterisk (*) include annotated answers.

What Is Intelligence?

1. Sir Francis Galton designed his intelligence test to evaluate his hypothesis concerning the

a. accuracy of the equation MA/CA $\times$ 100 = IQ.
b. inferiority of men.
c. superiority of the upper class.
d. negative effect of a disadvantage background.

*2. _____ is the psychologist who would believe that it may be appropriate to say of an individual, "He is highly intelligent" (or not intelligent) because there is a general or overall component of intelligence.

a. Sternberg
b. Gardner
c. Thurstone
d. Spearman

3. Thurstone believed that human intelligence

a. consists of a g-factor and s-factors.
b. contains componential, experiential, and contextual components.
c. is composed of seven independent mental abilities.
d. consists of 150 different kinds of intelligence.

4. Guilford used the term _content_ to describe

a. how we think.
b. what we think about.
c. how we apply our thinking.
d. primary ability.

5. The approaches of _____ provide models to describe the structure of intelligence. The approaches of _____ attempt to understand the process of intelligence.

a. Sternberg and Gardner | Spearman, Thurstone, and Guilford
b. Spearman, Thurstone, and Guilford | Sternberg and Gardner
c. Spearman and Guilford | Sternberg, Thurstone, and Gardner
d. Sternberg, Thurstone, and Gardner | Spearman and Guilford

6. Good problem solvers who score high on intelligence tests _____ than people who score low on intelligence tests.

    a. take a longer time to encode information
    b. take a shorter time to encode information
    c. arrive at the correct solution faster
    d. make more careless mistakes

7. Which of the following theoretical models of intelligence does *not* use the factor-analysis technique?

    a. Guilford's
    b. Thurstone's
    c. Spearman's
    d. Sternberg's

8. _____ is the psychologist who defines intelligence to include a number of abilities (such as musical ability and interpersonal abilities) that are not typically included in definitions of intelligence.

    a. Guilford
    b. Wechsler
    c. Gardner
    d. Sternberg

9. "The ability to think abstractly" is a definition of intelligence proposed by

    a. Sternberg.
    b. Binet.
    c. Wechsler.
    d. Terman.

Measuring Intelligence

*10. In developing his intelligence test Binet reasoned that a child with high intelligence would perform on the intelligence test similar to a(n)

    a. child of the same chronological age.
    b. older child of average intelligence.
    c. older child of below-average intelligence.
    d. child of the same age and of average intelligence.

*11. Who of the following would have the highest IQ?

    a. Mental age of 5, and chronological age of 5
    b. Mental age of 10, and chronological age of 8
    c. Mental age of 5, and chronological age of 6
    d. Mental age of 10, and chronological age of 10

12. A college student would most likely take which intelligence test?

    a. WAIS
    b. CAT
    c. Stanford–Binet
    d. Army Alpha

13. Which of the following is *not* an advantage of group-administered intelligence tests compared to individual intelligence tests?

    a. Can be given to a number of people at the same time

    b. Are quicker to administer

    c. Encourage the best possible performance from individuals

    d. Are more easily scored

14. Achievement tests are designed to

    a. predict ability to learn new information or new skill.

    b. measure what one has already learned.

    c. determine one's intelligence quotient.

    d. None of the above choices apply.

15. Which of the following is designed to measure a type of ability that is different from the type of ability measured by the other three tests?

    a. Aptitude tests

    b. Otis-Lennon School Ability Test (OLSAT)

    c. Achievement tests

    d. Wechsler Adult Intelligence Scale (WAIS)

Evaluating Intelligence Tests

16. Which of the following is *not* a step involved in developing an intelligence test?

    a. Calculating a child's IQ

    b. Establishing test norms

    c. Evaluating the test items

    d. Standardizing the test

*17. In the process of developing his intelligence test, Binet asked many French children of varying ages the test items to determine how these children performed on the test. Why did Binet do this?

    a. To develop standardization procedures

    b. To determine the numerical value of the average IQ

    c. To verify the reliability of the test

    d. To develop test norms

18. What percentage of people taking an IQ test achieve scores within the 85 to 115 range?

    a. 75 percent

    b. 68 percent

    c. 95 percent

    d. 50 percent

19. Because intelligence tests _____ one should receive the same IQ score regardless of who administers and scores the test.

    a. are standardized

    b. have established norms

    c. are valid

    d. are reliable

20. If a person wanted to evaluate the consistency of a test and decided to divide the test into half and scored each half separately to see if the two scores were similar, he or she would be

    a. assessing the concurrent reliability.
    b. assessing the concurrent validity.
    c. calculating the split-half reliability.
    d. calculating the split-half validity.

21. If a test measures what it is supposed to measure it has

    a. validity.
    b. norms.
    c. reliability.
    d. consistency.

22. To assess the _____ validity of a test, individuals' test scores are compared with their scores on other measures known to be good indicators of the skill or trait being assessed.

    a. alternate
    b. predictive
    c. concurrent
    d. standard

23. Which statement is *true*?

    a. Motivation is not a factor affecting IQ.
    b. Race is not a factor affecting IQ.
    c. Truly culture-fair IQ tests are available.
    d. Possibly no truly culture-fair or culture-free intelligence tests exist at this time.

What Determines Intelligence?

24. Studies of identical twins reared together and apart provide evidence to support

    a. only the hereditarian view.
    b. only the environmentalist view.
    c. the hereditarian view and, to a lesser degree, the environmentalist view.
    d. the environmentalist view and, to a lesser degree, the hereditarian view.

25. Which two people would you expect to have IQs that are most similar?

    a. A parent and child
    b. Fraternal twins reared together
    c. Two same-sex siblings
    d. Identical twins reared apart

26. Studies of children reared in orphanages lend support to the position of the

    a. hereditarians.
    b. environmentalists.
    c. humanists.
    d. behaviorists.

*27. Special enrichment programs, such as Head Start, would be

    a. most beneficial for school-age children.

    b. very beneficial for any child.

    c. most beneficial for children from disadvantaged environments.

    d. most beneficial for children from middle-class environments.

28. Concerning the contributions of nature and nurture in influencing human intelligence, most psychologists generally believe that

    a. the relative contribution of genetic factors is greater than that of environmental factors.

    b. the relative contribution of environmental factors is greater than that of genetic factors.

    c. genetic and environmental factors are equally important.

    d. genetic factors account for 75% of an individual's intelligence.

Racial Differences in Intelligence: Fact or Fiction?

29. _____ is the psychologist who proposed that the difference in average IQ scores between blacks and whites is due primarily to genetic factors.

    a. Jensen

    b. Skeels

    c. Sternberg

    d. Scarr

30. There is _____ overlap between the IQ scores of blacks and whites.

    a. no

    b. a small

    c. a moderate

    d. a large

31. A study in Minneapolis showed that black children adopted into white, middle-class families had IQs similar to the

    a. average IQ of black children.

    b. average IQ of white children.

    c. IQs of white children adopted into middle-class families.

    d. None of the above choices are correct.

Intelligence and Creativity

32. To be considered creative a product or ability should be

    a. novel or original.

    b. useful or valuable.

    c. Either of the above apply.

    d. Both a and b apply.

33. Answering a multiple-choice question is an example of _____ thinking.

    a. convergent

    b. abstract

    c. divergent

    d. trial-and-error

34. Which of the following traits has *not* been associated with creative people?

- **a.** They tend to express their feelings
- **b.** They are motivated by extrinsic rewards
- **c.** They have at least moderate intelligence
- **d.** They are nonconformists

Answer Key

1. c	**(481)**	8. c	**(486)**	15. c	**(493)**	22. c	**(496)**	29. a	**(506-507)**
*2. d	**(483)**	9. d	**(487)**	16. a	**(493)**	23. d	**(496-497)**	30. d	**(507)**
3. c	**(483-484)**	*10. b	**(489-490)**	*17. d	**(494)**	24. c	**(499-500)**	31. c	**(508)**
4. b	**(484)**	*11. b	**(491)**	18. b	**(494-495)**	25. d	**(500)**	32. d	**(508-509)**
5. b	**(484)**	12. a	**(491)**	19. a	**(494)**	26. b	**(501)**	33. a	**(509)**
6. a	**(484)**	13. c	**(493)**	20. c	**(495)**	*27. c	**(502)**	34. b	**(509)**
7. d	**(486)**	14. b	**(493)**	21. a	**(496)**	28. a	**(506)**		

Annotated Answers

2. The correct choice is d. Spearman proposed that intelligence is composed of a general factor and a number of specific abilities. A person could appropriately be described as highly intelligent because he or she would tend to consistently perform at a high level on many types of tests of mental ability.

- **a.** Sternberg's triarchic theory of intelligence proposes that intelligence consists of three different abilities and that a high (or average or low) level of one type of ability does not necessarily correspond with high (or average or low) levels of the other abilities.
- **b.** Gardner proposed a theory of multiple intelligences consisting of seven different kinds of intelligence. You would have to specify which type of intelligence you were talking about in order to describe an individual as highly intelligent.
- **c.** Thurstone proposed that intelligence is a composite of seven primary abilities that are independent. Because it is possible for an individual to be highly intelligent on one (or some) abilities and average or below average on other abilities, it would generally be inappropriate to say that that person is highly intelligent.

10. The correct choice is b. Binet reasoned that all children follow the same course of intellectual development, but differ on the rate at which they progress. A child of high intelligence (with a relatively rapid rate of progress) should perform similarly to an older child of average intelligence (with a slower rate of progress).

- **a.** A child of the same age would only show similar test performance if the other child was also highly intelligent. If the other child was of average intelligence, that child would not perform as well as the highly intelligent child.
- **c.** Although c is technically correct it is not the simplest, most logical, most informative, or "best" answer to the question. A child of average intelligence would also perform similarly to an older child with below-average intelligence.
- **d.** The highly intelligent child would perform at a higher level than a child of the same age who has average intelligence. The highly intelligent child would have an older mental age than the child with average intelligence.

11. The correct choice is b. Using the formula MA/CA $\times$ 100 = IQ, this child would have an IQ of 125, and (10/8 $\times$ 100 = 125).

- **a.** This child would have an IQ of 100, and (5/5 $\times$ 100 = 100).
- **c.** This child would have an IQ of 83, and (5/6 $\times$ 100 = 83).
- **d.** This child would have an IQ of 100, and (10/10 $\times$ 100 = 100).

17. The correct choice is d. Test norms refer to the average performance of a particular group of people. Binet was determining the average performance of 6-, 7-, 8- (and so on) year-old children.

  a. Standardization procedures refer to the way a test is administered and scored.

  b. Selecting the numerical value of the average IQ is unrelated to the performance of children of varying ages. Any numerical value could have been selected to correspond to the average IQ.

  c. The reliability or consistency of the test would be evaluated at a later stage in the test's development.

27. The correct choice is c. Enrichment programs are designed to compensate for a disadvantaged environment and are therefore most beneficial to children from disadvantaged environments.

  a. Because much intellectual development occurs in the early years, postponing an enrichment program until the school years begin would not be as beneficial as an early enrichment (preschool) program.

  b. Enrichment programs are designed to compensate for environments that are lacking in appropriate stimulation; therefore, if a child receives sufficient stimulation in his or her natural environment, an enrichment program would not really be "enriching" and no measurable intellectual advancement would result.

  d. The natural environment of a middle-class child would normally be sufficiently "enriched" so that a specific enrichment program would not be necessary.

PART VI. SUMMARY TABLES

To test your understanding of the material discussed in this chapter complete the following tables. Check your answers with those supplied in PART IX.

Research Suggesting Hereditary and Environmental Influences on IQ

Type of Research	Support for Hereditary Influence	Support for Environmental Influence
Twin		
Adoption		
Orphanage and enrichment		

Models of Intelligence

Psychologist/ Name of Model	Type of Model (Structural or Process)	Description
Gardner/ Multiple intelligences		
Guilford/ Structure of intellect		
Spearman/ Two-factor		
Sternberg/ Triarchic		
Thurstone		

PART VII. THOUGHT QUESTIONS/CRITICAL THINKING

Prepare answers to the following discussion questions.

1. Imagine that you are the parent of two children, a 5-year-old and a 10-year-old. You have only limited financial resources and realize that you have only enough money to send one child to college. You decide to designate the college fund for the more-intelligent child. Explain—in detail—how IQ tests would allow you to determine which child is more intelligent. What IQ score and how large of a difference in IQ scores between your two children would be large enough to justify sending only the more-intelligent child to college?

2. The text notes that there is only a moderate correlation between IQ and creativity. Discuss why highly creative people are not necessarily highly intelligent, and why high intelligence is not a prerequisite for being creative.

3. A psychology instructor teaches three sections of general psychology and is concerned that the students from classes that take their exams after other classes have already been tested are getting some overly helpful hints concerning the contents of the exam. In order to limit this information flow, the instructor decides that, for the next exam (covering three chapters) each class will receive an exam that will only contain questions from one of the chapters. Each class will be tested on a different chapter. Additionally, the instructor did not inform the students about the plan prior to administering the test. Evaluate this testing procedure by referring to the concepts of reliability and validity. Would this be an appropriate (or fair) way to test students' knowledge of the material? Why or why not?

4. You are the youngest child in your family and do not believe the research findings concerning birth order and IQ. You are very intelligent and regularly make the dean's list at college, your eldest sibling flunked out of college, and the middle child in your family barely graduated from college. Are you wrong to disregard this research because it is not consistent with your personal experience? Explain.

5. Should the older twin in a set of identical twins have a higher IQ than the second-born twin? Why or why not?

6. Jensen received a lot of negative publicity for proposing that the differences in IQs between blacks and whites is genetic (with blacks being genetically "inferior"). Similarly, in recent years a number of public individuals have received negative attention (and frequently been fired) as a result of proposing that blacks have a genetic advantage in athletic endeavors (for example, professional sports). The text discusses why Jensen's logic is flawed. Explain how the athletic-superiority-of-blacks argument is similarly flawed.

PART VIII. APPLICATIONS

1. The text distinguishes between aptitude tests (which are designed to measure ability to learn new information or skills) and achievement tests (which are designed to measure what one has already learned). By this point in the semester you have probably had several psychology-related achievement tests and should have a fairly good idea as to what psychology is about and what psychologists actually do. Imagine that you are the head of the Psychology Department at your college and are planning to develop a psychology aptitude test to give incoming freshmen planning on majoring in psychology. Your intent is to redirect to other majors those students who are unlikely to be successful as psychology majors. Describe the types or categories of questions you would include on this psychology aptitude test, and discuss why these would be included.

2. Imagine that, over college break, you get into a discussion with one of your parents' friends concerning IQ tests. Your parents' friend does not believe in IQ tests and has three points concerning IQ tests.

    a. He believes that the score a person gets on an IQ test depends more on luck than on anything else. He states that whether or not a person is in a good mood is a critical variable and doubts that a person would receive the same score if he or she took the test again a week or month later.

    b. He also believes that IQ tests for children are meaningless because children are continually learning new information. For example, an IQ test taken at the beginning of the school year would not be relevant at the end of the school year because the children would be able to correctly answer many more questions.

c. Finally, his major criticism involves the types of question that are on an IQ test. He states that IQ tests are meaningless because they do not ask questions related to what intelligence really is. He defines an intelligent person as an individual with common sense, who is creative, and well-rounded with music and athletic abilities.

Prepare a rebuttal to each of his criticisms.

PART IX. SUMMARY TABLES SOLUTIONS
Research Suggesting Hereditary and Environmental Influences on IQ

Type of Research	Support for Hereditary Influence	Support for Environmental Influence
Twin	Identical twins (reared together or apart) have a higher correlation of IQ scores than all other "pairs" of individuals	Correlation of IQs lower for identical twins reared apart than for identical twins reared together
Adoption	Correlation between adopted children and biological parents is higher than between adoptive children and adoptive parents	IQs of children adopted into upper socioeconomic status families is higher than for children adopted into lower socioeconomic families
Orphanage and enrichment	—	If orphanage's environment is disadvantaged, when environment is improved (even if enriched by mentally retarded adult women), child shows dramatic increase in IQ Enrichment programs (e.g., Head Start) result in at least short-term increase in IQ

Models of Intelligence

Psychologist/ Name of Model	Type of Model (Structural or Process)	Description
Gardner/ Multiple intelligences	Process	Broadly defines *intelligence* to include seven kinds of abilities: linguistic, logical-mathematic, spatial, musical, bodily kinesthetic, inter-personal, and intrapersonal
Guilford/ Structure of intellect	Structural	Intelligence consists of 150 separate abilities that are composed of combinations of operations (how one thinks), contents (what one thinks about), and products of applying a particular operation to a particular content
Spearman/ Two-factor	Structural	Intelligence is composed of an overall or general intelligence (g-factor) and specific intellectual abilities (s-factors) An individual with a high g-factor would tend to score higher on most tests than a person with a low g-factor
Sternberg/ Triarchic	Process	Intelligence is composed of three independent, different abilities: componential (ability to master the steps involved in problem solving), experiential (ability to combine experience in novel ways to solve problems), and contextual (proficient at adapting to the environment)
Thurstone	Structural	Intelligence is a composite of seven primary mental abilities: verbal comprehension, numerical ability, spatial relations, perceptual speed, word fluency, memory, and inductive reasoning

CHAPTER **14**

Personality: Theories and Assessment

PART I. LEARNING OBJECTIVES

When you finish studying this chapter you should be able to:

What Is Personality?

1. Define personality, and briefly discuss the differing perspectives of the two broad types of personality theory. **(513-514)**

Trait Theories

2. Describe Allport's trait theory, and define cardinal, central, and secondary traits. **(514-515)**

3. Describe Cattell's trait theory, define surface and source traits, and describe the 16 Personality Factors Questionnaire (16 PF). **(516)**

4. Evaluate the evidence concerning whether or not an individual's behavior is consistent as trait theorists would predict, and summarize two other criticisms of trait theories. **(517-518)**

Psychoanalytic Theory

5. Describe the historical context within which Freud developed the psychoanalytic theory of personality. **(519)**

6. Define and describe the importance of the unconscious mind to Freud's theory, and discuss what Freud believed to be man's primary drives. **(519, 521)**

7. Describe Freud's three structures of personality—the id, ego, and superego—and discuss how they are interrelated and interact. **(521-523)**

8. Describe events that result in anxiety, and how the ego shields itself from harsh aspects of reality. **(523-524)**

9. List and describe six defense mechanisms. **(524-526)**

10. Summarize Freud's theory of psychosexual development, and describe each of its five stages. **(526-528)**

11. Evaluate psychoanalytic theory by summarizing both criticisms of the theory and theoretical perspectives that are still utilized. **(528-529)**

12. Define the neo-Freudians, and describe three neo-Freudian theories of personality. **(530-531)**

Behaviorist and Social-Learning Theories

13. Describe Skinner's behaviorist approach to personality including how he would define personality, and discuss how behaviorist theory would explain consistencies and inconsistencies in a person's behavior. **(532-533)**

14. Discuss how the social-learning approach differs from the behaviorist approach, and describe Bandura's social-cognitive theory. **(533-535)**

15. Discuss the contributions of behaviorist and social-learning approaches to the field of personality research, and summarize the criticisms of the two approaches. **(535-536)**

Humanistic Theories

16. Discuss the basic assumptions common to humanistic personality theories. **(536)**

17. Describe Rogers' theory of personality, and discuss the importance of the relationship between our experiences and self-concept and between the ideal and real self. **(536-537)**

18. Describe the approach Maslow used in developing his theory of personality, and define and describe a self-actualized individual. **(537-538)**

19. Discuss the contributions of humanistic personality theories to the current view of personality, and summarize criticisms of these theories. **(538-539)**

Personality Assessment

20. Describe the type of information that is gained by using behavioral observation, and discuss the limitations of this approach to personality assessment. **(539-540)**

21. Describe the type of information that is gained by using interviews, and discuss the limitations of this approach to personality assessment. **(540-542)**

22. Describe how the Minnesota Multiphasic Personality Inventory (MMPI) and California Psychological Inventory (CPI) were developed, and the type of information provided by each of these assessment techniques. **(542-544)**

23. Discuss the assumptions underlying projective tests, and describe the Rorschach inkblot test and Thematic Apperception Test (TAT). **(544-546)**

PART II. OVERVIEW

Personality refers to the distinctive patterns of behavior shown by an individual. A number of personality theories are described. Trait theories attempt to describe dimensions of personality characteristics or traits. Allport proposed three categories of traits (cardinal, central, and secondary) that vary in how powerful and durable the traits are. Cattell proposed that surface traits (such as friendliness and tidiness) form clusters of 16 primary or source traits. Source traits exist in eight pairs of polar opposites. Trait theories only describe personality, whereas other personality theories attempt to explain personality and how personality develops.

Freud's psychoanalytic theory emphasizes the role of the unconscious and three structures of personality (id, ego, and superego). Freud maintained that man's primary motivations were sexual and aggressive in nature and viewed personality as shaped by the ongoing conflict between these urges and the demands of society. Personality is largely determined during childhood when an individual progresses through five stages of psychosexual development. At each stage the child experiences sexual gratification through a different erogenous zone. Psychoanalytic theories that accept some and reject other aspects of Freud's theory are neo–Freudian theories. Neo–Freudians believe that Freud overemphasized sexual and aggressive impulses. Jung, Adler, and Horney are three prominent neo–Freudians.

The behaviorist and social-learning personality theorists emphasize the role of external factors. Skinner's behaviorist approach completely ignores internal factors and cognition. Skinner believes that "personality" is the result of an individual's reinforcement history and if the environment were to change so would that individual's personality. Bandura and other social-learning theorists share many ideas with Skinner. However, unlike Skinner, they emphasize the interaction between cognitive factors and external events.

Humanistic theorists believe that man's primary motivation is to develop or grow in a positive manner. Rogers emphasizes the role of the self-concept and how people subjectively respond to experiences. Maslow studied exceptionally healthy and well-adjusted individuals and proposed that when all lesser needs are met people are motivated to reach their fullest potential or self-actualize.

Chapter 14 concludes with a discussion of a number of techniques psychologists use to describe or assess an individual's personality. Behavioral observation and interviews supply a wide variety of information of a global nature. For a more detailed view of an individual's personality psychologists use two types of personality tests. In paper-and-pencil questionnaires (or objective tests) such as the MMPI and the CPI, individuals respond to a number of objective questions (frequently true–false questions) and the answers are compared to the responses of groups of individuals known to show specific characteristics. Projective tests are designed to assess the unconscious and are open-ended and ambiguous. The Rorschach inkblot test and TAT are two well-known projective tests.

PART III. KEY TERMS/MATCHING EXERCISES

Match the following concepts and/or individuals with the appropriate descriptions. Check your answers against the Answer Key.

Personality (Theories: Overview)

Individuals

_____ 1. Adler (**530**)

_____ 2. Allport (**515**)

_____ 3. Bandura (**534**)

_____ 4. Cattell (**516-517**)

_____ 5. Freud (**518**)

_____ 6. Horney (**531**)

_____ 7. Jung (**530**)

_____ 8. Maslow (**538**)

_____ 9. Rogers (**537**)

_____ 10. Skinner (**532**)

Descriptions

a. Developed theory by studying healthy people; emphasized positive over negative qualities

b. Proposed that the primary force shaping personality was an individual's striving for superiority

c. Proposed that a person's personality is composed of central, surface, and for some individuals cardinal traits

d. Emphasized the social relationships of children with their parents and believed that faulty relationships may result in basic anxiety and hostility

e. Proposed that behavior (or personality) and cognitive factors show reciprocal determination

f. Proposed that surface traits cluster into 16 primary or source traits

g. Proposed tht personality "traits" only appear to exist because of the stability of an individual's environment and pattern of reinforcement

h. Proposed that the key to adjustment and happiness is a consistency or congruence between self-concept and experience

i. Developed psychoanalytic theory that depicts personality as shaped by an ongoing conflict between primary drives and societal pressures

j. Distinguished between the personal and collective unconscious and introduced the concepts of introversion and extroversion

Answer Key   1. b   2. c   3. e   4. f   5. i   6. d   7. j   8. a   9. h   10. g

Psychoanalytic Theory

Concepts

_____ 1. ego **(522)**

_____ 2. id **(521)**

_____ 3. defense mechanisms **(524)**

_____ 4. superego **(523)**

_____ 5. unconscious mind **(519)**

_____ 6. phallic stage **(527)**

_____ 7. oral stage **(527)**

_____ 8. latency period **(528)**

_____ 9. anal stage **(527)**

_____ 10. genital stage **(528)**

Descriptions

a. From age 3–5/6 during which boys experience the Oedipus complex and girls the Electra complex

b. Second component of personality to develop that operates according to the reality principle and acts as the personality's mediator

c. First 12–18 months of life during which a child receives pleasure through sucking, chewing, and biting

d. Involve(s) denying or distorting reality and used by the ego to protect it from anxiety

e. From puberty on when sexual feelings reemerge and an individual seeks to gratify these drives through sexual relations with people outside the family

f. "Storehouse" for repressed thoughts and feelings that is central to psychoanalytic theory

g. From age 5–6 until puberty during which sexual drives remain unexpressed

h. Biological component of personality that contains the libido and operates according to the pleasure principle

i. From age 1 or 1½–3 when the anal area is the center of pleasure feelings

j. Contains the moral values and standards of parents and society and consists of the conscience and ego ideal

Answer Key   1. b   2. h   3. d   4. j   5. f   6. a   7. c   8. g   9. i   10. e

Defense Mechanisms

Concepts

_____ 1. reaction formation (**526**)

_____ 2. rationalization (**525**)

_____ 3. sublimation (**525**)

_____ 4. repression (**524**)

_____ 5. projection (**525**)

_____ 6. regression (**526**)

_____ 7. displacement (**525**)

Descriptions

a. Involves denying unacceptable thoughts from consciousness and involved in all other defense mechanisms

b. Involves retreating to behavior associated with an earlier stage of development to gain a sense of security

c. Involves substituting a self-justifying excuse or explanation for the real reasons for one's behavior

d. Involves replacing unacceptable impulses with an acceptable opposite impulse

e. Involves attributing one's unacceptable impulses to someone else

f. Involves a redirection of impulses into a socially acceptable activity

g. Involves redirecting impulse-driven behavior from primary targets to secondary targets that arouse less anxiety

Answer Key   1. d   2. c   3. f   4. a   5. e   6. b   7. g

Personality Theories
(Neo-Freudian, Behaviorist, Social-Learning, Humanistic)

Concepts

_____ 1. reciprocal determination **(534)**

_____ 2. personal unconscious **(530)**

_____ 3. humanistic theory **(536)**

_____ 4. striving for superiority **(530-531)**

_____ 5. self **(537)**

_____ 6. neo-Freudian **(530)**

_____ 7. self-efficacy **(534)**

_____ 8. self-actualization **(537)**

_____ 9. behaviorist and social-learning theories **(532-533)**

_____ 10. collective unconscious **(530)**

Descriptions

a. Concept that is basically similar to Freud's view of the unconscious as a reservoir for repressed thoughts

b. Refers to one's beliefs that he or she can perform adequately and deal effectively with a particular situation

c. Principle that proposes that behaviors and personalities are shaped by an interaction between cognitive and environmental factors

d. Personality theories that maintain man's primary motivation is to strive to develop, change, and grow in pursuit of the full realization of human potential

e. Personality theories that agree with Freud in some areas (such as the role of the unconscious) but disagree regarding the emphasis he placed on aggressive and sexual conflicts

f. Personality theories that emphasize the role of external events in personality formation

g. Universal urge to achieve self-perfection through successful adaptation to life's circumstances, meeting and mastering challenges, and personal growth

h. Maslow's concept that refers to the needs to reach one's own highest potential and to do the things done best in one's own unique way

i. Basic core of one's being that glues the elements of personality together

j. Similar for all people; contains ancestral memories and archtypes

Answer Key   1. c   2. a   3. d   4. g   5. i   6. e   7. b   8. h   9. f   10. j

Personality Assessment

Concepts

_____ 1. MMPI **(542)**
_____ 2. projective tests **(544)**
_____ 3. CPI **(544)**

_____ 4. Rorschach inkblot test **(545)**
_____ 5. criterion-keyed test **(542)**
_____ 6. TAT **(545-546)**

Descriptions

a. Type of objective test in which each item is referenced or associated with one of the standardized groups that were used in developing the test

b. Best known and most widely used objective personality inventory that is appropriate for differentiating normal from disturbed individuals

c. Objective test designed for use with normal individuals

d. Loosely structured personality assessment tests containing ambiguous stimuli designed to tap unconscious thoughts and feelings

e. Involves having an individual describe what they "see" in a series of black blots

f. Involves having a person tell a "story" about what is going on in a series of cards depicting scenes

Answer Key   1. b   2. d   3. c   4. e   5. a   6. f

PART IV. TRUE-FALSE STATEMENTS

Fill in the blank before each statement with either a T (true) or an F (false). Check your answers against the Answer Key. Then go back to the items that are false and make the necessary change(s) to the statements to convert the items into true statements.

What Is Personality? | Trait Theories

_____ 1. Descriptive theories and theories that attempt to explain differences associated with individuals' personalities comprise the two main approaches of personality theories.

_____ 2. Allport developed the 16 PF questionnaire in order to measure cardinal, central, and secondary traits.

_____ 3. One main criticism of trait theories is that people do not behave as consistently from one situation to another as trait theories would tend to predict.

Psychoanalytic Theory

_____ 4. The ego operates according to the pleasure principle and seeks immediate gratification.

_____

_____

_____ 5. To Freud, the dynamics of personality center around conflict between the impulse-driven id, the guilt-inducing superego, and the ego or mediator.

_____

_____

_____ 6. Extraversion is expressed as shyness, reclusiveness, and innerdirectedness.

_____

_____

_____ 7. The concept of inferiority complex is associated with Horney's personality theory.

_____

_____

Behaviorist and Social-Learning Theories

_____ 8. To Skinner, one's personality is the sum total of overt and covert responses to the surrounding world.

_____

_____

_____ 9. Unlike the behaviorist approach, the social-learning approach emphasizes the role of cognitive processes in influencing personality.

_____

_____

Humanistic Theories

_____ 10. Humanistic theorists believe that man's primary motivation is to strive for superiority.

_____

_____

_____ 11. According to Maslow, self-actualized individuals tend to be conformists.

_____

_____

Personality Assessment

_____ 12. Both behavioral observation and interviews might be influenced by observer bias.

_____

_____

_____ 13. Criterion-keyed tests include the MMPI, CPI, and TAT.

_____

_____

Answer Key

1. T **(514)**	6. F **(530)**	10. F **(536)**
2. F **(517)**	7. F **(531)**	11. F **(538)**
3. T **(517)**	8. T **(532)**	12. T **(540-542)**
4. F **(522)**	9. T **(533)**	13. F **(544)**
5. T **(523-524)**		

PART V. MULTIPLE-CHOICE QUESTIONS

Choose the best answer to each question. Circle your choice. Check your answers against the Answer Key. Questions marked with an asterisk (*) include annotated answers.

What Is Personality?

1. A common theme in definitions of personality is that

    a. the unconscious mind plays a prominent role.
    b. the environment shapes our personalities.
    c. personality refers to distinctive patterns of behavior.
    d. man's primary motivations are negative in nature.

2. Personality psychology may best be described as the study of

    a. how much personality an individual has.
    b. individuals.
    c. the development of personality traits.
    d. the consistency of personality traits.

Evaluating the Trait Theories

3. Trait theories of personality attempt to _____ personality.

    a. predict
    b. describe
    c. explain
    d. describe and explain

4. Allport called traits that guide nearly all of a person's behavior _____ traits.

    a. cardinal
    b. central
    c. secondary
    d. surface

5. According to Allport, most people can be characterized by a relatively small number of generalized and enduring _____ traits.

   a. personality

   b. source

   c. cardinal

   d. central

6. The 16 Personality Factor Questionnaire was created by

   a. Maslow.

   b. Bandura.

   c. Cattell.

   d. Allport.

7. According to Catell, clusters of surface traits combine to give rise to _____ traits.

   a. source

   b. global

   c. central

   d. cardinal

8. Which of the following is *not* a common criticism of trait theories?

   a. These do not explain behavior but only label behavior as being the result of a personality trait.

   b. People's behavior is not as consistent from situation to situation as trait theories would have us believe.

   c. These do not attempt to describe behavior.

   d. These do not explain how personality develops.

Psychoanalytic Theory

9. Freud's psychoanalytic theory does *not* emphasize

   a. the influence of early childhood experiences on personality development.

   b. man's aggressive urges.

   c. the influence of the unconscious mind.

   d. man's striving to develop, change, and grow.

10. The storehouse of largely unconscious, biologically based, instinctive drives that provide the basic energy source for the entire personality system describes the

   a. superego.

   b. id.

   c. libido.

   d. ego.

11. The psychic structure, which seeks to delay gratification when satisfaction might bring disapproval from others, is the

   a. preconscious.

   b. id.

   c. ego.

   d. superego.

*12. Which concept does *not* belong with the other three?

    a. Reality principle
    b. Ego-ideal
    c. Superego
    d. Conscience

13. A person who tends to be selfish, demanding, and disregards the rights of other people, would appear to have a stronger _____ than _____ .

    a. ego | superego
    b. ego-ideal | conscience
    c. superego | id
    d. id | superego

14. The _____ uses _____ to protect itself from harsh aspects of reality.

    a. ego | fixations
    b. id | offense mechanisms
    c. superego | defense mechanisms
    d. ego | defense mechanisms

15. The most basic defense mechanism that underlies all other defense mechanisms is

    a. repression.
    b. distortion.
    c. regression.
    d. rationalization.

*16. A mother who unconsciously hates her child and says, "We have a bad relationship because the child hates me," would be using the defense mechanisms of

    a. displacement.
    b. reaction formation.
    c. regression.
    d. projection.

17. Which of the following pairs of terms do not belong together?

    a. anal stage | toilet training
    b. latency stage | Oedipus complex
    c. oral stage | sucking
    d. phallic stage | genital stimulation

18. Inadequate or excessive gratification during any psychosexual stage may cause

    a. the death wish.
    b. a fixation.
    c. repression.
    d. regression.

19. With the exception of one, all of the following Freudian concepts continue to influence personality psychology today. Which is the exception?

    a. That unresolved conflicts are central to many psychological problems

    b. Defense mechanisms

    c. That sex is the dominant motivating force throughout life

    d. The unconscious mind

20. _____ suggested that all people acquire a feeling of inferiority early in childhood.

    a. Adler

    b. Rogers

    c. Jung

    d. Horney

*21. Which of the following statements is *true*?

    a. Allport believed that man's primary motivation is striving for superiority.

    b. Horney believed that a child's primary need is for security.

    c. Adler first proposed the concepts of introversion and extroversion.

    d. Jung proposed that the personal unconscious contains ancestral memories of all mankind.

Behaviorist and Social-Learning Theories

22. Behaviorists are more interested in _____ than in _____ .

    a. the unconscious mind | the pattern of reinforcement

    b. behavioral consistencies | changes in behavior

    c. changes in behavior | behavioral consistencies

    d. describing personality | explaining personality

23. Skinner would explain why one student would respond positively to a B on a test while another student would respond negatively by saying that

    a. one student has a stronger superego than the other.

    b. one student has more self-efficacy than the other.

    c. the students have different personality traits.

    d. the students have different histories of reinforcement.

24. Behaviorists and social-learning theorists hold different perspectives concerning

    a. the importance of cognitive interpretation of external events.

    b. whether or not environmental factors influence personality.

    c. the importance of the libido.

    d. the existence of personality traits.

25. What principle is involved in the following situation? You find the students at your college to be friendly because most of them smile and say "Hi" when you greet them, whereas your roommate finds the students to be unfriendly and says no one ever smiles or says "Hi" to her.

    a. Rationalization

    b. Self-efficacy

    c. Reciprocal determination

    d. Basic anxiety

26. Bandura's concept of self-efficacy would suggest that a boy who thinks himself a bad athlete

   a. would not play many sports.
   b. would spend a great deal of time practicing alone in order to improve.
   c. Either of the above are true.
   d. Neither of the above are true.

Humanistic Theories

27. Personality theories that emphasize qualities such as creativity, spontaneity, joy, love, and striving for fulfillment are _____ theories.

   a. psychoanalytic
   b. social-learning
   c. trait
   d. humanistic

28. According to Rogers, if your self-concept is consistent with your experiences then you

   a. will probably self-actualize.
   b. have high self-efficacy.
   c. will be likely to show maladjustment.
   d. will be likely to show a healthy adjustment.

29. According to Rogers, the person that you would like to become is your _____ self.

   a. goal
   b. ideal
   c. real
   d. future

30. Maslow proposed that if all lesser needs are met a person would be motivated toward

   a. self-determination.
   b. self-actualization.
   c. self-esteem.
   d. the third force.

31. Which of the following is *not* a characteristic of a self-actualized person?

   a. Has a lively sense of humor
   b. Is creative
   c. Tends to require the company of others
   d. Is open and spontaneous

32. One main criticism of humanistic theories is that

   a. these emphasize the unconscious id more than the conscious superego.
   b. it is difficult to conduct experiments examining the concepts of humanistic theories.
   c. these do not emphasize negative influences on personality development.
   d. these completely ignore cognitive factors.

Personality Assessment

33. Which of the following is *not* an important method used to assess an individual's personality?

    a. Psychoanalysis
    b. Paper-and-pencil questionnaires
    c. Projective tests
    d. Behavioral observation

34. If your college has evaluation forms for students to complete at the end of the semester evaluating their instructors, your college is using a technique similar to

    a. criterion-keyed forms.
    b. projective tests.
    c. paper-and-pencil questionnaires.
    d. rating scales.

*35. With which type of assessment technique would you expect a number of psychologists to draw the most similar conclusions?

    a. Paper-and-pencil questionnaires
    b. Projective tests
    c. Behavioral observation
    d. Interviews

36. Which of the following is a limitation of the MMPI?

    a. It lacks the capacity to differentiate reliably within each of the categories of normal and disturbed individuals.
    b. It is unable to be used in diagnosing.
    c. It contains too few questions.
    d. It was normed on normal individuals.

37. Which paper-and-pencil questionnaire was recently revised?

    a. 16 PF
    b. WAIS
    c. MMPI
    d. CPI

38. If you are interested in objectively assessing or describing the personality of a normal individual, which of the following tests would be most appropriate to use?

    a. Rorschach inkblot test
    b. CPI
    c. MMPI
    d. TAT

*39. Which type of personality theorist would be *least* likely to utilize projective personality tests?

    a. Neo-Freudian
    b. Psychoanalytic
    c. Behaviorist
    d. All of the above would be equally likely to use projective tests.

40. If a psychologist asks you to tell a story concerning a scene on a card he or she shows you, that psychologist is giving you the

    a. CPI.
    b. TAT.
    c. 16 PF.
    d. Rorschach inkblot test.

41. Personality assessment techniques designed to tap unconscious thoughts and feelings are

    a. interviews.
    b. subjective tests.
    c. projective tests.
    d. objective tests.

Answer Key

1. c (513-514)	10. b (521-522)	18. b (528)	26. a (534)	34. d (540)
2. b (514)	11. c (522)	19. c (529)	27. d (536)	*35. a (542)
3. b (514-515)	*12. a (523)	20. a (531)	28. d (537)	36. a (543-544)
4. a (515)	13. d (522)	*21. b (531)	29. b (537)	37. c (543-544)
5. d (515)	14. d (524)	22. c (532)	30. b (537)	38. b (544)
6. c (517)	15. a (524)	23. d (532)	31. c (538)	*39. c (544)
7. a (517)	*16. d (525)	24. a (533)	32. b (538-539)	40. b (545-546)
8. c (517)	17. b (527-528)	25. c (534)	33. a (539)	41. c (544)
9. d (536)				

Annotated Answers

12. The correct choice is a. The ego is the structure of the personality that operates according to the reality principle.
    b. The ego-ideal is one subsystem of the superego.
    c. The superego has two subsystems.
    d. The conscience is the second subsystem of the superego.

16. The correct choice is d. Projection involves attributing your own unacceptable impulses (hating your child) to someone else (it's the child who hates me).
    a. Displacement refers to redirecting behavior from one person (your boss who reprimanded you unfairly) to another person (your child). You want to hit your boss but would instead hit your child.
    b. Reaction formation involves replacing an unacceptable impulse with its acceptable opposite impulse. If the mother in the example were to use reaction formation, she would say she loves her child and most likely would be an overly loving indulgent mother.
    c. Regression involves having your behavior revert to a less-mature stage of development and is not directly concerned with the person's impulses or thought processes. Perhaps a mother who hates her child would throw a temper tantrum and ask her child "Why do you make me hate you?"

21. The correct choice is b. Horney believed that a child's primary need is for security, which would be met if the child is reared in a home environment with love, caring, and good parenting practices.

  a. Adler (not Allport) believed that man's primary motivation is striving for superiority.

  c. Jung (not Adler) first proposed the concepts of introversion and extroversion.

  d. Jung proposed that the collective (not personal) unconscious contains ancestral memories of all mankind.

35. The correct choice is a. Because paper-and-pencil questionnaires (MMPI, CAT) are objective tests, these would be scored the same by all psychologists. In scoring a paper-and-pencil questionnaire the psychologist simply adds up or tallies an individual's responses to the questions.

  b. Because projective tests (Rorschach inkblot test, TAT) are ambiguous to take they are also ambiguous to score. The interpretation of these tests is subjective and psychologists do not always agree on how to properly score responses.

  c. Psychologists might not make similar observations or reach similar conclusions with behavioral observation because, even if the psychologists observed exactly the same behavior, each psychologist's observations would be subject to observer bias.

  d. As is the case with behavioral observations, interviews are subject to observer bias because the basic data of interviews is difficult to quantify and is therefore subject to the psychologist's individual or unique interpretation.

39. The correct choice is c. Projective tests are designed to tap unconscious thoughts and feelings, because the behaviorists reject the influence of inner forces (both conscious and unconscious) they would not use projective tests.

  a. Neo-Freudians would utilize projective tests because they are concerned with the unconscious.

  b. Psychoanalytic theorists (Freud and the neo-Freudians) would utilize projective tests. The unconscious mind is central to Freud's theory and a Freudian would utilize projective tests to help "unlock" the unconscious.

  d. This choice is incorrect because behaviorists (c) would not be at all likely to use projective tests.

PART VI. SUMMARY TABLES

To test your understanding of the material discussed in this chapter complete the following tables. Check your answers with those supplied in PART IX.

Summary of Personality Theories

Type of Theory	Individual(s)	Basic Assumptions or Description	Strengths	Criticisms and/or Limitations
Trait				
Psychoanalytic				

Neo-Freudian	Behaviorist	Social-learning	Humanistic

Personality Tests

Test	Projective or Objective	Description	Strengths	Weaknesses
MMPI				
CPI				
Rorschach Inkblot Test				
TAT				

PART VII. THOUGHT QUESTIONS/CRITICAL THINKING

Prepare answers to the following discussion questions.

1. Describe the id, ego, and superego by using an analogy to a company in which labor and management have just called in a mediator to resolve problems with the union contract agreement that is being negotiated.

2. Defense mechanisms are the ego's method of protecting oneself from the harsh aspects of reality. Think of the ego as frequently having a choice of which defense mechanism to use in a given situation. Describe how the ego could deal with each of the following situations by using at least three of the following: repression, rationalization, projection, displacement, regression, and reaction formation.
   a. A student gets a D on a test in a subject that is required for his or her major.
   b. A young man's fiancée just broke off their engagement.

3. You know yourself better than anyone else does. Which type of personality theory described in the text best accounts for your present personality (or distinctive pattern of behavior)? Explain.

4. If you were employed in the personnel department of a company and could give one personality test to potential employees, which of the tests described in the text would you use? Why did you choose that test over the other tests?

PART VIII. APPLICATIONS

1. Each of the types of personality theories described in the text have some aspects of personality that they account for in an adequate-to-good manner. However, no one theory supplies a complete and thorough explanation for all aspects of and influences on personality. To account for personality as a whole it may be necessary to mix and match from among the different theories, or to take the positives or strengths and reject the negatives or weaknesses of each theory. What do you see as the components of such a mixed-and-matched personality theory?

2. Describe each of the following individual's personalities from the psychoanalytic, behaviorist and/or social-learning and humanistic perspectives:
   a. John is a 24-year-old who has had a series of unsuccessful relationships with the opposite sex. His girlfriends typically break up with him after a couple of months. They state that he is unable to compromise and is selfish. John was the only child in an upper-middle-class family. John is planning a career in business because he believes that he should be fairly successful in that field and should make enough money to live comfortably.
   b. Diane is 35 years old, and now that her youngest child is in school, has decided to return to college and complete her teaching degree. She feels that she has a "calling" to teach young children. Her family is supportive of her plans, and her many friends feel that with her warm and caring personality she will make an excellent teacher.
   c. Tom is a 10-year-old problem child and his parents are at a loss as to what to do about the situation. Tom has a history of being disruptive at school and is a bully.

He takes no responsibility for his actions and says that the other children pick on him and start fights. Recently, some of the other children's belongings have been stolen, and Tom's teacher suspects him. Tom denies of any wrongdoing. His parents have always believed Tom's side of the story in the past and do so in this situation. Tom's dad, who feels that you should "Do what you have to do" and not let other people get in your way, is considering going to the school board to have the teacher reprimanded for falsely accusing Tom.

PART IX. SUMMARY TABLES SOLUTIONS

Summary of Personality Theories

Type of Theory	Individual(s)	Basic Assumptions or Description	Strengths	Criticisms and/or Limitations
Trait	Allport Cattell	Attempt to identify specific dimensions or characteristics associated with different personalities Traits account for consistency in the behavior of an individual and also account for differences in behavior between individuals	Provide methods (e.g., Cattell's 16PF) to assess basic characteristics	Describe, but do not explain, dynamics of personality or how personality develops An individual's behavior may not be consistent from one situation to the next
Psychoanalytic	Freud	Personality is shaped by an on-going conflict between primary urges (sexual and aggressive) and pressures of civilized society In other terms between the impulse-driven id and the guilt-inducing superego with the ego attempting to reconcile both with the demands of reality Personality is essentially formed during childhood as child pro-gresses through five stages of psychosexual development	Perspective concerning unconscious, defense mechanisms, and unre-solved conflicts being central to many psy-chological problems; still used today	Difficult to test experimentally because of lack of operational definitions and precise predictions Focuses on troubled individuals, therefore theory tends to emphasize negative components Too strong an emphasis on early childhood experiences determining personality

Theory	Theorists	Main ideas		Evaluation
Neo-Freudian	Jung Adler Horney	Agree with Freud regarding the role of the unconscious, importance of childhood experiences, and basic interpretation of the structure of personality. Disagree with Freud regarding the emphasis on sexual conflict and aggressive impulses, and importance of biological determinants of personality	With emphasis on social influences supply a broader framework than Freudian theory	Many of the same limitations as Freudian theory, but because some neo-Freudian theorist make more specific predictions concerning future behavior and personality, are more easily scientifically tested
Behaviorist	Skinner	Emphasizes the role of external events in personality formation. Personality is the sum total of individuals' overt and covert responses to the world around them. Personality "traits" are the result of stable environment and consistent patterns of reinforcement	Emphasis on behavior change and experimental research	Completely disregards not only the role of the unconscious, but also conscious cognitive processes
Social-learning	Bandura	Adds cognitive processes to behaviorist approach. Personality shaped by interaction between cognitive and environmental factors	Similar to behaviorist and more well rounded with the inclusion of cognitive factors	Tends to ignore the truly human dimensions of personality that are the focus of humanistic theories
Humanistic	Rogers Maslow	Man's primary motivation is to develop, change, and grow toward full realization of potential. Emphasizes individual's subjective view of reality	Focus on positive dimensions of personality (creativity, spontaneity, joy, love). Focus on healthy personality	Key terms subjective and lack operational definitions so is difficult to test experimentally. Largely ignores the influence of environmental factors

Personality Tests

Test	Projective or Objective	Description	Strengths	Weaknesses
MMPI	Objective	Designed for diagnosing psychological disorders. Contains 566 true–false statements about individuals' behaviors, thoughts, and emotional reactions. Scored on 10 clinical scales (e.g., depression, schizophrenia, paranoia) and also has four validity scales	Differentiates well between disturbed and normal individuals (between the two groups)	Does not reliably differentiate among disturbed and normal individuals (within each group). Low test–retest reliability
CPI	Objective	Designed for use with normal individuals. Format similar to MMPI. Scored on 15 "normal" personality traits (e.g., dominance, sociability, self-acceptance) and also has three response-bias scales	High test–retest reliability. Good predictive validity for a variety of purposes (e.g., job success, leadership, conformity)	Not appropriate for diagnosing disturbed individuals
Rorschach Inkblot Test	Projective	Consists of 10 cards with inkblots. Individual describes what inkblot looks like or brings to mind. Complex scoring system resulting in subjective interpretation	One of the most widely used techniques for clinical diagnosis and personality assessment	Interpretation is highly subjective, therefore is of questionable validity. However, the Rorschach is typically used along with other assessment procedures
TAT	Projective	Consists of 30 cards of vague and ambiguous scenes and one blank card. Individual tells a "story" related to the scene. Psychologist typically looks for common themes in the stories	Is a useful tool for research purposes and has adequate levels of validity	Similar to the Rorschach, interpretation is subjective. It is typically used for diagnostic purposes along with other assessment techniques

CHAPTER **15**

Psychological Disorders

PART I. LEARNING OBJECTIVES

When you finish studying this chapter you should be able to:

Defining Abnormality | Classifying Psychological Disorders

1. Discuss four criteria that may be used to distinguish normal from abnormal behavior. **(555-556)**

2. Summarize the development of the Diagnostic and Statistical Manual (DSM) classification system from DSM-I through DSM-III-R. **(556-557)**

Anxiety Disorders

3. Define anxiety, and list seven types of anxiety disorders. **(557-558)**

4. Describe panic disorder, and discuss the relationship between panic disorder and agoraphobia. **(558-559)**

5. Define phobia, and describe simple phobia and two types of social phobias. **(559)**

6. Describe obsessive–compulsive disorder. **(560-561)**

7. Describe posttraumatic stress disorder (PTSD), and explain how it differs from other anxiety disorders. **(561)**

8. Describe generalized anxiety disorder. **(561-562)**

9. Summarize the psychoanalytic, behavior/learning, and biological perspectives concerning anxiety disorders. **(562-563)**

Somatoform Disorders

10. Describe the general characteristics of somatoform disorders, and list three categories of somatoform disorders. **(566-568)**

11. Describe somatization disorder and hypochondriasis, and differentiate between the two. **(566-567)**

12. Describe conversion disorder. **(567-568)**

13. Summarize the psychoanalytic, behavior/learning, and biological perspectives concerning somatoform disorders. **(569)**

Dissociative Disorders

14. Describe the general characteristics of dissociative disorders, and list three types of dissociative disorders. **(569-570)**

15. Describe and differentiate between psychogenic amnesia and psychogenic fugue disorder. **(569)**

16. Describe multiple personality, and discuss what type of childhood experiences appear to be associated with this disorder. **(570-571)**

17. Summarize the psychoanalytic, behavior/learning, and biological perspectives concerning dissociative disorders. **(571)**

Mood Disorders

18. Describe the general characteristic of mood disorders, and list three mood disorders. **(572)**

19. Describe major depression (unipolar disorder). **(573)**

20. Describe bipolar disorder (manic-depressive disorder). **(573-574)**

21. Describe seasonal affective disorder (SAD). **(577)**

22. Summarize and evaluate the psychoanalytic, behavior/learning, and biological perspectives concerning mood disorders. **(579-581)**

23. Discuss the evidence that mood disorders involve an interaction of biological predispositions and psychosocial factors. **(584)**

24. Describe sex differences in incidence of depression, and discuss proposed explanations. **(585)**

Schizophrenic Disorders

25. Describe six primary symptoms of schizophrenia, and the three stages of the disorder. **(587-590)**

26. List the five subtypes of schizophrenia, and describe the secondary symptoms associated with each subtype. **(590-591)**

27. Summarize and evaluate the psychoanalytic, behavior/learning, and biological perspectives concerning schizophrenic disorders. **(591-592)**

28. Describe the interactional model that proposes that biological and environmental factors combine to influence the development of schizophrenia. **(594-595)**

Personality Disorders

29. List the characteristics that are common to the personality disorders, and describe the three clusters of personality disorders. **(595)**

30. Describe antisocial personality disorder, and summarize the psychoanalytic, behavior/ learning, and biological perspectives concerning antisocial personality disorder. **(595, 597-600)**

PART II. OVERVIEW

The term abnormal behavior relates to psychological disorders. The four criteria for abnormality are atypicality, maladaptivity, psychological discomfort, and social unacceptability. All four criteria do not need to be present for a behavior to be considered abnormal. This chapter discusses several categories of psychological disorders and a number of specific disorders in each category.

The anxiety disorders, which are the most common disorders in the United States, all involve anxiety (feelings of dread or apprehension) typically accompanied by physiological reactions such as an increased heart rate and muscle tension. The anxiety disorders differ in the ways or the situations in which individuals experiences anxiety. The anxiety disorders include panic disorder, agoraphobia, simple and social phobias, obsessive–compulsive disorder, posttraumatic stress disorder, and generalized anxiety disorder.

The primary symptoms of the somatoform disorders are physical in nature but there is no physical basis for these symptoms. Somatization disorder involves a number of chronic physical symptoms (such as aches and pains). Hypochondriasis is characterized by an individual believing that physical symptoms are indications of serious health problems. Conversion disorders involve a person experiencing sensory or motor disturbances (such as blindness or paralysis).

The dissociative disorders are characterized by thoughts and feelings that generate anxiety being dissociated (or removed) from conscious awareness. The dissociative disorders involve memory loss or a change in identity. Psychogenic amnesia, psychogenic fugue disorder, and multiple personality are dissociative disorders.

The primary symptom of the mood disorders is depression, which is characterized by feelings of sadness, dejection, and hopelessness, and physical symptoms (such as changes in activity level and eating and sleeping patterns). Major depression occurs when an individual is in a deep enduring depression. Bipolar disorder is characterized by periods of depression alternating with periods of mania (elation and euphoria). Recurrent episodes of depression that occur in either the winter or summer are diagnosed as seasonal affective disorders.

The schizophrenic disorders are very severe and disabling, with primary symptoms of disturbances of thought, emotion, perception, and behavior. A number of subtypes of schizophrenia exist that are differentiated according to the primary and secondary symptoms that are present and include disorganized, catatonic, paranoid, and undifferentiated. An additional subtype—residual schizophrenia—is used to describe the schizophrenic individual who is "recovered or in remission."

Personality disorders refer to long-term, well-developed styles of behavior or personality traits that are maladaptive. Individuals with personality disorders typically do not feel they "have a problem" and tend to refuse treatment. Antisocial personality disorder is very disruptive: These individuals show a chronic and continuous disregard for the rights of others and rules of society and do not experience quilt or remorse for their actions.

Throughout Chapter 15 the psychoanalytic, behavior/learning, and biological perspectives concerning the cause of psychological disorders are discussed. While the psychoanalytic perspective provides explanations for the disorders discussed in this chapter, these explanations are not supported by experimental evidence in a number of instances. The psychoanalytic perspective is most successful in explaining the dissociative disorders. The behavior/learning perspective offers explanations for a number of disorders that rely on classical and operant-conditioning models. The biological perspective concerning psychological disorders receives strong support in regards to the mood disorders and schizophrenia. People with a genetic predisposition regarding the mood disorders or schizophrenia are more likely to develop disorders when certain environmental influences or "triggers" are present.

PART III. KEY TERMS/MATCHING EXERCISES

Match the following concepts and/or individuals with the appropriate descriptions. Check your answers against the Answer Key.

Defining Abnormality | Classifying Psychological Disorders (Overview)

Concepts

_____ 1. somatoform disorders (**566**)

_____ 2. schizophrenic disorders (**586**)

_____ 3. abnormal behavior (**555**)

_____ 4. mood disorders (**572**)

_____ 5. anxiety disorders (**557**)

_____ 6. psychosis (**557**)

_____ 7. personality disorders (**595**)

_____ 8. neurosis (**557**)

_____ 9. DSM-III-R (**556-557**)

_____ 10. dissociative disorders (**569**)

Descriptions

a. Freud's term for severe psychological disorders characterized by reduced contact with reality, disturbances of thinking, and loss of ability to function socially

b. Disorders characterized by extreme disruptions of perceptions, thoughts, emotions, and behavior

c. Defined by emphasizing atypicality, maladaptivity, psychological discomfort, and social unacceptability

d. Disorders involving a separation of thoughts and feelings that cause anxiety from conscious awareness that are characterized by memory loss or a change in identity

e. Disorders characterized by rigid maladaptive behavior or personality traits that tend to develop at a young age; have a poor prognosis for treatment

f. Freud's term for psychological disorders that while distressing and often debilitating do not involve loss of contact with reality and inability to perform daily tasks

g. Disorders that have depression as the primary symptom

h. Characterized by feelings of dread or apprehension that are frequently accompanied by physiological reactions

i. Disorders that are expressed through physical symptoms

j. Used to classify and diagnose psychological disorders

Answer Key   1. i   2. b   3. c   4. g   5. h   6. a   7. e   8. f   9. j   10. d

Anxiety Disorders

Concepts

_____ 1. social phobia **(559)**

_____ 2. posttraumatic stress disorder (PTSD) **(561)**

_____ 3. agoraphobia **(558-559)**

_____ 4. generalized anxiety disorder **(561-562)**

_____ 5. phobias **(559)**

_____ 6. panic disorder **(558)**

_____ 7. simple phobias **(559)**

_____ 8. obsessive–compulsive disorder **(560)**

Descriptions

a. Characterized by fear and avoidance of being in open and public places

b. Characterized by reexperiencing and avoidance of stimuli associated with a traumatic event, or numbing of general responsiveness and increased arousal

c. Characterized by persistent unshakable thoughts frequently associated with irresistible repetitious behaviors

d. Characterized by sudden episodes of extreme anxiety with both psychological and physiological components that frequently occur for no apparent reason

e. May involve either an irrational fear of social situations or fear of performing specific behaviors (such as talking or eating publicly)

f. Characterized by persistent apprehension or anxiety in a wide range of situations

g. Relatively common irrational fears of specific objects or situations that are infrequently addressed in clinical settings because they are not very disruptive to the individual

h. Characterized by inappropriate fear and avoidance of specific situations or objects

Answer Key   1. e   2. b   3. a   4. f   5. h   6. d   7. g   8. c

Somatoform Disorders | Dissociative Disorders

Concepts

_____ 1. hypochondriasis **(567)**

_____ 2. psychogenic fugue disorder **(569-570)**

_____ 3. conversion disorder **(567-568)**

_____ 4. multiple personality **(570)**

_____ 5. somatization disorder **(566)**

_____ 6. psychogenic amnesia **(569)**

Descriptions

a. Involves a sudden loss of memory usually after a particularly stressful or traumatic event

b. Characterized by a variety of physical symptoms that the individual believes to be associated with serious illnesses

c. Characterized by multiple and recurrent physical symptoms (such as headaches, dizziness, and different bodily pains) that do not have a physical cause

d. Characterized by an alternation between an original or primary and one or more secondary or subordinate personalities

e. Typically of brief duration and involves a loss of memory during which the person travels from place to place

f. Manifested by either a sensory disturbance (such as blindness or loss of feeling to parts of the body) or a motor disturbance (such as paralysis) that do not have a physical cause

Answer Key   1. b   2. e   3. f   4. d   5. c   6. a

Mood Disorders | Schizophrenic Disorders | Personality Disorders

Concepts

_____ 1. catatonic schizophrenia **(590)**

_____ 2. seasonal affective disorder (SAD) **(577)**

_____ 3. residual schizophrenia **(591)**

_____ 4. disorganized schizophrenia **(590)**

_____ 5. antisocial personality disorder **(597)**

_____ 6. bipolar disorder **(573)**

_____ 7. undifferentiated schizophrenia **(591)**

_____ 8. major depression **(573)**

_____ 9. paranoid schizophrenia **(591)**

Descriptions

a. Characterized by an extended period of time during which the individual experiences a variety of psychological, psychomotor, and physical manifestations of depression

b. Subtype of schizophrenia, is diagnosed if the schizophrenic individual does not manifest specific symptoms associated with other subtypes of schizophrenia

c. Subtype of schizophrenia that shows the most severe personality disintegration, characterized by extreme disturbances of thought, speech, and constant mood changes

d. Subtype of schizophrenia with the dominant secondary symptom of well-organized delusional thought

e. Subtype of schizophrenia with secondary symptoms of extreme motor disturbances, which may range from stuporous immobility to agitation

f. Characterized by a history of chronic and continual disregard for the rights of others and rules of society, a lack of remorse, and very self-centered behavior

g. Characterized by extreme mood swings with episodes of depression and elation or euphoria alternating regularly

h. Subtype of schizophrenia applied during the third stage of schizophrenia when symptoms are markedly diminished or absent

i. Describes recurrent patterns of depression that are triggered or associated with seasonal changes (such as the decrease in exposure to light during the winter)

Answer Key   1. e   2. i   3. h   4. c   5. f   6. g   7. b   8. a   9. d

PART IV. TRUE-FALSE STATEMENTS

Fill in the blank before each statement with either a T (true) or an F (false). Check your answers against the Answer Key. Then go back to the items that are false and make the necessary change(s) to the statements to convert the items into true statements.

Defining Abnormality | Classifying Psychological Disorders

_____ 1. If a behavior is unusual or atypical it is sufficient to determine that the behavior is abnormal or disordered.

_____

_____

_____ 2. Unlike DSM-I and II, DSM-III-R's two main diagnostic categories are the neuroses and psychoses.

_____

_____

Anxiety Disorders | Somatoform Disorders | Dissociative Disorders

_____ 3. In the United States the most common psychological disorders are anxiety disorders.

_____

_____

_____ 4. A person who does not leave his or her house because of fear associated with being in public places suffers from social phobia.

_____

_____

_____ 5. Dissociative disorders include psychogenic amnesia, conversion disorders, and multiple personality.

_____

_____

_____ 6. Freud believed that somatoform disorders were the result of an individual dealing with anxiety by converting it into physical symptoms.

_____

_____

Mood Disorders | Schizophrenic Disorders

_____ 7. Major depression is much more common than bipolar disorder.

_____

_____

_____ 8. In most cases, major depression lifts over a period of months, even if the individual does not receive treatment.

_____

_____

_____ 9. Considerable evidence supports the psychoanalytic perspective concerning the mood disorders.

_____

_____

_____ 10. Undifferentiated schizophrenics show more severe personality disintegration than individuals with the other subtypes of schizophrenia.

_____

_____

_____ 11. Of the subtypes of schizophrenia, paranoid schizophrenics show the least impairment in ability to carry out daily functions.

_____

_____

Personality Disorders

_____ 12. Personality disorders typically develop in middle adulthood.

_____

_____

_____ 13. Intelligence and charm are two characteristics associated with antisocial personality disorder.

_____

_____

Answer Key			
	1. F **(555)**	6. T **(569)**	10. F **(590)**
	2. F **(556–557)**	7. T **(572–573)**	11. T **(591)**
	3. T **(557)**	8. T **(573)**	12. F **(595)**
	4. F **(558–559)**	9. F **(581)**	13. T **(597)**
	5. F **(569)**		

PART V. MULTIPLE-CHOICE QUESTIONS

Choose the best answer to each question. Circle your choice. Check your answers against the Answer Key. Questions marked with an asterisk (*) include annotated answers.

Defining Abnormality | Classifying Psychological Disorders

1. Which of the following criterion is *not* used to distinguish normal from abnormal behavior?

   a. Psychological discomfort
   b. Depression
   c. Atypicality
   d. Social unacceptability

*2. Which of the following statements is true?

  a. Most psychologists believe that atypicality is the most important criterion for distinguishing psychologically abnormal behavior.

  b. For an individual to be considered to be suffering from a psychological disorder it is necessary to have all four criteria of abnormality present.

  c. A behavior that is considered abnormal in one society may not be considered abnormal in other societies, eras, or cultures.

  d. Maladaptivity may manifest as anxiety, depression, or agitation.

3. The term _____ has historically been used to describe less severe disorders. The term _____ has been used to describe more severe disorders.

  a. psychological | psychiatric

  b. mood disorder | schizophrenia

  c. psychosis | neurosis

  d. neurosis | psychosis

4. When compared to DSM-II, the DSM-III-R has the advantage of

  a. specifying more precisely when a diagnosis should be made.

  b. greater diagnostic validity.

  c. being based completely on the social-learning model.

  d. addressing disorders that have only psychological causes.

Anxiety Disorders

5. Recurring episodes of intense anxiety that have a sudden onset for no apparent reason describes

  a. generalized anxiety disorder.

  b. panic disorder.

  c. obsessive–compulsive disorder.

  d. agoraphobia.

6. John attempts to control his anxiety by staying in the "safety" of his own home, the only place where he does not experience anxiety, John has

  a. social phobia.

  b. antisocial personality disorder.

  c. panic disorder.

  d. agoraphobia.

7. An anxiety disorder characterized by a persistent, irrational fear of performing some specific behavior (such as talking or eating) in the presence of other people is called a(n)

  a. simple phobia.

  b. social phobia.

  c. agoraphobia.

  d. triskaidekaphobia.

8. Kimberly constantly thinks her immaculate house is dirty and spends most of her time cleaning, scrubbing, and straightening up. She could be diagnosed as suffering from a(n)

   a. thought disorder.
   b. simple dirt phobia.
   c. obsessive–compulsive disorder.
   d. generalized anxiety disorder.

9. A person with a _____ experiences anxiety in only certain specific situations, whereas an individual with _____ experiences chronic anxiety in a wide variety of situations.

   a. phobia | generalized anxiety disorder
   b. generalized anxiety disorder | phobia
   c. social phobia | simple phobia
   d. agoraphobia | obsessive–compulsive disorder

10. Martin Seligman (1971) suggests that we develop phobias as a result of

   a. a biological predisposition to react fearfully to certain potentially dangerous stimuli.
   b. repressed hostility.
   c. classical conditioning.
   d. operant conditioning.

11. If you interpret your roommate's fear of asking a girl out for a date as a phobia resulting from the fact that the last three girls he asked out said no, your interpretation would be consistent with the _____ perspective concerning anxiety disorders.

   a. biological
   b. humanistic
   c. behavioral/learning
   d. psychoanalytic

Somatoform Disorders

12. A person who interprets every upset stomach as a sign of appendicitis would most likely be diagnosed as having

   a. a health phobia.
   b. somatization disorder.
   c. depression.
   d. hypochondriasis.

13. Which type of somatoform disorder typically develops soon after a specific serious stress or conflict?

   a. Multiple personality
   b. Conversion disorder
   c. Somatization disorder
   d. Hypochondriasis

14. An individual with _____ would most likely receive unnecessary medications or unnecessary surgery.

   a. somatization disorder
   b. conversion disorder
   c. psychogenic amnesia
   d. hypochondriasis

15. The _____ perspective proposes that the somatoform disorders result from anxiety associated with unresolved conflicts being converted into physical symptoms.

   a. behavior/learning
   b. biological
   c. humanistic
   d. psychoanalytic

Dissociative Disorders

16. Your careless smoking caused your family's home to burn down. You are most likely to develop

   a. panic disorder.
   b. multiple personality.
   c. psychogenic amnesia.
   d. psychogenic fugue disorder.

17. The police in your hometown pick up a man found loitering at the bus station at night who does not know his name. Most likely that person is suffering from

   a. paranoid schizophrenia.
   b. multiple personality.
   c. psychogenic fugue disorder.
   d. psychogenic amnesia.

18. Individuals, like Eve from *The Three Faces of Eve*, suffer from

   a. psychogenic amnesia.
   b. conversion disorder.
   c. schizophrenia.
   d. multiple personality.

19. Which of the following terms does *not* belong?

   a. Psychogenic fugue disorder
   b. Conversion disorder
   c. Dissociative disorder
   d. Multiple personality

20. A history of significant childhood trauma—primarily sexual abuse—is frequently associated with

   a. generalized anxiety disorder.
   b. multiple personality.
   c. psychogenic amnesia.
   d. schizophrenia.

*21. Freud's view that excessive application of defense mechanisms can lead to serious disorders is provided the best support by the _____ disorders.

  a. anxiety
  b. dissociative
  c. schizophrenic
  d. mood

Mood Disorders

22. Which of the following categories of symptoms are *not* characteristic of the mood disorders?

  a. Anxiety
  b. A marked change in activity level
  c. Feelings of sadness, hopelessness, and despair
  d. Insomnia or excessive sleep

23. People who become lethargic and sleep more than usual typify the mood disorder termed

  a. major depression.
  b. bipolar disorder.
  c. conversion disorder.
  d. schizophrenic disorder.

24. Jeff alternates periods of euphoria and frantic activity with periods of deep depression and is suffering from

  a. seasonal affective disorder.
  b. obsessive–compulsive disorder.
  c. major depression.
  d. bipolar disorder.

*25. The individual who would most likely suffer an episode of major depression in the future is a

  a. person who experienced an initial episode of major depression at age 17.
  b. person who experienced an initial episode of major depression at age 38.
  c. person with a history of bipolar disorder.
  d. 35-year-old who has never had a psychological disorder.

26. False perceptions that lack a sensory basis—such as hearing imaginary voices—are

  a. associated with unresolved sexual conflicts.
  b. illusions.
  c. hallucinations.
  d. delusions.

27. A disproportionately high incidence of _____ is found among creative individuals.

  a. psychosis
  b. bipolar disorder
  c. major depression
  d. panic disorder

28. If your therapist suggests that you should receive an increased exposure to artificial light, you most likely

    a. suffer from major depression.
    b. suffer from seasonal mania disorder.
    c. suffer from seasonal affective disorder.
    d. have a schizophrenic therapist.

29. Research suggests that brain level of melatonin may be related to

    a. major depression.
    b. bipolar disorder.
    c. schizophrenia.
    d. seasonal affective disorder.

30. According to the behavioral and learning theorists' perspective, mood disorders are

    a. caused by repressed love/hate relationships.
    b. the result of the loss of a primary source of reinforcement, such as the loss of a loved one or of a loss of any kind.
    c. the result of classical conditioning.
    d. caused by a deficiency of brain chemicals.

31. The interactive model of mood disorders proposes that _____ factors are responsible for an individual having a predisposition or tendency to develop a mood disorder and _____ factors help determine whether a disorder will develop.

    a. psychoanalytic | behavior/learning
    b. behavior/learning | psychoanalytic
    c. psychosocial or environmental | biological
    d. biological | psychosocial or environmental

Schizophrenic Disorders

32. Which of the following is *not* a primary symptom of schizophrenia?

    a. Emotional expression disturbances
    b. Social withdrawal
    c. Psychomotor disturbances
    d. Thought disturbances

33. It is common for schizophrenics to invent new words or

    a. neologisms.
    b. divergent vocabulary.
    c. echolalia.
    d. word salad.

34. The disturbances in emotional expression associated with schizophrenia are characterized

    a. by a blunted or flat affect.
    b. as inappropriate.
    c. Neither of the above apply.
    d. Either of the above apply.

35. Well-organized delusional thought characterizes _____ schizophrenia.

    a. paranoid
    b. residual
    c. catatonic
    d. disorganized

36. You observe a schizophrenic individual who remains in a bizarre position for several hours. That individual would be diagnosed as having _____ schizophrenia.

    a. residual
    b. disorganized
    c. paralyzed
    d. catatonic

*37. The _____ hypothesis suggests that schizophrenia is caused by either abnormally high levels of or an increased reactivity to a specific neurotransmitter.

    a. endorphin
    b. permissive amine
    c. dopamine
    d. norepinephrine

Personality Disorders

*38. Which of the following statements concerning personality disorders is true?

    a. Manifestations of or symptoms become more obvious during middle and old age.
    b. The prognosis for overcoming any of the personality disorders is poor.
    c. People with personality disorders are likely to request psychological treatment.
    d. Personality disorders usually develop during the mid-to-late 20s.

39. The charming con man, who allows rich young women to fall in love with him and then steals their money, might well be diagnosed as having

    a. multiple personality.
    b. paranoid schizophrenia.
    c. antisocial personality disorder.
    d. bipolar disorder.

40. The psychoanalytic perspective concerning antisocial personality disorder suggests that these individuals

    a. did not develop an id.
    b. did not develop an ego.
    c. did not develop a superego.
    d. have not learned to avoid punishment.

Answer Key

1. b	**(555)**	9. a	**(561)**	17. c	**(570)**	*25. a	**(573)**	33. a	**(588)**
*2. c	**(556)**	10. a	**(563)**	18. d	**(570)**	26. c	**(574)**	34. d	**(589)**
3. d	**(557)**	11. c	**(563)**	19. b	**(569)**	27. b	**(574-575)**	35. a	**(591)**
4. a	**(557)**	12. d	**(567)**	20. b	**(570)**	28. c	**(577)**	36. d	**(590-591)**
5. b	**(558)**	13. b	**(567-568)**	*21. b	**(591)**	29. d	**(584)**	*37. c	**(593)**
6. d	**(558-559)**	14. a	**(566)**	22. a	**(572)**	30. b	**(579-580)**	*38. b	**(595)**
7. b	**(559)**	15. d	**(569)**	23. b	**(572)**	31. d	**(584)**	39. c	**(595, 597)**
8. c	**(560)**	16. c	**(569)**	24. d	**(573)**	32. c	**(587)**	40. c	**(598)**

Annotated Answers

2. The correct choice is c. Each society decides what is considered abnormal or disordered. For example, our society views hallucinations as a sign of a serious disorder (frequently schizophrenia), while some societies in Polynesia and South America view hallucinations as a great gift.
   a. Atypicality alone is not sufficient to classify a behavior as abnormal. The text does mention that some psychologists view maladaptivity as the most important criterion.
   b. Although all disorders are considered atypical, any given disorder may show only one or a combination of maladaptivity, psychological discomfort, and social unacceptability.
   d. It is psychological discomfort (not maladaptivity) that may manifest as anxiety, depression, or agitation.

21. The correct choice is b. The dissociative disorders involve a memory loss (psychogenic amnesia, and fugue) or a change in identity (multiple personality). According to Freud, all involve an extreme use of the defense mechanism of repression to deal with (or deny) anxiety-producing situations. Freud's view makes sense on an intuitive level, and the behavioral/learning and biological perspectives do not offer well-developed or cohesive explanations for the dissociative disorders.
   a. Freud's explanation for the different anxiety disorders involves using defense mechanisms to deal with internal conflicts involving sexual and aggressive impulses, and proposes that different conflicts (Oedipal complex, anal fixation) result in different disorders. If you are a "true Freudian" these explanations may appear reasonable, however, the behavioral/learning perspective proposing a conditioning model offers a simpler explanation.
   c. Freud's explanation of the schizophrenic disorders centers around massive regression to the oral stage and receives little serious support today. The biological perspective is the focus of great attention today.
   d. Freud's explanation of the mood disorders stresses oral fixation that results in excessive self-hatred (depression) and self-love (mania). Research evidence does not support this view. As is the case with the mood disorders, the biological perspective has received far more experimental support.

25. The correct choice is a. One of the primary factors related to an occurrence (or relapse) of major depression is if the individual had had an initial episode of major depression prior to age 20.

    b. The age of this individual's initial episode of major depression occurred at an older age than the individual in choice a, therefore, this individual would be less likely to suffer another episode of major depression.

    c. Because major depression and bipolar disorder are two separate disorders a history of bipolar disorder would not increase the probability of developing major depression.

    d. Although a 35-year-old without a history of any psychological disorder is not immune from developing major depression, both the individuals described in choices a and b would be at a higher risk to develop a major depression.

37. The correct choice is c. The dopamine hypothesis of schizophrenia has received strong experimental support.

    a. There is no endorphin hypothesis of schizophrenia.

    b. The permissive amine theory is related to the mood disorders.

    d. The norepinephrine theory is also related to the mood disorders.

38. The correct choice is b. The prognosis for overcoming personality disorders is very poor, at least in part, because these individuals do not tend to believe that there is anything wrong with the way they are functioning and tend to refuse treatment.

    a. Symptoms of personality disorders become less (not more) obvious in middle and old age.

    c. Individuals with personality disorders are likely to refuse (not request) psychological treatment.

    d. Personality disorders generally develop in childhood or adolescence (not in the mid-to-late 20s).

PART VI. SUMMARY TABLES

To test your understanding of the material discussed in this chapter complete the following table. Check your answers with those supplied in PART IX.

Summary of Psychological Disorders

Disorder	Type of Disorder	Description
Agoraphobia		
Antisocial personality		
Bipolar disorder		
Catatonic schizophrenia		
Conversion disorder		
Disorganized schizophrenia		
Generalized anxiety disorder		
Hypochondriasis		
Major depression		

Multiple personality		
Obsessive–compulsive disorder		
Panic disorder		
Paranoid schizophrenia		
Psychogenic amnesia		
Psychogenic fugue disorder		
Posttraumatic stress disorder		
Residual schizophrenia		
Seasonal affective disorder		
Simple phobia		
Social phobia		
Somatization disorder		
Undifferentiated schizophrenia		

Theoretical Perspectives Concerning Psychological Disorders

Disorder	Psychoanalytic	Behavioral/Learning	Biological
Anxiety			
Somatoform			
Dissociative			
Mood			
Schizophrenic			
Antisocial personality			

PART VII. THOUGHT QUESTIONS/CRITICAL THINKING

Prepare answers to the following discussion questions.

1. The text defines a simple phobia as an irrational fear of a specific situation or object (for example, heights or spiders). The text defines a social phobia as an irrational fear of performing some specific behavior in the presence of other people (for example, talking or eating). At one level it seems appropriate to consider some social phobias to be simple phobias. Discuss why DSM-III-R considers social phobias a separate disorder.

2. It is very common for people (both educated and uneducated) to incorrectly use the terms *schizophrenia* and *multiple personality*. Differentiate between the two disorders and explain possible reasons why the terms are often confused or used incorrectly.

3. According to the psychoanalytic perspective the anxiety, somatoform, and dissociative disorders develop as a result of an individual's inability to adequately cope with anxiety associated with internal conflicts or unacceptable urges. If you accept this proposal, it would seem that, at least in some instances, an individual has some choice (at an unconscious level) as to which disorder they will develop. You won't ever have a conscious choice as to which type of anxiety, somatoform, or dissociative disorder you might develop. But if you did, which disorder would you choose to develop and which disorder would you be least likely to choose? Explain your selections. (You might want to determine how much disruption each disorder would cause in your life.)

4. Decide on a diagnosis as to what type of disorder each of the following individuals has. Cite specific information to justify your diagnoses.

   a. Linda, a 20-year-old college student, suffers from fatigue, frequent upset stomach, and difficulty sleeping. She is also having difficulty concentrating on her classes and can't seem to study for more than a few minutes at a time. She is worried about her grades, roommate, whether she will find a summer job, and so forth.

   b. Bill, who is in his 40s, is the local town's resident "crazy person." He spends much of his day stationed at an intersection in town where he directs traffic and frequently angrily lectures drivers for ignoring his commands to stop.

   c. Joy is a 32-year-old housewife who is depressed. She has finally decided to see a neurologist because of the headaches and blackouts she has suffered from for a number of years. She fears that she may have inherited some defect from her mother that is responsible for her problems. Her mother was an alcoholic who suffered from blackouts, usually after a drunken incident during which she abused Joy.

   d. John is 29-years-old and works in the same office as your mother. Your mother frequently discusses John's problems. He has been plagued with health problems for the entire year your mother has known him. John has a history of back problems, suffers from migraine headaches, and has been to three doctors about his "nervous stomach." None of the medication he has taken seems to have worked. It seems as though not a day goes by without John complaining about one of his health problems, and your mother feels sorry for him.

PART VIII. APPLICATIONS

1. Psychological disorders (or mental health problems) may be contrasted with physical health problems that have biological causes (disease, injury, etc.). However, the distinction between psychological and physical disorders is not always clear-cut. The somatoform disorders, which have primarily physical symptoms, are considered psychological disorders. Additionally, there is mounting evidence for a physical basis for the mood disorders and schizophrenia (also considered to be psychological disorders). Do you feel somatoform disorders should be considered psychological or physical disorders? Why or why not? Do you feel that mood disorders and schizophrenia should be considered psychological or physical disorders? Why or why not?

2. Decide on one or two possible psychological disorders that each of the following individuals would be most likely to develop. Cite evidence to support your choices.

   a. Bob, a 16-year-old adolescent, recently convinced his girlfriend to engage in sexual intercourse. He has mixed feelings concerning his behavior. Although he (and his girlfriend) found the experience to be satisfying he is also experiencing guilt.

   b. Cathy, as a young child, was subjected to recurrent sexual abuse by her older stepbrother.

   c. Tom, who was first described in application 2(c) in Chapter 14 (page 275).

PART IX. SUMMARY TABLES SOLUTIONS

The following solution corresponds to table on page 298.

Theoretical Perspectives Concerning Psychological Disorders

Disorder	Psychoanalytic	Behavioral/Learning	Biological
Anxiety	Defense mechanisms used to control anxiety associated with internal conflicts involving sexual or aggressive impulses fail or are overused	Classical conditioning, two-factor conditioning, and modeling are responsible	An autonomic nervous system that is more easily aroused or is hypersensitive
Somatoform	Unresolved sexual conflicts are converted into physical symptoms	Symptoms persist if reinforced and allow the person to escape or avoid anxiety	No evidence for biological factors
Dissociative	Repression is used to ward off unacceptable impulses (primarily sexual in nature)	Does not offer a comprehensive explanation Operant avoidance responses are reinforced by allowing the individual to avoid anxiety	No evidence for the biological perspective
Mood	Develops as a result of oral fixation No research evidence supporting this perspective	A loss of a primary source of reinforcement Learned helplessness if an individual believes he or she has little control over rewards and punishments	Genetic factors associated with levels of specific neurotransmitters (norepinephrine, serotonin), in the brain
Schizophrenic	Develops as a result of oral fixation Currently, not a seriously considered explanation	Follows extinction of normal patterns of responding (due to inadequate reinforcers or rewards)	Abnormally high levels of or reactivity to the neurotransmitter dopamine
Antisocial personality	Failure to develop a superego	Failure to learn to avoid punishment and/or punishment has little meaning for these individuals	Higher brain centers that control impulsive actions are slow to develop

The following solution corresponds to table on pages 296–297.

Summary of Psychological Disorders

Disorder	Type of Disorder	Description
Agoraphobia	Anxiety	Intense fear of being in places or situations from which escape might be difficult
Antisocial personality	Personality disorder	History of chronic and continual disregard for the rights of others and rules of society, a lack of remorse, and extreme self-centered behavior
Bipolar disorder	Mood	Extreme mood swings, from immobilizing depression to euphoria and frantic activity
Catatonic schizophrenia	Schizophrenic	Extreme psychomotor disturbances from stuporous immobility (waxy flexibility) to wild excitement and agitation
Conversion disorder	Somatoform	Manifested as sensory or motor-system disturbance for which there is no known organic cause
Disorganized schizophrenia	Schizophrenic	Disorganization and regression in thinking and behavioral patterns
Generalized anxiety disorder	Anxiety	Chronic state of pervasive anxiety (free-floating anxiety)
Hypochondriasis	Somatoform	Complain about a variety of physical symptoms and fear that symptoms indicate serious disease
Major depression	Mood	Deep enduring depression that impairs ability to function effectively

Multiple personality	Dissociative	Alternates between an original or primary personality and one or more secondary or subordinate personalities
Obsessive–compulsive disorder	Anxiety	Reflected in persistent, unwanted, and unshakable thoughts and/or irresistible, habitual, repeated actions
Panic disorder	Anxiety	Experiences four or more panic attacks in a four-week period
Paranoid schizophrenia	Schizophrenic	Dominant symptom is well-developed delusional thoughts
Psychogenic amnesia	Dissociative	Sudden loss of memory (typically, for all events for a specific period of time), usually after a particularly stressful or traumatic event
Psychogenic fugue disorder	Dissociative	Combines amnesia with a "flight" away from an intolerable situation
Posttraumatic stress disorder	Anxiety	Symptoms include reexperiencing a traumatic event, numbing of general responsiveness, and increased arousal
Residual schizophrenia	Schizophrenic	Label used when major symptoms are absent or markedly diminished
Seasonal affective disorder	Mood	Recurrent winter or summer depression
Simple phobia	Anxiety	Irrational fear of a specific situation or object
Social phobia	Anxiety	Irrational fear of performing some specific behavior in the presence of other people
Somatization disorder	Somatoform	Multiple and recurrent physical symptoms for which medical attention is sought, but which have no physical cause
Undifferentiated schizophrenia	Schizophrenic	"Catch-all" category for individuals who are schizophrenic but do not manifest the specific symptoms associated with the other subtypes of schizophrenia

CHAPTER 16

Therapy

PART I. LEARNING OBJECTIVES

When you finish studying this chapter you should be able to:

Psychoanalysis

1. Describe the primary goal of psychoanalysis, and describe four techniques Freud developed to accomplish this goal. **(605, 607-608)**

2. Discuss the similarities and differences between Freud's psychoanalysis and modern psychoanalytic therapy. **(609)**

Humanistic Therapies

3. Describe the primary goal and general focus of humanistic therapies. **(609)**

4. Discuss three elements of the "definable climate" that Rogers' person-centered therapy advocates. **(609)**

5. Describe the primary goal and general focus of Perls' Gestalt therapy, and discuss techniques used to facilitate these goals. **(611-612)**

Cognitive Therapies

6. Discuss the basic premise and approach of the cognitive therapies. **(612-614)**

7. Describe the primary focus of Ellis' rational-emotive therapy (RET), and discuss how a faulty belief system may be challenged. **(613)**

8. Describe the primary focus of Beck's cognitive restructuring therapy, and discuss techniques utilized to counteract negative self-images. **(615-616)**

Behavior Therapies

9. Discuss how the central thesis of behavior therapy differs from traditional methods of therapy, and the basic techniques utilized by behavior therapies. **(616)**

10. Describe two types of behavior therapy that are based on classical conditioning—Wolpe's systematic desensitization and aversion conditioning—and discuss situations in which each approach would be appropriate. **(616-619)**

11. Describe three types of behavior therapy based on operant conditioning—positive reinforcement, extinction, and punishment—and discuss situations in which each approach would be appropriate. **(619)**

12. Describe how modeling can be a helpful therapy technique, and give two examples of two types of behaviors that can be acquired or altered through modeling. **(622)**

Group Therapy

13. Define and describe several advantages of group therapy, and list a number of problems that may be successfully treated in group therapy. **(622-624)**

14. Discuss the premise upon which family therapy is based, and describe several techniques that are used to change maladaptive patterns in disturbed families. **(624-625)**

15. Discuss how couple therapy is similar to and different from family therapy. **(625)**

Evaluating Psychotherapy

16. Summarize the research concerning whether receiving psychotherapy is more beneficial than not receiving therapy. **(626-627)**

17. Summarize research comparing the success rates of different types of psychotherapy. **(627, 629)**

18. Describe four features that are shared by most types of psychotherapy. **(629-630)**

Biomedical Treatment of Psychological Disorders

19. Summarize the history of psychosurgery, and describe the lobotomy procedures and the effects this procedure has on an individual. **(630-631, 633)**

20. Summarize the history of electroconvulsive therapy (ECT), and discuss its current status. **(633-635)**

21. Describe the effects, since the 1950s, the psychoactive drugs have had on the number of individuals hospitalized and the length of hospitalization. **(635-636)**

22. List four major categories of psychoactive drugs, and describe the uses of these drugs in controlling the symptoms of psychological disorders. **(636-638)**

PART II. OVERVIEW

A number of different psychotherapy techniques for treating psychological disorders exist. Freud's psychoanalysis attempts to help individuals first gain insight into their unconscious conflicts and then to resolve these conflicts. Psychoanalysis uses the techniques of free association, dream analysis, and interpretation of resistance and transference. Contemporary psychoanalytically oriented therapists utilize a modified version of Freud's technique.

Humanistic therapies are concerned with fostering the psychological growth of individuals. Rogers' person-centered therapy attempts to provide an appropriate environment (a definable climate) to facilitate self-understanding and changes in self-concept. Rogers emphasizes the therapist's genuineness, unconditional positive regard, and empathic understanding to promote the client's growth. The goals of Perls' Gestalt therapy is to help a person combine or integrate the various parts of their personalities into a well-organized whole. Gestalt therapists utilize role playing, and training an individual to speak in the first person, and will not hesitate to confront a client when there is a discrepancy between what the client says and does.

Cognitive therapies define psychological disorders as arising from irrational or distorted beliefs or cognitions and attempt to replace these irrational cognitions with more appropriate beliefs. Ellis' rational-emotive therapy (RET) attempts to force individuals to confront and challenge irrational self-defeating belief systems. Beck's cognitive restructuring therapy focuses on the negative self-images and self-labels of disturbed individuals. Cognitive restructuring therapy attempts to alter these inappropriate beliefs by using "experiments" or real-life exercises that will contradict an individual's negative self-labels.

Behavior therapies—based on the principles of classical conditioning, operant conditioning, and modeling—are designed to teach individuals appropriate behaviors to replace the inappropriate or disturbed behaviors they previously learned. Two behavior therapies based on classical conditioning are systematic desensitization (which is very effective in treating phobias) and aversive conditioning (which may be used to alter an individual's previously acquired positive response to a harmful substance, such as alcohol). Techniques based on operant conditioning are used to induce desired behaviors (positive reinforcement) and eliminate undesirable behaviors (extinction and punishment).

In addition to treating people individually, many therapy approaches are also conducted in group therapy situations. Unique advantages of group therapy include such factors as the group members receive feedback from a number of individuals beside the therapist, and also group members offer support and suggestions to others that may result in increases in their self-esteem. Frequently an individual's problems are addressed in family therapy because the behavior and interaction of family members affect the functioning of other members of the family. Couple therapy is the most common approach for treating relationship problems within couples.

Many people with psychological problems recover without the benefit of therapy (spontaneous remission), but psychotherapy has been shown to be more effective and result in better outcomes than not receiving therapy. Research attempts to evaluate the relative effectiveness of the different types of therapies indicate that no one technique is significantly superior to the others. Almost all therapy techniques share four common features: (1) combatting the client's demoralization, (2) providing a rationale for symptoms and treatment, (3) providing a warm supportive relationship, and (4) providing a professional setting.

In addition to psychotherapy techniques a number of biomedical (or biologically based) treatments for psychological disorders exist. The lobotomy (the severing of connections between the frontal cortex and lower regions of the brain), which was once used to "treat" schizophrenia, is the best-known psychosurgery technique. Although the lobotomy was successful in calming agitated patients, this technique did not have generally beneficial consequences for the individual. Today other more specific forms of psychosurgery exist and are used in some circumstances. Electroconvulsive therapy (ECT), which had its beginnings at about the same time as the lobotomy, is still in use today. ECT is used primarily to treat major depression when an individual does not respond to other treatments. Psychoactive drugs comprise the most commonly used biomedical technique currently used. Four different categories of psychoactive drugs are used to control (but not cure) a variety of psychological disorders: (1) neuroleptics (for schizophrenia), (2) antidepressants (for major depression), (3) antimanics (for bipolar disorder), and (4) antianxiety drugs (for anxiety and tension).

PART III. KEY TERMS/MATCHING EXERCISES

Match the following concepts and/or individuals with the appropriate descriptions. Check your answers against the Answer Key.

Therapies (Overview)

Concepts

_____ 1. cognitive therapy (**612**)   _____ 5. humanistic therapy (**609**)

_____ 2. psychoanalysis (**605**)   _____ 6. group therapy (**623-624**)

_____ 3. biomedical treatment (**630**)   _____ 7. behavior therapy (**616**)

_____ 4. psychotherapy (**605**)

Descriptions

a. Attempts to allow an individual to gain insight or conscious awareness of repressed conflicts so that the conflicts can be resolved

b. Assumes that distorted or irrational thoughts contribute to psychological difficulties

c. Based on one or both assumptions that many psychological problems result from biological abnormalities, and physiological intervention will reduce symptoms

d. Any nonbiological, noninvasive psychological technique or procedure to improve a person's adjustment to life

e. Believes that because maladaptive behavior is learned it can also be unlearned

f. Attempts to encourage psychological growth by focusing on the present and individual's conscious thoughts

g. Offers the advantage of providing a more true-to-life environment for trying out new behaviors and ways of relating to others

Answer Key   1. b   2. a   3. c   4. d   5. f   6. g   7. e

Individuals

_____ 1. Beck **(615)**

_____ 2. Ellis **(613-614)**

_____ 3. Freud **(605)**

_____ 4. Perls **(611)**

_____ 5. Rogers **(610)**

_____ 6. Wolpe **(617)**

Descriptions

a. Believes therapy should focus on the here and now, utilizes role playing and may point out a discrepancy between what the client says and does

b. Developed systematic desensitization to treat phobias

c. Developed techniques of free association, dream analysis, and interpretation of resistance and transference

d. Believes that disturbed people typically have very negative self-images based on highly negative self-labels

e. Believes therapy should focus on the here and now and challenges the individual to find flaws in their irrational belief systems

f. Believes that a therapist should let the client know that he or she understands and accepts what they are saying

Answer Key   1. d   2. e   3. c   4. a   5. f   6. b

Psychoanalysis | Humanistic Therapies

Concepts

_____ 1. transference **(607-608)**

_____ 2. empathic understanding **(610)**

_____ 3. dream analysis **(607)**

_____ 4. Gestalt therapy **(611)**

_____ 5. free association **(607)**

_____ 6. person-centered therapy **(609)**

_____ 7. unconditional positive regard **(610)**

_____ 8. resistance **(607)**

Descriptions

a. Involves being encouraged to say whatever comes to mind

b. proposes that if a definable climate is provided, an individual will be able to "tap" resources to alter his or her self-concept

c. Proposes that psychological problems often arise from an individual's inability to integrate the various aspects of his or her personality into a healthy well-organized whole

d. Process in which people relate to their therapist in a manner similar to the way they relate to other important people in their life

e. To Freud, the "royal road to the unconscious"

f. Facilitated by active listening

g. Viewed as a sign that the therapist is getting close to the "problem"

h. Refers to a therapist (or other individual) who offers a totally accepting attitude

Answer Key   1. d   2. f   3. e   4. c   5. a   6. b   7. h   8. g

Cognitive Therapies | Behavior Therapies

Concepts

_____ 1. aversive conditioning **(618)**

_____ 2. cognitive restructuring therapy **(615-616)**

_____ 3. operant conditioning therapies **(619)**

_____ 4. systematic desensitization **(617)**

_____ 5. rational-emotive therapy (RET) **(613)**

Descriptions

a. Use(s) techniques based on positive reinforcement, extinction, and punishment; also referred to as behavior modification

b. Involve(s) substituting a negative response for a positive response to an inappropriate or harmful stimuli

c. Confrontative method that involves challenging irrational beliefs and substituting more logical thoughts

d. Treat(s) phobias by training individuals to relax when confronted with a fear-inducing stimuli

e. Experiential method(s) that involve(s) altering negative self-images and self-defeating behaviors

Answer Key   1. b   2. e   3. a   4. d   5. c

Biomedical Treatments of Psychological Disorders

Concepts

_____ 1. antianxiety drugs **(638)**

_____ 2. electroconvulsive therapy (ECT) **(633-634)**

_____ 3. antidepressants **(637)**

_____ 4. psychoactive drugs **(635)**

_____ 5. lobotomy **(630)**

_____ 6. neuroleptic drugs **(635)**

_____ 7. psychosurgery **(633)**

_____ 8. antimanics **(637)**

Descriptions

a. Newer techniques relieve specific symptoms of some psychological disorders as a result of the destruction of limited amounts of tissue located in specific brain structures

b. Describe(s) lithium carbonate useful in controlling the symptoms of bipolar disorder

c. Also referred to as antipsychotics or major tranquilizers; most effective in managing the symptoms of schizophrenia

d. Also referred to as minor tranquilizers; used to reduce symptoms of anxiety and tension

e. Involve(s) disconnecting the frontal cortex from lower brain structures that mediate emotional responses

f. Since the 1950s the most common form of biomedical treatment of psychological disorders

g. Involves inducing a convulsive seizure that is associated with a reduction of the symptoms of depression

h. Consist(s) of tricyclics, MAO inhibitors, and other types of drugs; primarily used to treat major depression

Answer Key   1. d   2. g   3. h   4. f   5. e   6. c   7. a   8. b

PART IV. TRUE-FALSE STATEMENTS

Fill in the blank before each statement with either a T (true) or an F (false). Check your answers against the Answer Key. Then go back to the items that are false and make the necessary change(s) to the statements to convert the items into true statements.

Psychoanalysis

_____ 1. Resistance occurs when an individual undergoing psychoanalysis begins to respond to the therapist in much the same manner as they respond to other important people in their lives.

_____   2. Freud believed that a therapist's interpretation of patients' experiences, resistances, transferences, and dreams would help to break through their defenses and provide them with insight into the causes of their behavior.

_____

_____

Humanistic Therapies

_____   3. Rogers believes that genuineness, unconditional positive regard, and empathic understanding are the three major elements of a definable climate.

_____

_____

_____   4. Role playing and being taught to speak in the first person are two techniques used in Gestalt therapy.

_____

_____

Cognitive Therapies

_____   5. As (activating events), Bs (belief systems), and Cs (emotional consequences) are related to Beck's cognitive restructuring therapy.

_____

_____

_____   6. Ellis' rational-emotive therapy (RET) is primarily concerned with irrational beliefs, whereas Beck's cognitive restructuring therapy is concerned with negative self-images and self-labels.

_____

_____

Behavior Therapies

_____   7. Systematic desensitization is useful in stopping people from continuing to engage in "bad habits" such as smoking and alcohol abuse.

_____

_____

_____   8. The behavior therapy techniques of positive reinforcement, aversive conditioning, and extinction are all based on operant conditioning.

_____

_____

Group Therapy

_____   9. Group therapy groups almost always consist of individuals with the same basic problem.

_____

_____

_____ 10. Family therapy assumes that individual pathology is rooted in a disturbed family and that changing the interactions of the family will affect those individuals displaying pathology.

_____

_____

Evaluating Psychotherapy

_____ 11. Eysenck's (1952) finding that approximately two-thirds of disturbed people improve markedly whether they receive psychotherapy or not has been supported by additional research.

_____

_____

_____ 12. Research examining the success rate of different types of psychotherapy has shown that no particular type of psychotherapy is significantly superior to the others.

_____

_____

Biomedical Treatment of Psychological Disorders

_____ 13. Today, psychosurgery is the most common biomedical treatment of psychological disorders.

_____

_____

_____ 14. Like lobotomies, discussion of electroconvulsive therapy is mostly "historical" in nature because both of these treatments are no longer in use.

_____

_____

Answer Key

1. F **(607-608)**	6. T **(615)**	11. F **(626)**
2. T **(607-608)**	7. F **(617)**	12. T **(627)**
3. T **(609)**	8. F **(619)**	13. F **(635)**
4. T **(611)**	9. F **(623)**	14. F **(635)**
5. F **(613)**	10. T **(625)**	

PART V. MULTIPLE-CHOICE QUESTIONS

Choose the best answer to each question. Circle your choice. Check your answers against the Answer Key. Questions marked with an asterisk (*) include annotated answers.

Psychoanalysis

1. The basic aim of psychoanalysis can be described as to

a. weaken the id.

b. make the conscious unconscious.

c. make the unconscious conscious.

d. provide unconditional positive regard.

2. Which of the following is *not* one of the therapeutic techniques of Freud's psychoanalysis?

　　a. Interpretation of transference
　　b. Active listening
　　c. Interpretation of resistance
　　d. Free association

3. Sometimes an individual decides to terminate therapy at a time the therapist feels is premature and at a point when therapy is about to make significant progress. This patient's behavior illustrates

　　a. repression.
　　b. reaction formation.
　　c. transference.
　　d. resistance.

4. It is not uncommon for clients to "fall in love" with their therapists. This type of client behavior illustrates

　　a. attachment.
　　b. resistance.
　　c. transference.
　　d. projection.

*5. Compared to classical (Freudian) psychoanalytic therapists, contemporary psycho-analytically oriented therapists

　　a. pay more attention to a patient's current life and relationships.
　　b. tend to desire a longer duration of therapy.
　　c. sit out of view of a patient.
　　d. attempt to gain insight into the unconscious roots of a patient's problems.

Humanistic Therapies

6. The therapist who would most likely provide an individual with continual messages of acceptance as opposed to approval and/or disapproval is

　　a. Ellis.
　　b. Rogers.
　　c. Perls.
　　d. Freud.

*7. Which of the following statements concerning humanistic therapies is true?

　　a. Therapy tends to focus on the past relationships and experiences of a client.
　　b. Psychological disturbances are believed to be the result of self-defeating beliefs.
　　c. Therapy involves restructuring an individual's entire personality.
　　d. Responsibility for the success of therapy is placed more on the shoulders of the client than the therapist.

8. To Rogers, a definable climate

    a. provides the client a sample environment in which to role play or act out current situations or conflicts.

    b. involves the therapist defining the client's strengths and weaknesses.

    c. encourages unconditional positive regard and transference.

    d. provides an environment that facilitates self-understanding.

9. Gestalt therapy strives to help a person

    a. resolve unconscious conflicts and repressed urges.

    b. confront self-defeating, irrational beliefs.

    c. interpret the meaning of his or her dreams.

    d. bring together the alienated fragments of self.

10. A client is asked to role play his or her parent while the therapist role plays the client. The therapy being practiced is probably that of

    a. psychoanalysis.

    b. Gestalt therapy.

    c. person-centered therapy.

    d. rational-emotive therapy.

11. _____ therapists would directly confront a client with a discrepancy in what he or she says and does. _____ therapists would tend to allow an individual to notice this discrepancy for himself or herself.

    a. Gestalt | Person-centered

    b. Person-centered | Gestalt

    c. Behavior | Cognitive

    d. Person-centered | Psychoanalytic

Cognitive Therapies

12. According to Ellis' rational-emotive therapy (RET), psychological problems arise as a result of

    a. specific activating events (A).

    b. the individual's belief system (B).

    c. emotional consequences (C).

    d. negative self-images.

13. Rational-emotive therapy tends to focus on _____ . Cognitive restructuring therapy focuses on _____ .

    a. thoughts | behavior

    b. behavior | thoughts

    c. irrational beliefs | negative self-images

    d. negative self-images | irrational beliefs

14. _____ is the therapist who would most likely instruct a 40-year-old secretary, who feels she is inferior and unworthy of a job with greater responsibility, to enroll in a course at her local community college.

    a. Beck
    b. Wolpe
    c. Perls
    d. Ellis

Behavior Therapies

15. Developing a hierarchy of fears is a component of

    a. aversive conditioning.
    b. cognitive restructuring therapy.
    c. extinction technique.
    d. systematic desensitization.

16. Systematic desensitization involves

    a. training one to relax when confronted with fearful stimuli.
    b. interpreting fearful stimuli to be less fearful.
    c. changing misconceptions regarding fearful stimuli.
    d. uncovering repressed feelings regarding fearful events.

*17. The classical conditioning behavior therapy of _____ would effective treat an individual suffering from a spider phobia, whereas the _____ technique would be appropriate to treat alcohol abuse.

    a. aversive conditioning | systematic desensitization
    b. systematic desensitization | aversive conditioning
    c. extinction | punishment
    d. punishment | extinction

18. Behavior modification

    a. is most successful in treating mood disorders.
    b. refers to behavior and cognitive therapies.
    c. involves the application of classical conditioning techniques.
    d. involves changing behavior by manipulating reinforcers.

19. The type of therapy in which a chronic drinker is given a drug that induces nausea when combined with alcohol is called

    a. systematic desensitization.
    b. aversive conditioning.
    c. chemotherapy.
    d. counterconditioning.

20. Which type of behavior therapy technique would be most appropriate in order to convert a nonassertive individual into an assertive person?

    a. Positive reinforcement
    b. Aversive conditioning
    c. Punishment
    d. Client-centered therapy

*21. Which of the following pairs of techniques and problem behaviors do *not* go well together?

   a. modeling and mouse phobia
   b. punishment and fingernail biting
   c. systematic desensitization and assertiveness
   d. aversive conditioning and cocaine abuse

Group Therapy

22. Which of the following group therapy compositions would you expect to be *least* successful?

   a. A group composed of individuals who have different problem areas
   b. A group composed entirely of victims of child abuse
   c. A group composed entirely of depressed individuals
   d. A group composed entirely of nonassertive individuals

23. Which of the following is an advantage of group therapy?

   a. An individual may receive a feeling of superiority compared to the other group members.
   b. An individual realizes that he or she is not alone and that other people also have problems.
   c. An individual receives more individual attention from the therapist.
   d. An individual does not have to be concerned with the reasons for his or her behavior.

24. Family therapy involves attempting to

   a. instruct family members in how to accept the disturbed family member "as they are."
   b. support the other family members during the disturbed member's "illness."
   c. change maladaptive patterns of interaction between family members.
   d. All of the above choices apply.

25. The most common approach for treating relationship problems within a primary couple is

   a. couple therapy.
   b. having one person receive individual therapy.
   c. having both people receive individual therapy from the same therapist.
   d. having both people receive individual therapy from different therapists.

Evaluating Psychotherapy

26. Which statement is *false*?

   a. Whether a person receives individual or group therapy has little impact on the therapy's effectiveness.
   b. More-experienced psychotherapists tend to achieve better results than less-experienced psychotherapists.
   c. People who receive therapy are more likely to show marked improvement than similarly disturbed people who do not receive therapy.
   d. Person-centered therapy is significantly more effective than cognitive therapy.

27. One reason why researchers have found little difference in the effectiveness of various psychotherapy approaches is that

  a. all therapists are well trained.
  b. all therapists must take the same licensing exam.
  c. most approaches began as one approach anyway.
  d. almost all styles of therapy share certain common features.

28. Eclecticism refers to

  a. the use of electroconvulsive therapy.
  b. the therapist using a pragmatic application of a number of clinical techniques.
  c. the use of magnetic resonance imaging.
  d. a new type of cognitive therapy.

29. Which of the following is *not* a common feature shared by almost all styles of therapy?

  a. Focusing on an individual's early experiences
  b. Providing a warm, supportive relationship
  c. Providing a rationale for symptoms and treatment
  d. Combating a client's demoralization

Biomedical Treatment of Psychological Disorders

30. Following a lobotomy a person could be expected to

  a. show an inability to plan ahead.
  b. be lethargic and unmotivated.
  c. show memory loss.
  d. All of the above choices apply.

31. Electroconvulsive therapy is most effective for the treatment of

  a. schizophrenia.
  b. major depression.
  c. bipolar disorder.
  d. generalized anxiety disorder.

⁺32. Psychoactive drugs

  a. all tend to have a calming effect on an individual.
  b. control the symptoms of psychological disorders.
  c. are a second-line treatment modality used only if first-choice treatments fail.
  d. cure psychological disorders.

33. Depressed patients given drugs and psychotherapy conjointly as compared to patients given drugs only

  a. took much longer to recover.
  b. had a comparable relapse rate.
  c. had a higher relapse rate.
  d. had a lower relapse rate.

34. Jeff is an out-patient who suffers from muscle tension, sleeplessness, and feelings of impending doom. What drug would Jeff's doctor possibly prescribe for him?
- **a.** Lithium
- **b.** Thorazine
- **c.** Librium and Valium
- **d.** Mellaril

Answer Key

1. c	**(602)**	8. d	**(609)**	15. d	**(617)**	22. c	**(624)**	29. a	**(629)**
2. b	**(605)**	9. d	**(611)**	16. a	**(617)**	23. b	**(623)**	30. d	**(631)**
3. d	**(607)**	10. b	**(611)**	*17. b	**(618)**	24. c	**(625)**	31. b	**(634)**
4. c	**(607-608)**	11. a	**(611-612)**	18. d	**(619)**	25. a	**(625)**	*32. b	**(635)**
*5. a	**(609)**	12. b	**(615)**	19. b	**(618-619)**	26. d	**(627)**	33. d	**(637)**
6. b	**(610)**	13. c	**(615)**	20. a	**(619-620)**	27. d	**(627, 629)**	34. c	**(638)**
*7. d	**(609)**	14. a	**(615-616)**	*21. c	**(617)**	28. b	**(629)**		

Annotated Answers

5. The correct choice is a. While Freud basically ignored a patient's current life and relationships and concentrated instead on early experiences, contemporary psychoanalytically oriented therapists emphasize a patient's current situation much more so than Freud.
- **b.** Contemporary psychoanalysis tends to be briefer in duration than Freudian psychoanalysis.
- **c.** Freud had patients lie on a couch and remained out of their view (to reduce distractions); contemporary psychoanalysts have patients sit on a chair and face them.
- **d.** Both Freudian and contemporary psychoanalysts attempt to gain insight into the unconscious roots of a patient's problems.

7. The correct choice is d. Humanistic therapists attempt to foster a client's psychological growth and to help him or her take responsibility for their life and actions. Thus responsibility for the success of therapy would basically fall on a client's shoulders.
- **a.** Humanistic therapists tend to focus on the present (not the past).
- **b.** It is cognitive therapists (not humanistic therapists) that state psychological disorders are the result of self-defeating beliefs.
- **c.** It is psychoanalysis (not humanistic therapists) that attempts to restructure an individual's entire personality.

17. The correct choice is b. Systematic desensitization is perhaps the most effective treatment for phobias, and aversive conditioning is designed specifically to treat problems such as alcohol abuse.
- **a.** This choice has the two classical conditioning-based behavior therapies listed, but they are incorrectly associated with the problem behaviors.
- **c.** Both extinction and punishment are operant conditioning-based behavior therapy techniques.
- **d.** The explanation for c above applies.

21. The correct choice is c. Systematic desensitization is a treatment for phobias (not nonassertiveness).

a. Modeling is an appropriate treatment for phobias and to establish other new adaptive behaviors.

b. Punishment is an appropriate treatment to eliminate voluntary maladaptive responses such as fingernail-biting.

d. Aversive conditioning is designed to substitute a negative response for a positive response to an inappropriate or harmful stimulus (such as cocaine abuse).

32. The correct choice is b. Psychoactive drugs control the symptoms of a variety of psychological disorders. For example, lithium carbonate controls the manic symptoms associated with bipolar disorder.

a. Different psychoactive drugs vary considerably in their effects: some calm, some energize, and some promote an emotional lift.

c. For some psychological disorders (such as schizophrenia and bipolar disorder) psychoactive drugs would be the treatment of choice. The text refers to electroconvulsive therapy as a second-line treatment modality.

d. Psychoactive drugs do not cure psychological disorders, but temporarily control or manage the symptoms of the disorders.

PART VI. SUMMARY TABLES

To test your understanding of the material discussed in this chapter complete the following tables. Check your answers with those supplied in PART IX.

Summary of Therapy Techniques

Therapy	Individual(s)	Cause(s) of Disorder(s)	Goal of Therapy	Methods of Therapy
Psychoanalysis				
Humanistic Person-centered				
Gestalt				
Cognitive Rational-emotive				
Cognitive restructuring				
Behavior				
Biomedical				

Summary of Psychoactive Drugs

Category	Types	Specific Drugs	Disorder(s) Prescribed for	Effect
Neuroleptics				
Antidepressants				
Antimanics				
Antianxiety				

PART VII. THOUGHT QUESTIONS/CRITICAL THINKING

Prepare answers to the following discussion questions.

1. The text discusses several general features common to most psychotherapeutic approaches. There are also a number of more specific features or techniques that are shared by some (but not all) approaches. Decide which of the psychotherapy approaches described in the text (psychoanalysis, person-centered, Gestalt, rational-emotive therapy, cognitive restructuring, and behavior therapy) share each of the following emphases or techniques.

   a. An emphasis on an individual's current situation (the here and now)
   b. Encourage a gaining of insight into the causes of an individual's difficulties or problems
   c. Therapist uses a confrontative approach or style
   d. Utilizes specific situations or experiences to encourage an individual to alter behavior or reasoning

2. Imagine that your mother is currently hospitalized for a psychological problem and her doctor recommends that she receive electroconvulsive therapy (ECT). What questions would you ask the doctor before you would give your consent for the treatment?

3. Discuss the advantages and disadvantages of individual and group therapy. Which approach would you most likely select if you were to decide to receive psychotherapy? Explain.

4. While none of the psychotherapy approaches has been shown to be significantly superior to the other approaches, they do differ considerably in the theoretical orientation and techniques employed. Additionally, no one type of therapy would be "right" for everyone. If you were to decide to enter therapy, which type of therapy would you most likely select? Why? Which type of therapy would you least likely select? Why?

PART VIII. APPLICATIONS

1. During the last couple of years many organizations providing psychological services (hospitals, independent clinics, stress units, etc.) have started to advertise their programs through newspapers, mass mailings, radio, and television. A typical advertisement might be:

   > Do you have . . . feelings of hopelessness? . . . a sense of worthlessness? . . . constant fatigue? . . . sleep problems? . . . a loss of appetite? If your answer is yes to two or more of these questions you may be suffering from depression. Here at the ABC Institute we specialize in the treatment of depression and other psychological problems. Our treatment is proven to be effective. The majority of our clients experience marked improvement after just a few short weeks of treatment. The effects of depression are devastating and it is no longer necessary for you to continue to suffer. Call us at the ABC Institute today for a free evaluation of your problem.

   Assume that you answered yes to several of the questions mentioned in the advertisement. Prepare a list of questions that you would want to know the answers to before you decide to enter treatment at the ABC Institute. Explain the reasons why you would ask each question.

2. Imagine that a close friend of yours is experiencing each of the following psychological difficulties:

   a. His main problem concerns interpersonal relationships. He has difficulty in maintaining friendships, and frequently gets into disagreements with friends, and is often disappointed by the actions of his friends.

   b. She is a chronic procrastinator and, as a result, is in danger of flunking out of college.

   c. He is afraid to drive his car after dark.

   d. She is very anxious and insecure and tends to feel that she cannot compete effectively with others in college, in relationships, and in life in general.

   e. He had an unhappy childhood and believes that if his childhood had been happier his life would be better today.

Select one or two types of therapy (psychoanalysis, person-centered, Gestalt, rational-emotive therapy, cognitive restructuring, behavior therapy) that you would recommend to your friend. Explain the reasons why you selected each therapy.

PART IX. SUMMARY TABLES SOLUTIONS
Summary of Therapy Techniques

Therapy	Individual(s)	Cause(s) of Disorder(s)	Goal of Therapy	Methods of Therapy
Psychoanalysis	Freud	Unconscious conflicts and repressed urges, most of which are rooted in childhood experiences	To help individuals gain insight or conscious awareness of repressed conflicts and then to resolve those conflicts	Free association, dream analysis, and interpretation of resistance and transference
Humanistic Person-centered	Rogers	An incongruence between an individual's self-concept and experiences	Enhance an individual's potential for self-examination, personal growth, and self-fulfillment	Genuineness, unconditional positive regard, and empathic understanding
Gestalt	Perls	Inability to integrate the various parts of the personalities into a healthy, well-organized whole	Bring together the alienated fragments of self into a unified whole	Role playing, training clients to speak in the first person
Cognitive Rational-emotive	Ellis	Self-defeating irrational beliefs	Challenge or dispute irrational beliefs and then to substitute more logical or realistic thoughts	Confrontation, persuasion, role playing, interpretation, behavior modification, and reflection of feelings
Cognitive restructuring	Beck	Irrational beliefs concerning negative self-images and self-labels	Help client's restructure his or her thinking, especially negative self-labels	Experiential method to disprove a client's misguided self-impressions
Behavior	Wolpe Bandura	Result from learning	Help clients unlearn maladaptive behavior while learning more adaptive behavior	Systematic desensitization, aversive conditioning, positive reinforcement, extinction, and punishment
Biomedical	de Egas Moniz Watts Cerletti Bino	Result from biological abnormalities	Elimination of symptoms through physiological intervention	Psychosurgery, electroconvulsive therapy, and psychoactive drugs

Summary of Psychoactive Drugs

Category	Types	Specific Drugs	Disorder(s) Prescribed for	Effect
Neuroleptics	Also called antipsychotics, major tranquilizers Phenothiazine derivatives	Thorazine	Schizophrenia	Blocks dopamine receptor sites (CNS)
Antidepressants	Tricyclics, monamine oxidase (MAO) inhibitors, and newer agents	Elavil Nardil Marphan (and others)	Major depression and severely depressed individuals	Increases level of or sensitivity to norepinephrine and serotonin (CNS)
Antimanics	Inorganic salts	Lithium carbonate (Lithane, Lithonate)	Bipolar disorder	Increases reuptake of norepinephrine and serotonin (CNS)
Antianxiety	Also called minor tranquilizers Propanediols and benzodiazepines	Miltown Librium Valium Xanax	Anxiety and tension (especially generalized anxiety disorder)	Relaxes skeletal muscles

CHAPTER **17**

Social Psychology

PART I. LEARNING OBJECTIVES

When you finish studying this chapter you should be able to:

Social Perception

1. Define social perception, and list three factors that influence it. **(646-649)**

2. Describe the importance of first impressions on social perception, and discuss differences in the formation and maintenance of positive and negative first impressions. **(647)**

3. Define person schemas, and explain how person schemas influence social perception. **(647-648)**

4. Define implicit personality theories, and describe how central traits and the halo effect are associated with implicit personality theories. **(648-649)**

Attributing Causes to Behaviors

5. Discuss the basic premise of attribution theory, and differentiate between dispositional and external causes. **(649)**

6. Describe Jones' correspondent inference theory approach to understanding attribution, and discuss three variables related to making correspondent inferences. **(649-650)**

7. Describe Kelley's covariation principle approach to understanding attribution, and discuss three dimensions that are analyzed in making attributions. **(651-652)**

8. List and describe three attribution biases that cause errors to be made in the inferences people draw concerning the behavior of others. **(652-654)**

Attitudes

9. Define attitude, and discuss five types of experiences that influence the attitudes people develop. **(654)**

10. List and describe five functions that attitudes serve. **(656-657)**

11. Summarize the research concerning the consistency between attitudes and behavior, and discuss three variables influencing whether attitudes are predictive of behavior. **(657-659)**

12. Describe two consistency theories (balance theory and cognitive dissonance theory) that explain how attitudes are changed. **(659, 661-662)**

13. Define persuasion, and discuss three elements that are important in persuasive communication. **(662-665)**

Prejudice

14. Define prejudice, stereotypes, and discrimination, and discuss the interrelationships between these three terms. **(665)**

15. Define and differentiate between outgroups and ingroups, and discuss three factors that may influence the development of prejudice. **(666-667)**

16. Describe the prejudiced or authoritarian personality, and discuss common features in the manner in which these individuals were reared. **(667, 669)**

Social Influence

17. Define conformity, and differentiate between informational and normative social influences. **(669-670)**

18. Summarize Sherif and Asch's research concerning conformity, and discuss several factors that increase an individual's tendency to conform. **(670-672)**

19. Define compliance by contrasting it with conformity, and describe two techniques to increase compliance. **(672-673)**

20. Define obedience by contrasting it with conformity and compliance, and summarize Milgram's study of obedience. **(673-674)**

21. Discuss three reasons why people may respond to social influence in the form of destructive obedience. **(674)**

Interpersonal Attraction: Liking and Loving

22. Discuss four factors that influence interpersonal attraction. **(674-678)**

23. Discuss Rubin's love scale, and describe the three components of love it measures. **(678)**

24. Describe and differentiate between passionate and companionate love. **(678-680)**

Interpersonal Aggression

25. Describe the biological perspective concerning aggression, and summarize the research regarding this biological perspective. **(680-681)**

26. Describe the psychosocial perspective concerning aggression, and discuss three major areas this perspective focuses on. **(681, 683-686)**

PART II. OVERVIEW

Social psychology is concerned with how a variety of social factors influence thoughts, beliefs, feelings, and behaviors. Social perception relates to how one forms judgments about the qualities of people they meet. The primacy effect results in one's first impressions of an individual having a strong and frequently lasting influence on their perception of them. Both person schemas and implicit personality theories result in one inferring a person's overall personality or traits from a limited amount of information. In addition to having such a "personality profile" of individuals one meets people also attempt to understand the reasons behind the behavior of others. According to attribution theory people attribute another's behavior to either dispositional causes (or internal traits) or external causes (such as environmental or situational factors). The tendency exists to attribute the behavior of others to dispositional causes while we frequently explain our own behavior by referring to external causes.

Attitudes are learned, relatively enduring predispositions to respond in a consistent way to certain people, groups, ideas, and situations. Attitudes serve a variety of functions from providing one with a frame of reference and information concerning others to identifying with or gaining approval from one's peers. The attitudes and behaviors of a person are related, but may not be consistent in specific situations. Two theories related to attitude change and overall cognitive consistency are balance theory and cognitive dissonance theory. Balance theory proposes that the attitudes of other people (who we like or dislike) play a significant role in determining whether we maintain or modify our attitudes. Cognitive dissonance theory proposes that we experience discomfort when we are aware of a conflict between two attitudes or an attitude and behavior. This conflict is then reduced by changing our attitude. Persuasion involves direct attempts to change another person's attitudes. The attitude of prejudice is discussed in depth.

Conformity, compliance, and obedience all relate to altering feelings, beliefs, and behavior as a result of social influence. Conformity refers to simply modifying one's behavior so that it is consistent with the behavior of others. Compliance refers to modifying one's behavior in response to direct requests from others to do so. Finally, obedience refers to modifying one's behavior in response to direct commands or orders from people perceived as having power to do so. Research examining conformity (Sherif and Asch), compliance, and obedience (Milgram) shows that social influence is very strong and frequently difficult to resist.

Interpersonal attraction focuses on factors that influence the people we choose to like and love. Four general factors that influence interpersonal attraction are proximity, similarity, reciprocity, and physical attractiveness. Love relationships are frequently divided into two categories. Passionate love is characterized by intense feelings of excitement, generalized physiological arousal, and strong sexual desire. Intense passionate love typically does not last very long and may evolve into companionate love, which is characterized by friendly affection and deep attachment.

Chapter 17 concludes with a discussion of interpersonal aggression (any physical or verbal behavior intended to hurt another person). Biological factors (which have been linked to human aggression) include levels of prenatal androgens, structures in the limbic system, and genetic factors (from twin studies). The psychosocial perspective concerning aggression has focused on three areas: the association between frustration and aggression, social learning, and the influence of mass-media violence.

PART III. KEY TERMS/MATCHING EXERCISES

Match the following concepts and/or individuals with the appropriate descriptions. Check your answers against the Answer Key.

Social Perception| Attributing Causes to Behaviors

Concepts

_____ 1. covariation principle (651)

_____ 2. person schemas (647)

_____ 3. false consensus bias (653)

_____ 4. social perception (646)

_____ 5. attribution theory (649)

_____ 6. implicit personality theories (648)

_____ 7. primacy effect (647)

_____ 8. illusion of control (653)

_____ 9. halo effect (649)

_____ 10. fundamental attribution error (652)

_____ 11. correspondent inference theory (649)

Descriptions

a. Propose(s) that people tend to believe that behavior is caused by either dispositional or external causes

b. Tendency to overestimate dispositional causes associated with the behavior of others, and to overestimate external causes to one's own behavior

c. Suggest(s) several factors that determine whether people make dispositional attributions

d. Generalized assumptions about certain classes of people

e. Belief that we control events in our lives that are in fact controlled by external causes

f. Suggest(s) that one considers the situation, the persons involved, and the stimuli toward which a behavior is directed when making attributions

g. Tendency to infer other positive (or negative) traits from one's perception of one central trait

h. Refer(s) to the first information received about a person that often seems to count the most

i. Often organized around central traits that one tends to associate with many other characteristics

j. Assumption that one's own attitudes and behaviors are shared by most people

k. Describe(s) the ways we perceive, evaluate, categorize, and form judgments about the qualities of people we encounter

Answer Key 1. f   2. d   3. j   4. k   5. a   6. i   7. h   8. e   9. g   10. b   11. c

Attitudes | Prejudice

Concepts

_____ 1. cognitive dissonance theory **(661)**

_____ 2. ingroup **(666)**

_____ 3. impression management **(654)**

_____ 4. authoritarian personality **(667)**

_____ 5. persuasion **(662)**

_____ 6. prejudice **(665)**

_____ 7. attitudes **(654)**

_____ 8. discrimination **(665)**

_____ 9. outgroup **(666)**

_____ 10. balance theory **(659)**

_____ 11. stereotypes **(665)**

Descriptions

a. Negative, unjustifiable and inflexible attitude toward a group and its members based on erroneous information

b. Tendency to carefully select what information to reveal concerning personal attitudes

c. Individuals perceived as different as a result of them not sharing the same characteristics

d. Preconceived and oversimplified beliefs and expectations about the traits of members of a particular group that do not account for individual differences

e. Propose(s) that other people play a significant role in determining whether one maintains attitudes or changes them

f. Measured by the F Scale and associated with prejudicial attitudes

g. Propose(s) that an individual experience(s) a state of discomfort whenever two related cognitions are in conflict

h. Associated with a tendency to see one's own group in a favorable light

i. Learned, relatively enduring predispositions to consistently respond in favorable or unfavorable ways to people, groups, ideas, or situations

j. Behavioral consequence of prejudice

k. Three important elements related to this concept are the communicator, the message, and the audience

Answer Key 1. g 2. h 3. b 4. f 5. k 6. a 7. i 8. j 9. c 10. e 11. d

Social Influence

Concepts

_____ 1. compliance **(672)**

_____ 2. normative social influence **(670)**

_____ 3. door-in-the-face technique **(673)**

_____ 4. conformity **(669-670)**

_____ 5. obedience **(673)**

_____ 6. informational social influence **(670)**

_____ 7. foot-in-the-door technique **(672)**

Descriptions

a. Tends to increase compliance by first making a relatively large or significant request, which is likely to be refused

b. Tendency to modify one's own beliefs or behaviors often associated with a perceived social pressure to do so

c. Associated with altering one's behavior in response to direct requests from others

d. Tends to increase compliance by first getting a person to agree to a relatively minor or trivial request

e. Refers to accepting a group's beliefs or behaviors as providing accurate information about reality

f. Refers to the belief that one will benefit in some way if beliefs or behaviors are modified

g. Associated with altering one's behavior in response to commands or orders from people perceived as having power or authority

Answer Key   1. c   2. f   3. a   4. b   5. g   6. e   7. d

Interpersonal Attraction: Liking and Loving | Interpersonal Aggression

Concepts

_____ 1. reciprocity (**676**)

_____ 2. frustration-aggression hypothesis (**681**)

_____ 3. companionate love (**679**)

_____ 4. similarity (**675**)

_____ 5. interpersonal aggression (**680**)

_____ 6. passionate love (**678**)

_____ 7. proximity (**675**)

Descriptions

a. Principle that states that when one receives expressions of liking and loving, the tendency is to respond with similar expressions

b. Any physical or verbal behavior intended to hurt another person

c. State of extreme absorption in another person

d. Associated with the mere exposure effect

e. Psychosocial perspective concerning aggression that links frustration and aggression

f. Refers to the observation that people are attracted to others who often share common beliefs, values, attitudes, interests, and intellectual ability

g. Based on extensive familiarity; characterized by friendly affection and deep attachment

Answer Key   1. a   2. e   3. g   4. f   5. b   6. c   7. d

PART IV. TRUE-FALSE STATEMENTS

Fill in the blank before each statement with either a T (true) or an F (false). Check your answers against the Answer Key. Then go back to the items that are false and make the necessary change(s) to the statements to convert the items into true statements.

Social Perception

_____ 1. Negative first impressions are more easily altered in response to additional information than are positive first impressions.

_____

_____

_____ 2. The halo effect would predict that you perceive a well-mannered child as more attractive than his less-polite identical twin.

_____

_____

Attributing Causes to Behaviors

_____ 3. According to correspondent inference theory, if you observe a person behaving in a socially acceptable manner, you would not make a correspondent inference.

_____

_____

_____ 4. The fundamental attribution error occurs when a person falsely believes that they have control over an event in their life.

_____

_____

Attitudes | Prejudice

_____ 5. LaPiere's study involving a Chinese couple found a high level of consistency between individuals' attitudes and behaviors.

_____

_____

_____ 6. Balance theory suggests that if you like your roommate, you would also like their boyfriend or girlfriend.

_____

_____

_____ 7. Providing accurate information that contradicts a prejudiced individual's viewpoint is an effective way to alter that person's negative attitude.

_____

_____

Social Influence

_____ 8. The less familiar a person is with an attitude object, the more likely they are to conform.

_____

_____

_____ 9. Conformity involves simply modifying behaviors so that these are consistent with those of others; compliance involves modifying behavior in response to direct requests from others.

_____

_____

Interpersonal Attraction: Liking and Loving

_____ 10. Proximity, similarity, the halo effect, and physical attractiveness are four primary variables contributing to interpersonal attraction.

_____

_____

_____ 11. Companionate love is generally more enduring than passionate love.

_____

_____

Interpersonal Aggression

_____ 12. Berkowitz suggests that frustration will not result in aggression unless suitable environmental cues are present.

_____

_____

_____ 13. Sociobiologists support the psychosocial perspective concerning aggression.

_____

_____

Answer Key
1. F **(647)**	6. T **(659, 661)**	10. F **(674-675)**
2. T **(649)**	7. F **(665)**	11. T **(679)**
3. T **(649-650)**	8. T **(672)**	12. T **(683)**
4. F **(652)**	9. T **(669, 672)**	13. F **(680)**
5. F **(657)**		

PART V. MULTIPLE-CHOICE QUESTIONS

Choose the best answer to each question. Circle your choice. Check your answers against the Answer Key. Questions marked with an asterisk (*) include annotated answers.

Social Perception

1. Darley and Latane (1968) found that one would be more likely to help another person in trouble if

a. paid to do so.
b. they were the same sex.
c. they thought they were the only person present.
d. there were several bystanders.

2. First impressions are most directly related to

a. impression management.
b. the halo effect.
c. the mere exposure effect.
d. the primacy effect.

3. A person believes that elementary schoolteachers are nurturing people. This is an example of

a. a person schema.
b. an attribution.
c. prejudice.
d. an implicit personality theory.

*4. A friend tells you about the clumsy person who sits next to them in class who is always dropping their pencil and stepping on your friend's feet. As a result of _____ , you expect that the person is also not very bright.

a. person schemas
b. prejudice
c. implicit personality theories
d. balance theory

5. Which term is *not* directly associated with the other three terms?

    a. Halo effect
    b. Person schemas
    c. Implicit personality theories
    d. Central trait

Attributing Causes to Behaviors

6. The theory that describes how one decides if another person's behavior is a result of internal or external factors is the _____ theory.

    a. decision
    b. attribution
    c. balance
    d. social influence

7. An assumption that behavior is determined by internal causes, such as personal attitudes or goals, is referred to as

    a. consensus.
    b. fundamental attribution.
    c. situational attribution.
    d. dispositional attribution.

8. When would you be most likely to attribute a person's behavior to a correspondent inference or dispositional cause?

    a. When that behavior is focused on achieving a unique outcome that would unlikely occur as the result of some other behavior.
    b. When that behavior is fairly common.
    c. When that behavior illustrates conformity.
    d. When that behavior is socially desirable.

9. According to Kelley's covariation principle, which of the following is *not* one of the three potential causes of a behavior we examine when making an attribution?

    a. Persons involved
    b. Stimuli or objects toward which the behavior is directed
    c. Consistency of the behavior
    d. Situation or context

*10. If your professor believes that anyone who doesn't find psychology as fascinating as he or she does must be an idiot, your professor would be

    a. committing the fundamental attribution error.
    b. a "victim" of the false consensus bias.
    c. prejudiced.
    d. using a person schema.

Attitudes

11. Which of the following is included in the definition of attitudes?

   a. Attitudes involve predispositions to respond in a consistent way.
   b. Attitudes are learned.
   c. Attitudes are enduring.
   d. All of the above are included in the definition.

12. If a child earns a nod of approval from a parent when he or she makes a racially derogatory comment, he or she is likely to develop a negative attitude toward the group through

   a. direct experience.
   b. classical conditioning.
   c. operant conditioning.
   d. observation.

13. At times the attitudes we express allow us to identify with or gain approval from our peers. This statement describes the _____ function of attitudes.

   a. social identification
   b. social adjustment
   c. conformity
   d. value-expressive

14. According to _____ , the attitudes of other people play a significant role in determining whether we maintain our attitudes or change them.

   a. balance theory
   b. attribution theory
   c. the covariation principle
   d. cognitive dissonance theory

15. When people whom we dislike do not agree with us, we probably will be in a state of

   a. nonbalance.
   b. imbalance.
   c. balance.
   d. dissonance.

16. According to cognitive dissonance theory, people are motivated to

   a. achieve consistency between attitudes and behavior.
   b. behave inconsistently.
   c. avoid unconscious conflicts.
   d. avoid people who are similar to themselves.

17. According to cognitive dissonance theory, which individual would most likely undergo a change in attitude concerning the death penalty (which they were originally opposed to)? An advertising/public relations expert who

   a. wrote a brief anti-death penalty piece as a favor for a friend.
   b. wrote a brief anti-death penalty piece for a client and was paid to do so.
   c. wrote a brief pro-death penalty piece as a favor for a friend.
   d. wrote a brief pro-death penalty piece for a client and was paid to do so.

18. A used-car salesman tells you, "That's a fine car at an outstanding price." This salesman is not effective in persuading you to buy the car, in large part because
    a. there is little prestige associated with being a used-car salesman.
    b. the salesman is unattractive.
    c. you doubt that the salesman is trustworthy.
    d. you doubt that the salesman has any expertise concerning cars.

19. Attempts to change attitudes are often most successful if there is _____ discrepancy between the individual's original attitude and the attitude that is being encouraged.
    a. a small
    b. a moderate
    c. a large
    d. no

Prejudice

*20. Preconceived and oversimplified beliefs and expectations about the traits of members of a particular group that do not account for individual differences defines
    a. person schemas.
    b. an outgroup.
    c. prejudice.
    d. stereotypes.

21. We divide our world into two groups of people, "us" and "them." You and I belong to the
    a. outgroup.
    b. ingroup.
    c. minority group.
    d. known group.

22. The slogan from the youth movement of the late 1960s and early 1970s, "Don't trust anyone over 30," is an example of
    a. the ingroup bias.
    b. the outgroup bias.
    c. discrimination.
    d. social perception.

23. Attitudes are composed of beliefs, feelings, and behaviors. Regarding prejudiced attitudes these three components—in order—relate to
    a. discrimination, stereotypes, and prejudice.
    b. prejudice, stereotypes, and discrimination.
    c. stereotypes, prejudice, and discrimination.
    d. ingroup, outgroup, and compliance.

24. Overt acts of prejudice tend to increase during periods of
    a. isolation between the groups.
    b. voluntary cooperation.
    c. forced cooperation.
    d. frustration.

25. Which personality trait is *not* included in the profile of the authoritarian personality?

    a. High self-esteem
    b. Emotional coldness
    c. Rigidity
    d. Intolerance

Social Influence

*26. Changing your behavior to be consistent with the behavior of a group because you believe that the group is more knowledgeable than you, illustrates _____ influence.

    a. social identification
    b. normative social
    c. value-expressive
    d. informational social

27. In Sherif's experiment asking subjects to estimate how far a light moved in group-testing situations, subjects' estimates became progressively more similar. Following the group test, when tested alone subjects made judgments similar to those made in the group situations indicating the _____ influence.

    a. social identification
    b. normative social
    c. value-expressive
    d. informational social

28. Who would be *least* likely to exhibit conforming behavior in Asch's experiment involving line-comparison judgments?

    a. An individual with low self-esteem
    b. An architectural draftsman
    c. A college freshman in a group of college seniors
    d. The last individual to answer in a group of seven subjects

29. A career woman would like her husband to help a little more with the housework. If she first requests that her husband do 50 percent of the work she would be using the _____ technique.

    a. settle-for-less
    b. door-in-the-face
    c. foot-in-the-door
    d. foot-in-the-mouth

30. Milgram's study examined

    a. obedience.
    b. the authoritarian personality.
    c. conformity.
    d. compliance.

31. A teenage gang member murders a member from a rival gang but denies being to blame because "The gang leader told me to do it." This teenager's statement would support the _____ explanation of destructive obedience.

    a. diffusion of responsibility
    b. graduated demands
    c. visible symbols of power
    d. reduced personal accountability

Interpersonal Attraction: Liking and Loving

32. Probably the most basic reason you will not fall in love with and marry a Russian citizen is:

    a. conformity.
    b. proximity.
    c. reciprocity.
    d. similarity.

33. Regarding interpersonal attraction, which of the following old adages is most correct?

    a. Birds of a feather flock together.
    b. Don't take any wooden nickels.
    c. Two's company, three's a crowd.
    d. Opposites attract.

34. A cross-cultural study of sex differences in mate selection found that

    a. men and women both place very high values on physical attractiveness.
    b. women place greater value on physical attractiveness than men.
    c. men place greater value on physical attractiveness than women.
    d. men and women in industrial societies place less value on physical attractiveness than men and women in more primitive societies.

35. The three components of Rubin's love scale are

    a. respect, responsibility, and commitment.
    b. intensity, duration, and exclusiveness.
    c. passionate, companionate, and platonic.
    d. attachment, caring, and intimacy.

36. Most enduring love relationships begin with _____ love that only later may evolve into _____ love.

    a. emotional | physical
    b. physical | emotional
    c. passionate | companionate
    d. companionate | passionate

Interpersonal Aggression

37. Lorenz believes that

  a. all species have a "fighting instinct."
  b. there is survival value associated with aggression directed toward members of the same species.
  c. unlike most other species, man does not have an innate inhibition that prevents us from killing other men.
  d. All of the above choices are correct.

38. Which of the following describes the most recent revision of the frustration-aggression hypothesis?

  a. In order for frustration to result in aggression a readiness to act aggressively and environmental cues must both be present.
  b. Frustration can produce a number of possible responses beside aggression.
  c. Aggression is always a consequence of frustration.
  d. Frustration always leads to aggression.

39. Regarding the effect of television violence on children, the consensus of opinion among psychologists is that

  a. no consensus has been reached.
  b. violence on TV has a cathartic effect and reduces aggressive behaviors.
  c. violence on TV has a negative effect on boys but not on girls.
  d. violence on TV does lead to aggressive behavior.

Answer Key

1. c	**(645)**	9. c	**(651)**	17. c	**(662)**	25. a **(667, 669)**	33. a **(675-676)**
2. d	**(647)**	*10. b	**(653)**	18. c **(662-663)**		*26. d	**(669)**	34. c	**(677)**
3. a	**(647)**	11. d	**(654)**	19. b	**(663)**	27. d	**(670)**	35. d	**(678)**
*4. c	**(648)**	12. c **(655-656)**		*20. d	**(665)**	28. b	**(672)**	36. c	**(680)**
5. b	**(649)**	13. b	**(656)**	21. b	**(666)**	29. b	**(673)**	37. d	**(680)**
6. b	**(649)**	14. a	**(659)**	22. a	**(666)**	30. a	**(673)**	*38. a	**(683)**
7. d	**(649)**	15. c **(659-661)**		23. c	**(665)**	31. d	**(674)**	39. d **(685-686)**
8. a	**(650)**	16. a **(661-662)**		24. d	**(667)**	32. b	**(675)**	

Annotated Answers

  4. The correct choice is c. Implicit personality theories are assumptions about personality traits that go together. Clumsy is a "bad intellectual" trait that would be associated with a lack of intelligence.
  a. Person schemas relate to generalized assumptions about certain classes of people; whereas implicit personality theories are based around the traits of individuals.
  b. Prejudice involves negative attitudes toward an entire group.
  d. Balance theory is associated with attitude changes and not with social perception.

  10. The correct choice is b. The false consensus bias is the tendency to assume that most people share your attitudes and behaviors and to conclude that a person who does not share your attitudes and behaviors is abnormal. Thus, someone who doesn't find psychology fascinating has something wrong with them (they're an idiot).
  a. The fundamental attribution error involves attributions concerning the behavior of another person: specifically, overestimating dispositional and underestimating external causes.

    c. Prejudice is a negative attitude toward an entire group and not an assumption concerning the personality traits of an individual.

    d. Person schemas are generalized assumptions about *classes* of people (for example, lawyers) and not people who just happen not to find psychology fascinating.

20. The correct choice is d. This is the definition of stereotypes.

    a. Person schemas is a related term, however, stereotypes may be more specific than the generalized assumptions of a person schema. Additionally, person schemas refer to classes of people (lawyers) while stereotypes refer to groups of people (blacks).

    b. Outgroups are the "them" in the "us versus them" category. They are frequently subject to prejudice.

    c. The definition of stereotypes relates to the belief component of a prejudicial attitude. Prejudice also involves feeling and behavior components.

26. The correct choice is d. This question relates to conformity and describes the informational social influence of conformity. If you're at a fancy dinner party and do not know which fork to eat your salad with, you will probably wait until others start to eat and then use the same fork as they.

    a. Social identification refers to a function of attitudes that provides us with information about other people's attitudes.

    b. The normative social influence of conformity relates to altering our behavior because we think it is to our advantage (such as gaining the approval of others, and avoiding disapproval) without an actual change in our beliefs. Even if you really believe that it is correct to eat your salad with your fingers, you would probably still use a fork at a fancy dinner party.

    c. Value-expressive refers to a function of attitudes that involves expressing your attitudes and values that have a central importance in your life.

38. The correct choice is a. This statement summarizes Berkowitz's (1978) view of the frustration-aggression hypothesis.

    b. This statement summarizes Miller's (1941) view of the frustration-aggression hypothesis.

    c. This choice (and choice d) are the two sides of Dillard's (1939) original view of the frustration-aggression hypothesis.

    d. See c above.

PART VI. SUMMARY TABLES

To test your understanding of the material discussed in this chapter complete the following tables. Check your answers with those supplied in PART IX.

Attribution Theory

Attribution of Causes	Theories	
	Correspondent Inference	Covariation Principle
Dispositional		
External		

Types of Social Influence

Type	Definition	Examples of Experiments	Influencing Factors
Conformity			
Compliance			
Obedience			

PART VII. THOUGHT QUESTIONS/CRITICAL THINKING

Prepare answers to the following discussion questions.

1. Discuss the advantages (or benefits) and disadvantages (or costs) of person schemas and implicit personality theories. Refer to the discussion of heuristics in Chapter 8 (Thinking and Language). Are person schemas and implicit personality theories heuristics? Why or why not?

2. Prejudiced attitudes between two groups frequently exist bilaterally as opposed to unilaterally. For example, some soldiers may be prejudiced toward sailors and sailors toward soldiers and some whites may be prejudiced toward blacks and blacks toward whites. Discuss principle(s) of social psychology that would explain this observation.

3. Discuss how you would approach each of the following situations. Explain why you would use the approaches you selected.

   a. You are a consultant hired by the president of a local company that has been negatively affected by economic conditions. This company is experiencing major labor–management conflicts.
   b. You have been appointed chairperson of your dormitory to collect contributions for the victims of a natural disaster in a nearby state.
   c. Your younger brother will be a college freshman next fall at a college where he does not know any other students. Based on the material in this chapter, what advice would you give him that would result in a successful (both academically and interpersonally) adjustment to college?

4. Try to be completely honest here. When you first read about Asch's line-comparison judgment experiment and Milgram's obedience experiment, what did you think about the individuals who were the subjects in these experiments? Did you attribute their behavior to dispositional or external causes? Did you fall victim to the fundamental attribution error? Now that you have read the discussion of factors influencing conformity and obedience, predict what you think your behavior would have been had you been a subject in the Asch and Milgram studies.

5. The textbook describes three types of social influence. These three influences may be viewed as blending together. *Conformity* is modifying one's behavior to be consistent with the behavior of others. *Compliance* is modifying one's behavior as a result of a direct request from others. *Obedience* is modifying one's behavior in response to a command or order from a person perceived as having power or authority. Describe an example of conformity, compliance, and obedience that could be observed in each of the following situations:

   a. Junior-high-age adolescents at school
   b. The employees in an office
   c. A group of individuals who live in a neighborhood (or apartment, or dormitory).

PART VIII. APPLICATIONS

1. Ideally naturalistic observation would be the research method I would choose for this application, but due to time constraints we're going to develop a new research method—the naturalistic interview. The fundamental attribution error is to over-estimate external causes and underestimate external causes when accounting for the

behavior of others (and to do the opposite when accounting for our own behavior). Select two or three individuals with whom you have frequent contact. Over the next few days casually slip into your conversation a number of questions asking your friends to make attributions concerning the behavior of others (for example, "Why do you think she piles so much food on her plate?") and themselves ("Why did you go to the movies last night?"). Make sure that you ask each person a number of questions concerning both themselves and others. Remember their answers and write them down as soon as you get a chance. When you have finished your data collection, examine the answers to determine whether or not you see evidence of the fundamental attribution error.

2. You decide to design an experiment illustrating conformity for the lab section of general psychology that you are in charge of. You are interested in showing that larger groups result in an increased tendency to show conformity than smaller groups. So that your students will be less likely to "see through" your experimental procedure, you decide to do the experiment the week before the class reads the social psychology chapter in the text. Assume that you can come up with an acceptable reason for the students to come to the lab at different times (in order to give you a number of smaller groups). You would also probably hand out written material for the class to read. For all but one of the students this written hand-out would be instructions for the "script" they should follow as confederates in the experiment. The remaining student—the subject—would read material concerning an experiment or lab exercise that he or she will falsely believe to be the focus of the lab session. You may choose either to design an experiment replicating Asch's line-comparison judgment task or some other situation (suggestions: trying to talk the instructor into having class outdoors because it's such a nice day; complaining about the lab instructor for being unreasonable).

    a. What is your hypothesis?

    b. Write a paragraph explaining exactly what procedure you will use to conduct the experiment.

    c. Identify the independent variable.

    d. Identify the dependent variable and explain how it will be measured.

    e. Identify the experimental group(s).

    f. Identify the control group.

    g. Explain how you would assign subjects to the experimental and control groups.

    h. Provide any necessary operational definitions.

    i. Evaluate your experiment in regards to the APA's ethical guidelines. Even though this experiment is only a classroom exercise and not a "real" experiment, you must adhere to the guidelines.

    j. How would you compare the experimental and control groups on their performance on the dependent variable? Using only descriptive statistics, how would you present the results (that is, would you calculate means, percentiles, or whatever)?

    k. Predict what differences in behavior you would find if your hypothesis was confirmed by the results of the experiment.

PART IX. SUMMARY TABLES SOLUTIONS

Attribution Theory

Attribution of Causes	Theories	
	Correspondent Inference	Covariation Principle
Dispositional	Socially undesirable behaviors Focused on a unique outcome (or noncommon effect) Free will	Behavior typical for the individual (low distinctiveness) Behavior different from that of others (low consensus)
External	Socially acceptable behaviors Focused on a common outcome Presence of social or other influence (lack of free will)	Behavior unusual or atypical for the individual (high distinctiveness) Behavior similar to that of others (high consensus)

Types of Social Influence

Type	Definition	Examples of Experiments	Influencing Factors
Conformity	Behavior or beliefs are modified so that they are consistent with those of others	Sherif: stationary light Asch: line-comparison judgments	Increased tendency to conform when majority group is unanimous, perceive group members acting independently, size of group is larger, unfamiliar with attitude object, low self-esteem, and believe group members have higher status
Compliance	Behavior is altered in response to direct requests from others	Cialdini et al.: college students asked to interact with delinquent youths	Foot-in-the-door technique Door-in-the-face technique
Obedience	Behavior is altered in response to commands or orders from people perceived as having power or authority	Milgram: subjects instructed to shock another individual for incorrect responses	Increased tendency to be obedient as a result of diminished personal accountability, authority figure has highly visible symbols of power or status, and if individual is presented with a series of graduated demands

CHAPTER **18**

Applying Psychology

PART I. LEARNING OBJECTIVES

When you finish studying this chapter you should be able to:

Environmental Psychology

1. Discuss the focus of environmental psychology, and list two broad areas studied by environmental psychologists. **(691, 693-696)**

2. Describe the effects excessive noise has on humans, and summarize research findings concerning the effects of noise on the cognitive functioning of children. **(691, 693)**

3. Describe the effects of heat on human productivity and aggressive behavior. **(694-695)**

4. Define environmental toxins, and discuss the adverse consequences associated with lead and carbon monoxide (CO), also discuss environments where lead and CO exist at high levels. **(695-696)**

5. Define architectural psychology, and summarize research concerning how the design of dormitories influences residents. **(696-698)**

6. Discuss territoriality, and differentiate between primary and secondary territories. **(698-699)**

7. Discuss personal space, and describe three different interpersonal distances that vary depending on the type of social interaction. **(700-701)**

8. Describe and summarize the findings of Calhoun's (1962) study concerning overpopulation in a group of rats. **(701)**

9. Describe the relationship in humans between urban population density and socially disruptive behaviors and explain why it would be inappropriate to infer a cause-and-effect relationship. **(702)**

10. Differentiate between density and crowding. **(702-703)**

Industrial/Organizational Psychology

11. Discuss the focus of industrial/organizational psychology and list several areas in which industrial/organizational psychologists are active. **(703)**

12. Discuss the personnel selection process describing job analysis and four techniques used in the selection process. **(703-707)**

13. Describe subjective and objective techniques for evaluating worker performance, and discuss limitations of each technique. **(707-708)**

14. Discuss Maslow's hierarchy-of-needs perspective concerning worker motivation. **(708)**

15. Discuss Herzberg's two-factor theory concerning worker motivation. **(708-709)**

16. Summarize the research related to job satisfaction and productivity. **(709-711)**

17. Describe Theory Y and Theory X management styles, and contrast their effects on workers. **(712-713)**

Health Psychology

18. Discuss the focus of behavioral medicine and health psychology, and list three areas with which health psychologists are concerned. **(713-714)**

19. Discuss four reasons why health-damaging behaviors are widespread. **(714-715)**

20. Discuss approaches that attempt to change health-damaging behaviors by changing health attitudes. **(715-716)**

21. Discuss two psychological therapy approaches that are well suited for changing health-damaging behaviors. **(716-717)**

PART II. OVERVIEW

This chapter examines three areas of applied psychology: environmental psychology, industrial/organizational psychology, and health psychology. Environmental psychology focuses on how the physical environment affects psychological processes. A variety of environmental conditions adversely affect psychological processes: excessive noise (impaired intellectual functioning and other effects), excessive heat (decreased productivity and increased aggressive behaviors), and environmental toxins (a variety of neurotoxins affect the nervous system). Lead and carbon monoxide are two widespread neurotoxins. Environmental psychology also studies the effects of space on behavior. Architectural psychology studies the behavioral implications of building design. Humans and other species establish territories that are their special domain. People have both primary and secondary territories. Personal space refers to the space that surrounds us. The size of one's personal space varies from situation to situation. Crowding is associated with adverse behavioral consequences, but it is necessary to distinguish between population density—number of people per unit of space, and crowding—psychological feelings of discomfort associated with lack of space.

Industrial/organizational psychology applies psychological principles to improve the functioning of businesses and industrial organizations and encompasses a wide range of activities from personnel selection to the effects of different styles of management. Two theories of how to motivate workers are Maslow's hierarchy-of-needs theory and Herzberg's two-factor theory. Maslow's approach suggests that employees differ in their dominant needs and thus are motivated by different aspects of their work. Herzberg describes two types of needs: hygiene needs are related to extrinsic motivators (such as salary), and motivator needs are related to intrinsic motivators (such as a desire for challenge). Meeting only hygiene needs may not be sufficient to motivate workers. The relationship between worker job satisfaction and productivity is not simple. Employee-centered management styles (Theory Y), which emphasize the psychological efficiency of workers, are more effective in inducing both increased productivity and job satisfaction than are the job-centered or scientific-management styles (Theory X), which emphasize work efficiency.

Behavioral medicine examines the relationship between behavioral factors and illness. Health psychology examines the relationship between psychological factors and physical health. Health-damaging behaviors such as smoking, overeating, and lack of adequate exercise are widespread and often difficult to change. Health psychology attempts to reduce the unhealthy attitudes and behaviors of individuals. Health psychology uses a number of techniques (described in the previous chapter) to attempt to change unhealthy attitudes. Because changing attitudes does not necessarily result in changes in behavior, health psychologists and other professionals use psychotherapy techniques to assist in behavior change. Many behavior therapy and cognitive therapy techniques are well suited to assist people in changing their health-damaging behaviors.

PART III. KEY TERMS/MATCHING EXERCISES

Match the following concepts and/or individuals with the appropriate descriptions. Check your answers against the Answer Key.

Environmental Psychology

Concepts

_____ 1. interpersonal distance **(700)**

_____ 2. territoriality **(699)**

_____ 3. behavioral toxicology **(695)**

_____ 4. crowding **(703)**

_____ 5. environmental psychology **(691)**

_____ 6. architectural psychology **(698)**

_____ 7. primary territory **(699)**

_____ 8. density **(702-703)**

_____ 9. environmental toxins **(695)**

_____ 10. personal space **(700)**

_____ 11. secondary territories **(699)**

Descriptions

a. Visual relatively fixed boundaries of a given space that one considers to be a special domain for his or her own use

b. Physical attribute that is reflected in the number of people in a given amount of space

c. Examine(s) the adverse effects of neurotoxins

d. Examine(s) how the physical environment affects psychological processes

e. Space that is not rigidly defined which people are not very protective of

f. Varies from situation to situation according to a number of factors such as the nature of the relationship and context

g. Psychological response to a lack of space, characterized by feelings of over-stimulation, distress, and discomfort

h. Study of the behavioral implications of building design

i. Private space defined by people as for their use only

j. Imaginary circle of space surrounding an individual and into which others are not supposed to enter without an invitation

k. Hazardous substances people come into contact with, in a variety of situations

Answer Key   1. f   2. a   3. c   4. g   5. d   6. h   7. i   8. b   9. k   10. j   11. e

Industrial/Organizational Psychology | Health Psychology

Concepts

_____ 1. motivator needs **(709)**

_____ 2. two-factor theory **(709)**

_____ 3. health psychology **(714)**

_____ 4. job analysis **(704)**

_____ 5. Theory Y **(712)**

_____ 6. participant management **(712)**

_____ 7. industrial/organizational psychology **(703)**

_____ 8. Maslow's hierarchy of needs **(708)**

_____ 9. assessment centers **(706)**

_____ 10. behavioral medicine **(713)**

_____ 11. Theory X **(712-713)**

_____ 12. hygiene needs **(709)**

_____ 13. job description index (JDI) **(710)**

Descriptions

a. Suggests that what is motivating for one employee may not motivate other employees

b. Necessary to conduct in order to determine job specifications

c. Studies and attempts to understand how behavior affects physical disease processes

d. Applies psychological principles to improve the functioning of businesses and industrial organizations

e. Assesses five dimensions of job satisfaction

f. Relate(s) to system–maintenance needs, such as job security and fair company policies, that are related to job context

g. Satisfied primarily through job control and include a desire for challenge and autonomy

h. Studies the relationship between psychological factors and physical health and applies findings to real-life problems

i. Strategy in which all levels of employees are included in decision making

j. Use(s) techniques, such as the in-basket technique and leaderless group discussions

k. Proposes that employers should consider both intrinsic and extrinsic factors to motivate employees

l. Job-centered or scientific management style that offers little or no opportunity for employee involvement in decision making

m. Employee-centered management style that allows employees considerable latitude and personal discretion in carrying out job functions

Answer Key 1. g 2. k 3. h 4. b 5. m 6. i 7. d 8. a 9. j 10. c 11. l 12. f 13. e

PART IV. TRUE-FALSE STATEMENTS

Fill in the blank before each statement with either a T (true) or an F (false). Check your answers against the Answer Key. Then go back to the items that are false and make the necessary change(s) to the statements to convert the items into true statements.

Environmental Psychology

_____ 1. Car exhaust fumes can be a source of both lead and carbon monoxide.

_____

_____

_____ 2. *Primary territory* refers to the imaginary circle of space with which we surround ourselves.

_____

_____

_____ 3. A relatively high population density is not always perceived as stressful.

_____

_____

Industrial/Organizational Psychology

_____ 4. Measuring the number of absences an employee has from work is a subjective technique for evaluating worker performance.

_____

_____

_____ 5. An employer applying the hierarchy-of-needs approach to worker motivation might offer employees a choice of cafeteria benefits.

_____

_____

_____ 6. Increasing a worker's job satisfaction results in an increase in productivity.

_____

_____

_____ 7. Job-centered management styles are more effective than employee-centered management styles in increasing productivity and job satisfaction.

_____

_____

Health Psychology

_____ 8. *The second revolution* in medicine refers to information about how psychological, social, and behavioral factors contribute to physical illness.

_____

_____

_____ 9. One reason that health-damaging behaviors are common is that these damaging behaviors are often reinforcing.

_____ 10. Mass-media health campaigns are generally more effective in changing behavior than changing health attitudes.

Answer Key	1. T **(695)**	6. F **(711)**
	2. F **(700)**	7. F **(713)**
	3. T **(703)**	8. T **(713)**
	4. F **(707-708)**	9. T **(715)**
	5. T **(708)**	10. F **(716)**

PART V. MULTIPLE-CHOICE QUESTIONS

Choose the best answer to each question. Circle your choice. Check your answers against the Answer Key. Questions marked with an asterisk (*) include annotated answers.

Environmental Psychology

1. An environmental psychologist would be least likely to

   a. study the effects of food preservatives on the behavior of children.
   b. work to change people's attitudes and behaviors related to conserving natural resources.
   c. study the effect of barometric pressure on behavior.
   d. assist city planners in designing neighborhoods.

2. Excessive noise has been associated with

   a. impaired intellectual functioning.
   b. increased aggression.
   c. high levels of stress.
   d. All of the above choices are correct.

3. In one study children living on the _____ floors of a 32-story, high-rise apartment complex were shown to have better performance on a reading test than children living on other floors.

   a. 5th–11th
   b. 12th–18th
   c. 19th–25th
   d. 26th–32nd

*4. The relationship between temperature and aggressive behaviors can be summarized best by which of the following?

   a. Temperatures at either extreme are associated with aggressive behaviors.
   b. As temperature increases so does aggressive behaviors.
   c. As temperature increases aggressive behaviors decrease.
   d. Aggressive behaviors are most likely to occur when the temperature is between 69°–74°F.

5. Hazardous substances that have a damaging effect on the nervous system, and that frequently first result in behavioral changes as opposed to physical symptoms, are

   a. neurotoxins.
   b. controlled substances.
   c. carcinogens.
   d. environmental toxins.

*6. The child who would most likely show an impairment in IQ is a

   a. child living in an urban environment that is excessively noisy.
   b. child growing up in a humid environment.
   c. child suffering from lead contamination.
   d. child suffering from carbon monoxide exposure.

7. Which of the following describes students who live in dormitories with corridors and suites?

   a. Suite residents were more inclined to avoid contact with others.
   b. Suite residents made more visits to the campus health center.
   c. Corridor residents felt they experienced overexposure to unwanted social situations.
   d. Corridor residents spent more time in lounge areas.

8. The primary reason humans use territoriality is to

   a. achieve a degree of privacy.
   b. achieve status.
   c. avoid social interaction.
   d. avoid unwanted responsibility.

9. The type of interpersonal distance that typically ranges from 18 inches to 4 feet is _____ distance.

   a. conversational
   b. intimate
   c. personal
   d. social

10. You would most likely have feelings of crowding and psychological discomfort

   a. on a five-day cross-country bus trip.
   b. while attending the seventh game of the World Series.
   c. while attending your general psychology class in a packed lecture hall.
   d. at a New Year's Eve party at the "in" nightspot in town.

Industrial/Organizational Psychology

11. You are in charge of hiring a new secretary for your office. On the first morning after your newspaper ad appeared, 25 candidates were at the office when you arrived. What would you do first?

    a. Give everyone a secretarial aptitude test.
    b. Give everyone a vocational interest test.
    c. Conduct a brief interview with everyone.
    d. Give everyone an application form.

12. Which personnel-selection technique, according to validity studies, is a poor predictor of ultimate job success?

    a. The application form
    b. The interview
    c. Testing
    d. Assessment centers

13. The truly unique feature of assessment centers is that these

    a. use a wide variety of aptitude, vocational interest, and personality tests.
    b. use simulated work situations.
    c. conduct extensive interviews.
    d. All of the above are unique features of assessment centers.

14. The aspect of personnel work that is an important basis for decisions regarding salary increases, promotions, terminations, and the selection of workers for special training is

    a. personnel selection.
    b. evaluating worker performance.
    c. evaluating worker motivation.
    d. implementing management decisions.

15. Two major potential problems associated with subjective techniques for evaluating worker performance are

    a. subjective bias and objective bias.
    b. personal bias and the employee's nervousness during the interview.
    c. the halo effect and the employee's nervousness during the interview.
    d. the halo effect and personal bias.

16. Job enrichment and job enlargement programs are most closely related to

    a. flextime.
    b. Theory X.
    c. Maslow's hierarchy of needs.
    d. Herzberg's two-factor theory.

17. Kathy considers her work stimulating, rewarding, and feels challenged. Herzberg would say that Kathy's _____ needs are being met.

    a. motivator
    b. hygiene
    c. context
    d. contingency

18. When measuring job satisfaction, how do most employees usually rate money?

  a. First on the list
  b. Second only to work conditions
  c. Second only to social relations
  d. After challenging work, autonomy, and good social relations with coworkers

*19. The job description index (JDI)

  a. describes the exact nature of a job and the tasks that must be performed.
  b. is an objective technique to measure worker performance.
  c. is used to assess job satisfaction.
  d. is used to assess worker productivity.

*20. Workers who have a high degree of job satisfaction typically

  a. are no more likely to stay with a company than are workers with low job satisfaction.
  b. have low absenteeism rates.
  c. show low productivity.
  d. show high productivity.

21. Research has *not* linked flextime to

  a. reduced productivity.
  b. reduced absenteeism.
  c. increased job satisfaction.
  d. improved relations between line workers and management.

22. Which of the following statements is *false* concerning an American Honda plant that uses participant management?

  a. Meeting of workers and managers are held daily.
  b. Executives do not have private offices.
  c. The plant has low rates of absenteeism and low employee turnover.
  d. Labor and management employees each wear distinctive uniforms.

23. Theory Y or employee-centered management assumes that

  a. when allowed some autonomy, workers are willing to accept responsibility and will be more productive.
  b. workers produce more if management focuses on production and improving work efficiency.
  c. focus on salary, fringe benefits, and nonmonetary rewards improve workers' productivity.
  d. None of the above are correct.

24. Which term does *not* belong with the other terms?

  a. Scientific management
  b. Theory X
  c. Participant management
  d. job-centered management

Health Psychology

25. The study of how behavior and state of mind can influence physical health is

    a. psychobiology.
    b. environmental medicine.
    c. behavioral medicine.
    d. sociobiology.

26. It has been estimated that _____ percent of mortality from the 10 leading causes of death in the United States is largely behaviorally determined.

    a. 10–20
    b. 30–40
    c. 50–70
    d. 80–90

27. The speciality field of psychology that links psychology with behavioral medicine is _____ psychology.

    a. forensic
    b. health
    c. medical
    d. environmental

28. Widespread, health-damaging behaviors are associated with the observation that the association between unhealthy behaviors and chronic-illness risks (for example, smoking and lung cancer) are unlikely to surface until many years have elapsed. Which of the following best describes why this is so?

    a. People often have little incentive to practice good health behaviors
    b. People believe that medical advances will offer a way of avoiding the future consequences of their behaviors
    c. Health-damaging behaviors are often quite rewarding and enjoyable while one is indulging in them
    d. Observational learning

29. While people tend to _____ the risks associated with their own unhealthy habits, they tend to _____ the potential ill-effects of such unhealthy behaviors in others.

    a. underestimate | overestimate
    b. overestimate | underestimate
    c. underestimate | have a much clearer impression of
    d. have a much clearer impression of | underestimate

*30. Moderate fear appeals to encourage people to change their health-damaging behaviors tend(s) to

    a. use case histories to present the message.
    b. primarily motivate an individual to want to change his or her behavior.
    c. be relatively unsuccessful.
    d. All of the above choices are correct.

31. The success of mass media informational appeals, encouraging people to engage in healthier behavior, has been associated with the use of all of the following *except*

  a. presenting a strong message at both the beginning and end of the message.
  b. using statistics to emphasize or document the message.
  c. stating conclusions explicitly.
  d. using case histories to present the message.

32. Which two types of psychotherapy techniques are generally most well suited to help people change health-damaging behaviors?

  a. Behavior therapy and biomedical techniques
  b. Cognitive therapy and humanistic therapy
  c. Behavior therapy and cognitive therapy
  d. Humanistic therapy and biomedical techniques

33. A _____ would suggest to a heavy drinker who says, "I am a weak person, and can't just say no," that he or she is incorrect.

  a. cognitive therapist
  b. psychoanalyst
  c. behavior therapist
  d. person-centered therapist

Answer Key

1. b	**(691)**	8. a	**(699)**	15. d	**(707)**	22. d	**(712)**	28. a	**(715)**
2. d	**(691, 693)**	9. c	**(700)**	16. d	**(709)**	23. a	**(712)**	29. c	**(715)**
3. d	**(693)**	10. a	**(703)**	17. a	**(709)**	24. c	**(712-713)**	*30. b	**(715-716)**
*4. b	**(694)**	11. d	**(704)**	18. d	**(710)**	25. c	**(713)**	31. b	**(716)**
5. a	**(695)**	12. b	**(705)**	*19. c	**(710)**	26. c	**(713)**	32. c	**(716)**
*6. c	**(696)**	13. b	**(706)**	*20. b	**(712)**	27. b	**(714)**	33. a	**(716-717)**
7. c	**(697)**	14. b	**(707)**	21. a	**(712)**				

Annotated Answers

  4. The correct choice is b. A variety of evidence supports the positive relationship between temperature and aggressive behaviors: violent crimes increase during warmer months and the higher the temperature the more likely riots are to occur.
   a. Extremely cold temperatures are not associated with an increase in aggressive behaviors.
   c. This choice describes a negative correlation between temperature and aggressive behaviors that is the opposite of the actual positive correlation.
   d. It is performance that tends to be optimal at moderate temperatures between 67°–74° F.

  6. The correct choice is c. Childhood exposure to even low levels of lead has been shown to impair the IQ of children.
   a. Excessive noise is associated with a decrease in cognitive functioning (for example, proofreading and reading skills) but has not been associated with long-term impairment of IQ.
   b. Humidity has not been associated with an impairment of IQ.
   d. Similar to excessive noise, carbon monoxide does effect cognitive functioning, but has not been associated with an impairment of IQ.

19. The correct choice is c. The JDI assesses five dimensions of job satisfaction: supervision, coworkers, promotions, pay, and the work itself.
   a. This statement describes job analysis.
   b. Objective techniques to measure worker performance would include measures of absenteeism and productivity.
   d. Productivity would be measured by either the quantity or quality of work completed.

20. The correct choice is b. One of the major findings concerning job satisfaction is that employees with high job satisfaction have low rates of absenteeism.
   a. The second major finding concerning job satisfaction is that employees with high job satisfaction tend to have low turnover rates.
   c. The relationship between job satisfaction and productivity is not simple. Some employees with high job satisfaction show high productivity and others show low productivity.
   d. The explanation for c above applies.

30. The correct choice is b. Fear appeals often add to an individual's motivation to change behavior by changing his or her attitudes concerning that behavior.
   a. Although some fear appeals do use case studies, this is not the only way to induce fear. "Scary" statistics also induce fear, and may be used.
   c. Moderate fear appeals tend to be more successful than some other approaches (for example, low and high fear appeals).
   d. This statement is incorrect because a and c are incorrect.

PART VI. SUMMARY TABLES

To test your understanding of the material discussed in this chapter complete the following tables. Check your answers against those supplied in PART IX.

Theories for Motivating Workers

Theory	Assumptions	How Implemented	Current Status
Maslow's need theory			
Herzberg's two-factor theory			

Management Styles

Style	Also Referred to as	Assumptions and Concerns	How Implemented	Effectiveness
Theory Y				
Theory X				

PART VII. THOUGHT QUESTIONS/CRITICAL THINKING

1. The text described Cohen's (1973) study, which showed a positive correlation between children's performance on a reading test and how high they lived in a 32-story apartment complex. Cohen interpreted the correlation as supporting evidence for the relationship between excessive noise (the higher the apartment, the lower the noise level) and cognitive skills. Here, the intent is not to dispute Cohen's conclusion, but to discuss his general finding concerning the correlation between reading test performance and floor level in relation to other environmental factors. Would other relevant environmental factors (toxins, crowding) exist at different levels (higher, lower) on the different floors of the apartment complex that might be related to Cohen's findings? Explain.

2. Use the house or apartment you lived in while growing up to evaluate, from an environmental psychology perspective, the following. Describe the territories that exist(ed) in the house or apartment and who has (had) "access" to each territory. Also, from an architectural psychology perspective, could the floor plan of the house or apartment be improved? What additions (another bathroom, another door) or subtractions (knock down a wall) would you suggest? Explain the reasoning behind your suggestions.

3. Just like everyone else, your professors are workers. How should their job performance be evaluated? Suggest a number of specific subjective and objective techniques that could (and might already be conducted at your college) be used to evaluate faculty members.

4. If you are like most college students today, you probably have some work experience. It is appropriate to also think of your high school and college courses as work experience. You probably have had a wider variety of "work" experiences in a classroom than on a job. You also most likely have had some courses you liked more than others, some you learned more in, some you worked harder in, some you participated more in, some you attended more regularly, some you attended less regularly, and so on. Discuss the following topics in relation to a number of different courses you have taken: worker performance, worker motivation, worker satisfaction, worker productivity, and management styles. Predict the type of employment situation in which you would perform best as a full-time employee.

5. Antidrug, antismoking, and antidrinking programs are now being presented to very young schoolchildren. Explain why this is so.

PART VIII. APLICATIONS

1. For this application, watch television and listen to the radio. Pay close attention to the public-service announcements and commercials encouraging healthy behaviors (for example, eating high-fibre foods) or offering methods to change unhealthy behaviors (weight-loss programs). Evaluate each public-service announcement and commercial individually. If it is a fear appeal, does it contain all the components associated with a successful fear appeal? If it is an informational campaign, does it contain all the components associated with a successful informational campaign? Describe one or two messages that you feel will be relatively successful, and explain why. Describe one or two messages that you feel will not be successful, and explain why.

2. For this application, go to the college library—on two separate occasions—to study territoriality: once during a low-use period (perhaps in the morning or on Friday night) and once during a high-use period (perhaps at 8 o'clock on a weeknight). Find the section that has a number of study tables with several chairs at each table. Now, sit down and observe. Are students widely separated or are they sitting close together? What, if any, strategies are students using to mark their own territories? Watch as a couple of students enter the area and sit down. Do they sit at an empty table or at a table that is already occupied? Is the size of an individual's territory different during low- and high-use periods? Describe how you would feel if someone came in and sat at "your" table during a low-use period. During a high-use period.

PART IX.   SUMMARY TABLES SOLUTIONS

Theories for Motivating Workers

Theory	Assumptions	How Implemented	Current Status
Maslow's need theory	Human needs exist at five levels: physiological, safety or security, belongingness, esteem, and self-actualization Different people have different dominant needs that are satisfied by different aspects of their work	Different dominant needs are satisfied in different ways To motivate an employee, one should know their dominant need and try to satisfy it Cafeteria benefits allow worker choices so that he or she can select how to meet those needs	Not considered to be an optimal model
Herzberg's two-factor theory	Two types of needs: hygiene needs are extrinsic motivators (e.g., equitable pay and job security); motivator needs are intrinsic motivators (e.g., desire for challenge and autonomy) It is in the best interest of an organization if workers are motivator seeking	Job enrichment or job enlargement to make job more intrinsicly rewarding	One of the most popular theories in business and industry for the past 15 years

Management Styles

Style	Also Referred to as	Assumptions and Concerns	How Implemented	Effectiveness
Theory Y	Employee-centered management	Workers are willing to accept responsibility Workers are more productive if they have some autonomy and independence Concerned with psychological efficiency	One application is participant management in which all employees have a say in important decisions	Related to increased productivity and increased job satisfaction
Theory X	Job-centered or scientific management	Emphasizes production and concerned with increasing work efficiency	Emphasizes policy, job specialization, quotas, rigid chain of command Employee has little or no opportunity for involvement in decision making	Less effective than employee-centered regarding productivity and job satisfaction

Elementary Statistics

PART I: LEARNING OBJECTIVES

When you finish studying this chapter you should be able to:

Descriptive Statistics

1. Discuss the function of measures of central tendency, and describe three measures of central tendency. **(A-0-A-3)**

2. Discuss the function of measures of variability, and describe three measures of variability. **(A-3-A-6)**

3. Describe the normal distribution, and explain how z-scores are related to the normal distribution. **(A-6-A-7)**

4. Discuss how correlation is used to describe the relationship between two variables, and describe the Pearson product-moment correlation coefficient. **(A-9-A-11)**

5. Explain how regression is related to correlation, and discuss how regression is used. **(A-11-A-13)**

Inferential Statistics

6. Discuss how a sample is used to estimate characteristics of a population. **(A-13-A-14)**

7. Explain why researchers need to use hypothesis testing, and differentiate between the null hypothesis and the working hypothesis. **(A-14-A-15)**

8. Discuss how t-tests allow researchers to interpret the results of their experiments, and describe Type I and Type II errors. **(A-15-A-17)**

9. Discuss how analysis of variance is similar to the t-test and discuss when it is necessary to use analysis of variance. **(A-17)**

10. Describe factor analysis, and list two areas of psychology in which factor analysis has been extensively used. **(A-17-A-18)**

PART II: KEY TERMS/MATCHING EXERCISES

Match the following concepts and/or individuals with the appropriate descriptions. Check your answers against the Answer Key.

Descriptive Statistics (Measures of Central Tendency and Variability)

Concepts

_____ 1. range (**A-3**)   _____ 5. mean (**A-0**)

_____ 2. mode (**A-3**)   _____ 6. variance (**A-4**)

_____ 3. standard deviation (**A-6**)   _____ 7. median (**A-1**)

_____ 4. frequency distribution (**A-6**)

Descriptions

a. Table showing how many individuals actually received each possible score on a test

b. Measure of variability that is computed by subtracting the lowest score from the highest score

c. Measure of variability that is the average of the squared distances of the scores from the mean

d. Measure of central tendency that is computed by adding up all the scores and dividing by the number of scores

e. Measure of central tendency that is the middle score in a list of scores that have been arranged in increasing order

f. Measure of variability that is the square root of the average of the squared distances of the scores from the mean

g. Measure of central tendency that is the most frequently occurring score in a group of scores

Answer Key 1. b   2. g   3. f   4. a   5. d   6. c   7. e

Descriptive Statistics
(Normal Frequency Distribution, Correlation, and Regression)

Concepts

_____ 1. probability (**A-8**)   _____ 5. normal distribution (**A-6**)

_____ 2. scatter plot (**A-9**)   _____ 6. Pearson product-moment

_____ 3. z-scores (**A-6**)   correlation coefficient (**A-11**)

_____ 4. regression (**A-12**)   _____ 7. correlation coefficient (**A-9**)

Descriptions

a. Graph used to visualize the relationship between two variables
b. Proportion of cases that fit a certain description
c. Measure of the degree to which two variables covary
d. Used to predict a score on a variable from the individual's score on another variable
e. Bell-shaped curve in which scores near the mean are most common
f. Measure of correlation that is used most often and varies from -1.0 to $+1.0$
g. Standard deviation scores

Answer Key 1. b   2. a   3. g   4. d   5. e   6. f   7. c

Inferential Statistics | Advanced Statistical Techniques

Concepts

_____ 1. analysis of variance **(A-17)**   _____ 5. null hypothesis **(A-15)**

_____ 2. working hypothesis **(A-14)**   _____ 6. Type I error **(A-17)**

_____ 3. Type II error **(A-17)**   _____ 7. t-test **(A-15)**

_____ 4. factor analysis **(A-17)**

Descriptions

a. Incorrectly concluding that the independent variable has no effect when it does
b. Incorrectly concluding that the independent variable has an effect when it has none
c. Statistical procedure that is conceptually similar to the t-test and examines differences between the means of two or more groups
d. Statistical technique used to determine if there is a significant difference between the means of two groups
e. Highly sophisticated correlational technique used to identify the basic factors underlying psychological phenomena
f. Predicts that the independent variable will have an effect on the dependent variable
g. Predicts that the independent variable will have no effect on the dependent variable

Answer Key 1. c   2. f   3. a   4. e   5. g   6. b   7. d

Statistical Symbols

Concepts

_____ 1. s^2 **(A-4)**   _____ 6. $\overline{X}$ **(A-0)**

_____ 2. Σ **(A-0)**   _____ 7. r_{xy} **(A-11)**

_____ 3. X **(A-0)**   _____ 8. N **(A-0)**

_____ 4. f **(A-3)**   _____ 9. s **(A-6)**

_____ 5. z **(A-6)**

Descriptions

a. Variable that can take on many values

b. "Add up these scores"

c. Mean

d. Number of scores

e. Frequency

f. Variance

g. Standard deviation

h. Standard deviation score

i. Pearson product-moment correlation coefficient

Answer Key 1. f   2. b   3. a   4. e   5. h   6. c   7. i   8. d   9. g

PART II: TRUE-FALSE STATEMENTS

Fill in the blank before each statement with either a T (true) or an F (false). Check your answers against the Answer Key. Then go back to the items that are false and make the necessary change(s) to the statements to convert the items into true statements.

Descriptive Statistics

_____ 1. A distribution of scores that is asymmetrical and unbalanced is said to be a normal distribution.

_____

_____

_____ 2. The variance and standard deviation reflect the degree of spread or fluctuation of scores around the mean.

_____

_____

_____ 3. A z-score of $+2.0$ corresponds to a score two standard deviations above the mean.

_____

_____

_____ 4. In a distribution of scores the mean is unaffected by extreme scores.

_____

_____

_____ 5. A scatter plot is used to visualize a frequency distribution.

_____

_____

Inferential Statistics | Advanced Statistical Techniques

_____ 6. In a random sample, everyone in the specified population has the same chance of being in the sample.

_____

_____

_____ 7. If tests of statistical significance indicate that the null hypothesis would only happen five percent of the time or less by chance, then psychologists would conclude that it was not a chance event but a real effect.

_____

_____

_____ 8. Researchers try to minimize the probability of making Type II errors.

_____

_____

_____ 9. Factor analysis is a highly sophisticated correlational procedure.

_____

_____

Answer Key

1. F **(A-6)**	4. F **(A-2)**	7. T **(A-16)**
2. T **(A-4)**	5. F **(A-9–A-10)**	8. F **(A-17)**
3. T **(A-7)**	6. T **(A-14)**	9. T **(A-17)**

PART V: MULTIPLE-CHOICE QUESTIONS

Choose the best answer to each question. Circle your choice. Check your answers against the Answer Key. Questions marked with an asterisk (*) include annotated answers.

Descriptive Statistics

1. _____ statistics are used to summarize the results of research. _____ statistics are used to draw conclusions about the research.

  a. Central tendency | Variability
  b. Descriptive | Inferential
  c. Inferential | Descriptive
  d. Regression | Correlational

2. Descriptive statistics include all of the following concepts *except*

  a. measures of variability.
  b. correlation.
  c. hypothesis testing.
  d. measures of central tendency.

3. A type of average calculated by dividing the sum of scores by the number of scores is the

  a. mean.
  b. median.
  c. mode.
  d. range.

4. In the distribution of scores 1, 1, 2, 3, 5, 6 the median is

   a. 1.
   b. 2.
   c. 2.5.
   d. 3.

5. In a distribution of scores it is possible to have more than one

   a. median.
   b. standard deviation.
   c. mean.
   d. mode.

6. The standard deviation is a better estimate of the variability of a distribution than the range because the standard deviation

   a. is easier to compute.
   b. is about the same as the mean, anyway.
   c. relies on the median.
   d. is less influenced by extreme scores.

7. To calculate a z-score for an individual score you need to know the _____ of the distribution of scores.

   a. median and variance
   b. variance and standard deviation
   c. mean and standard deviation
   d. median and standard deviation

8. In a normal distribution of scores, more individuals would fall between z-scores from _____ than in the other three choices.

   a. 0 to +1.0
   b. +1.0 to +2.0
   c. +2.0 to +3.0
   d. +1.0 to +3.0

9. According to the normal distribution statistic, _____ percent of Wechsler IQ scores fall between 85 and 115.

   a. 50
   b. 68
   c. 84
   d. 98

10. The correlation coefficient describes the

   a. probability that scores very together.
   b. Pearson product-moment score.
   c. relationship between individual scores.
   d. degree of relationship between variables.

11. Most likely there is a _____ correlation between a person's time on a half-mile run and their time on a mile run.

    a. zero

    b. positive

    c. negative

    d. unsystematic

12. The Pearson product-moment correlation measure of correlation can take on any numerical value from −1.0 to +1.0. The size of the correlation represents the _____ of the relationship, and the sign of the correlation represents the _____ of the relationship between two variables.

    a. degree | direction

    b. direction | range

    c. range | degree

    d. direction | degree

13. Regression is most closely related to

    a. variability.

    b. factor analysis.

    c. correlation.

    d. hypothesis testing.

14. If you know an individual's score on one variable (e.g., height) you would use _____ to predict his or her score on a second variable (e.g., weight).

    a. estimation

    b. regression

    c. the median

    d. the correlation coefficient

Inferential Statistics

15. A random sample is representative because

    a. everyone in the specified sample has an equal chance of being chosen.

    b. it is scientific

    c. it is used by experts.

    d. it leaves nothing to chance.

16. Inferential statistics, such as the *t*-test, actually test the

    a. experimental hypothesis.

    b. working hypothesis.

    c. null hypothesis.

    d. either the null or working hypotheses.

17. You conduct an experiment and calculate a *t* ratio and find that the chance probability of obtaining a *t* as large as you found is 10 percent. You would conclude that

    a. you had miscalculated the *t* ratio because it is always at the .05 level or less.

    b. the null hypothesis was incorrect.

    c. there is a real difference between the groups.

    d. there is no real difference between the groups.

18. A statistic commonly used to decide if there is a statistically significant difference between the means of two groups is the

   a. z-score.
   b. Pearson product-moment correlation coefficient.
   c. t-test.
   d. F-test.

Read the following and then respond to questions 19–21:

You conduct an experiment on the effects of caffeine on resting heart rate. You have four groups of subjects who receive different dosages of caffeine (no caffeine, low dose, medium dose, and high dose).

19. The null hypothesis is that the

   a. higher the dosage of caffeine the higher the heart rate.
   b. caffeine groups will have different heart rates than the no-caffeine group.
   c. three caffeine groups will not differ on heart rate.
   d. four groups will not differ on heart rate.

20. You should use a(n) _____ to analyze the results of your study.

   a. factor analysis
   b. analysis of variance
   c. t-test
   d. correlation

21. If you incorrectly interpret the results of your study and make a Type I error, you would

   a. reject the null hypothesis when it is, in fact, false.
   b. not reject the null hypothesis when it is, in fact, false.
   c. reject the null hypothesis when it is, in fact, true.
   d. not reject the null hypothesis when it is, in fact, true.

22. A statistical technique that attempts to find clusters of tests that correlate with one another is

   a. covariance.
   b. factor analysis.
   c. regression.
   d. F-test.

Answer Key

1. b	(A-0)	6. d	(A-3–A-4)	11. b	(A-9)	16. c (A-16–A-17)	21. c	(A-17)
2. c	(A-14)	7. c	(A-6)	12. a	(A-11)	17. d (A-17–A-18)	22. b	(A-17)
3. a	(A-0)	8. a	(A-8)	13. c (A-11–A-12)		18. c (A-16–A-17)		
4. c	(A-1)	9. b	(A-8)	14. b	(A-12)	19. d	(A-15)	
5. d	(A-3)	10. d	(A-9)	15. a	(A-14)	20. b	(A-18)	